WITH ALL MY MIGHT

With All My MIGHT

ERSKINE

AN AUTOBIOGRAPHY

CALDWELL

PEACHTREE PUBLISHERS, LTD.

Published by
PEACHTREE PUBLISHERS, LTD.
494 Armour Circle, N.E.
Atlanta, Georgia 30324

Manufactured in the United States of America

1st printing

Library of Congress Catalog Card Number 86-63528

ISBN 0-934601-11-9

ISBN 0-934601-21-6 (signed and limited edition)

for Virginia

With All My MIGHT

Chapter One

MY ACTUAL RECOLLECTIONS OF earliest childhood—some particulars still vague and others glowingly vivid—did not have a beginning until sometime between my second and third birthdays. All else until then is hearsay.

Prior to that indeterminate age, according to my mother's often told tales, there were some incidents in the beginning of my existence which I wish I had the ability to recall.

It is possible that first-hand knowledge of such happenings would lead to speculations of some significance in the events that followed in my life. In fact, during most of my adult years I have often sought signs and manifestations from the past that might enable me to make wise decisions that would lead to personal happiness or, at the other extreme, to avoid damaging disaster. This has brought me to wonder if our entire life is spent in a subconscious search for that mysterious lost phase of existence.

When I was a babe in arms—what follows here of course is according to my mother's own recollections and recounted on occasion by her with delight in the presence of family or strangers alike—then it was that I was said to have rebelled against being held in arms and restrained in any manner. As a result, I always struggled free and proceeded to crawl on the church floor during my father's Sunday sermon.

While tolerated by some members of the congregation and severely criticized by others, my freedom to wander at will was undoubtedly aided and abetted by the permissiveness of my parents. My father, for his part, believed that forcibly constraining a small boy-baby was a denial of freedom of action and stiffled the growth of independence. The reason for my mother's acquiescence was not made known although it may be presumed that she was glad to be relieved of the hopeless task of trying to confine me.

It was said that my tireless crawling on hands and knees, performed in silence and without causing disconcerting sounds at the outset, took me up and down the aisles, under row after row of the straight-back pews, and even to the pulpit where my father stood while conducting the service.

My conduct was disturbing enough during a religious service, but there was another phase of my permissive wanderings under the pews that was understandably even more of an annoyance to the congregation of more than a hundred men, women, and children. After exploring the whole width and breadth of the church floor, my next objective was the tickling of the bare legs of the small girls in short dresses whose dangling feet were a tempting lure. For whatever reason, the legs of the boys were usually left untouched. And as might be expected, the ticklish little girls often giggled or shrieked so loudly that my father would have to pause in the delivery of his sermon until silence could be restored throughout the church.

After a season, there came the time when, still with no recollection of my own, my career as a crawler was abruptly ended with my advancement to the stage of a beginning toddler. Soon, with the experience then of one who had taken a few tottering steps without incident, I ventured all the way across the kitchen to the cooking stove. There, flushed with accomplishment and in a moment of eagerness, my fateful introduction to the toddling stage of life was signified by my tipping over a large pan of boiling grease at the glowing-hot iron stove. The flesh-searing liquid spilled down my chest and over my stomach with the burning of my body deep under the skin that was to leave lifelong scars and wales.

Following an extended period of surgical and medical treatment, the local doctor said to my parents, as quoted by my mother, that he had feared from the outset that I would never recover from such a damaging accident at my tender age.

"This child must have been intended by the Good Lord to live for some worthwhile purpose," the doctor had said, "because otherwise he would have been dead by now."

At this stage in life, having survived the likelihood of a fatal injury, though still without the benefit of rememberance, it would be necessary to rely completely upon hearsay in order to be confident that actually I had been born and was a native of the land. Reliance on hearsay was necessary for a long time because there was no provision in effect for recording births by the county or state.

Consequently, I was never able to obtain an official birth certificate. The lack of such a document was of no concern to me until many years later. Then it was, in order to fulfill the requirements for obtaining a passport from the Department of State for travel abroad, that I looked in all directions for possible help for my cause. The doctor who had attended my mother at my birth and later treated my burns had been dead for a number of years. All the few neighbors had died or moved to places unknown. Moreover, my parents had moved from place to place in intervals of two or three years during my youth and nobody could be found to attest to the fact that I was known to have come into the world.

Fortunately, in the end, the United States Bureau of the Census determined, after lengthy and diligent search, that I had in fact been officially enumerated in the census of 1910 with legal name, known parentage, and place and date of birth.

And so here and now it can be stated with sufficient authority that I was born on December 17, 1903, in a three-room manse in the pine-and-cotton country of the White Oak community near the village of Moreland, Coweta County, State of Georgia.

My father was Ira Sylvester Caldwell, an Associate Reformed Presbyterian minister, and my mother was Caroline Bell Caldwell, formerly a teacher of English and Latin in seminaries and colleges for girls and young women in the Carolinas and Virginia. At the time of my birth, my father was pastor of the White Oak A.R.P. Church and was paid a yearly salary of three hundred and fifty dollars. He had been born in North Carolina where his father was a cotton farmer. My mother was a native of Virginia and the daughter of a railroad telegrapher. Each of my parents had six brothers and sisters. I was the only child of my parents.

= 2 =

At the age of three, I was old enough to have my first playmate and, according to my father's wish, was permitted to play outside our house without supervision by a parent. In our rural neighborhood of widely-scattered families, both black and white, my only playmate was a chubby-faced mulatto boy of my own age whose parents were sharecroppers living in a one-room log cabin on an adjoining tenant farm.

Whatever my playmate's real name may have been, it always sounded to me like "Bisco". Even years later when I wrote about him at length in a book with the title of *In Search of Bisco*, I was still in doubt about his actual given name and had to speculate that it may have been Brisco or Frisco or perhaps derived from the cookie with the brand name of Nabisco.

During the next two years following our first meeting, Bisco and I played almost daily in summer and winter alike with only minor disruptions in friendship. When disagreements did occur, they would last only momentarily and then disappeared completely after a casual shove or nudge of the elbow by either one of us. A slight shove or nudge was the gesture that indicated all was forgiven and that no hurt feelings had been engendered.

Our favorite pastime was friendly rough-and-tumble wrestling. Our tussling usually lasted for several hours of tireless activity during the day and took place on a sandy patch of ground between our two houses in fair weather and on the sandy earth under the elevated breezeway of my house on rainy days. Often when we wrestled, cockleburrs or sawdust or weedchaff would cling to Bisco's close-cropped kinky black hair and he had a habit of calling quits long enough to brush the annoying burrs and chaff from his head with quick flailing motions of his hands as if fighting gnats and mosquitoes.

Both Bisco and I would grunt and groan with exaggerated sounds of effort while trying to get a better hold. With no rules to guide us, nevertheless first one and then the other would acknowledge defeat or claim victory. And, willingly taking turns of winning and losing as we did, at no time was there a flaring of anger to lead to painful blows and gouging. Without words spoken at the end of day, it was as if actually we had said we were pleased with our friendly wrestling and looked forward to the coming of the next day for another bout between us.

There came a time when there was a change in our routine of play, however, and this was when long before nightfall of a cold and rainy day in early autumn that Bisco began shivering and said he wanted to stop playing and

4

not wanting to leave Bisco and have to go into my house before it was dark, I followed him up the long path to his house. Once before I had followed him home and on that occasion his mother had taken me down the path to where my mother was anxiously waiting for me. This time I hoped I could stay with Bisco and not be sent home.

There were blazing pine logs in the fireplace when we got to the small cabin on the hillside and Bisco's mother took us both to the brick hearth and told us to sit there in the warmth and glow of the fire until all our shivering had stopped.

Presently, since it was soon to be Bisco's suppertime, she brought each of us a large tin cup filled with steaming-hot collard pot-likker and, to share between us, a big plate of sliced chitterling bread. When we had finished drinking the pot-likker and eating all the chitterling bread we could, Bisco's mother sat down in her rocking chair and lifted both of us to her broad lap. She was a large, wide-hipped, ample-fleshed woman with a beaming smile and glowing mulatto coloring. She usually wore a brightly-colored shawl during most of the year and her gleaming black hair was always in a long braid dangling down her back.

As she held Bisco in a tight embrace while tucking his bare feet against her stomach for warmth, with her other arm she drew me into the soft cushion of her bosom. Soon after that she began singing as though to herself while swaying slowly in her rocking chair. Drowsy in the warmth of the cabin and lulled by the soft sounds of her voice, I must have been wondering if anywhere else there could be another place as cozy and comforting as the cradle of her warm and gently heaving bosom.

Presently, in the flickering firelight, Bisco's mother left me in the rocking chair and placed him on the quilt-covered bed. He had already fallen asleep while she was undressing him for the night and that was when I began taking off my clothes so I could get under the covers with him. While I was still struggling to get undressed, there was a loud knocking on the cabin door and I recognized my father's voice when he called to me a moment later.

A shivering blast of cold night air came into the room when my father walked inside even though he had quickly closed the door behind him. His dark thick hair had been tousled in the wind and his coat collar had been turned up for protection against the coldness. He held a kerosene lantern that swung back and forth in his hand as he came across the room to me in the rocking chair.

What my father was telling me when he reached for my hand and drew

5

me to my feet was that it was late and time for me to go home. I may have thought he would scold me for being in Bisco's house without permission, as my mother had done previously, but all he said was that it was nighttime and getting colder outside and that my mother was worried about my not being at home.

Carrying me tightly in his arm and holding the swinging lantern with his other hand, he went down the long path in the darkness of the windy night with eerie shadows cast by the lantern light suddenly looming on all sides and then quickly disappearing from sight. At first, I must have been frightened by the weird display of the shadowy shapes and figures, but I tightened my arms around my father's neck and all fear quickly vanished. After that I was glad he had come for me and was taking me to the warmth of home where I would soon be in my own familiar bed.

= 3 =

When I was six years old, and certainly with little more than a vague comprehension of what was to follow, I was told by my parents that we were going to pack all our clothes into suitcases and leave the house where I had been born and go on a long trip on a train to a new home.

My immediate reaction, which became a lengthy one not easily endured, must have been one of overwhelming agony, because it brought tears to my eyes day after day. My acute unhappiness had nothing to do with the fact that I was to be taken away from my birthplace and the only home I had ever known. Instead, I was in a state of abject misery because I feared I was going to be parted forever from my friend Bisco.

Soon the day came when we were to leave on our trip by train from Georgia to South Carolina. All our clothing and other belongings had been packed into three large suitcases and two trunks while the small amount of furniture and kitchenwares had been left for the use of the next pastor and his family to live in the manse. One of the members of my father's congregation had arranged to take us in his two-horse surrey to the railroad station in Moreland a few miles away.

It was midmorning of a mild spring day with large, billowy, white clouds in the sky when we were ready to leave in the surrey. Early in the evening before, Bisco's mother had come to our house to help my mother cook a small picnic meal to take with us for eating on the train during our trip. They had prepared my father's favorite food, and which I liked more than any other. This consisted of biscuit-and-sausage-patty sandwiches and small wedge-shaped fried pies. Both apple and peach fried pies had been made and, together with the sausage sandwiches, our picnic meal was carried in a sturdy shoe box with a heavy cord to secure it.

As we drove away in the surrey with the horses trotting almost silently down the soft sand-clay road and, while our small, unpainted, plank-sided house was slowly disappearing from sight, I looked back and saw Bisco standing beside our mail box waving good-by with his hand held high above his head. As long as I could see Bisco, I waved to him. And even after we had gone around a curve of the road and he could no longer be seen, I kept on waving good-by for a while. Presently, with no tears in my eyes, all I could do was stare blankly at the roadside in my loneliness with the feeling that the sorrow of parting would never end.

My sadness was soon to vanish, however. The moment we were within sight of the Moreland railroad station and, hearing the sound of a switching engine on a sidetrack, I became so excited that all I could think about was that I was going to ride on a train to a strange place somewhere far away.

There and then I felt for the first time the call of the unknown beyond the horizon. In all my life thereafter, even though not every result came to be as joyous as the prospect had been in the beginning, a journey by train, automobile, steamship, or airplane was never to become commonplace.

On this day in the farm-country village of Moreland, where the railroad station stood gleaming in the sunlight like a small castle newly colored with bright yellow paint, the faint whistle of the train that was to carry us to Atlanta on the first part of our trip to South Carolina was heard in the distance. Just as the train came around the bend, the steam whistle of the locomotive blasting its arrival, the stationmaster pulled on the long chain of the red-painted semaphore board high above the station to signal the engineer to stop for passengers. The thundering monster, looming bigger and more threatening each moment, looked as if it would sweep us from the earth.

Suddenly, with the screeching of brakes and a loud hissing of steam, the monstrous engine trailing a mail-express-baggage car, a coach for black passengers, and a similar coach for white people came to a jarring stop at the station platform. Nobody left the train, but several mail sacks and express packages were unloaded.

As my parents and I hurried from the waiting room to board the train, I

7

could see our three suitcases and two trunks being loaded on the baggage car. While we were still in the aisle of the passenger coach, the train started with a violent jerk at the same time that the steam whistle blew several times in quick succession.

We stayed in the Atlanta railroad station for almost six hours waiting for the train that would take us to Greenville, South Carolina. The waiting-room seats were hard wooden benches and for row after row they looked like the pews in the White Oak Church. While we waited through the afternoon, my father bought bottles of milk and a large sack of red apples for us so we could save our biscuit-and-sausage sandwiches and fried fruit pies for our supper on the train to Greenville.

Our train left at dusk while the lights of the city began twinkling on both sides of the passenger coach. The train ran faster and faster as it left the city and the sound of the *click-clacking* of the wheels on the rail joints was much louder than had been made by the short three-car train from Moreland to Atlanta. The steam whistle on our train of many cars was much louder than the earlier one and it was blown longer and more often at road crossings as we passed through numerous small towns in the night.

I could not stay awake very long after eating so much for supper and I soon went to sleep on the prickly red-plush seat. During the night, I woke up only a few times when the screaming whistle of the engine filled the coach with its sounds of urgent warning.

It was barely in the light of dawn when we arrived in Greenville and went into the station waiting room to stay until our train to Prosperity, South Carolina, was ready to leave at eight o'clock that morning.

I remember well hearing my father say there would not be a barbershop open nearly in time for him to get a shave and that he wished he would not have to arrive as the new pastor of the church in Prosperity looking like Bluebeard. My mother made light of his appearance by saying he could not make himself any more handsome than he was by patronizing a barbershop in Greenville or anywhere else. My father smiled at my mother but said nothing in reply.

Chapter Two

OUR HOME IN PROSPERITY WAS a dilapidated, unpainted, wooden structure with a slanting hallway and narrow porches front and rear. It had been the unoccupied manse of the local A.R.P. Church for several years and only a few days before our arrival had a section of the leaky roof been reshingled and several broken window panes replaced. There was a brick chimney with a fireplace to heat one of the four rooms and a crumbling plaster flue for the kitchen stove.

At first sight, the house in Prosperity was similar to the manse that had been our home in the White Oak community near Moreland. After a while, though, in some manner it did appear to be different. And that may have been because it was situated on a large lot about two acres in size with a sodded lawn in front and an even larger area devoted to a vegetable garden and peach orchard behind the house.

The old house had been built facing the unpaved street—actually a dirt road—midway between the church and the cemetery. It was a short distance from the railroad station and at least a half-mile from the shantytown on the other side of the railroad tracks where the black people were required to live. Our outhouse was a two-seat privy with a rusty tin roof and it had been built at the farthest reach of the garden. Just as it had been in the Georgia countryside, there was no running water, no electricity, and no other utility in the town of more than three hundred persons.

Soon after we had moved into the manse, in what she later called an unguarded moment, my mother made a bold remark in the presence of a female member of the congregation concerning the small space and cramped living conditions in the house and stressed the fact that I had to sleep on a folding cot in my father's study. In response to my mother's forthright comment, she was told that a good Christian minister and his wife should use restraint in their private lives and not let themselves become burdened with a large family.

As if in answer to a prayer, although our lives were endangered, in the middle of the night between one and two o'clock, and about a month after our arrival in town, the manse burst into flames. The building burned to the ground so quickly that by the time the half-dozen members of the Prosperity volunteer fire department could assemble and get there with their hose and water wagon they could do no more than wet down the embers to prevent sparks from setting one of the nearby houses on fire.

Fortunately, my father had been awakened by the glare of the flames and the three of us were able to escape through the front door. The rear part of the building was the first to burn, evidently having been set on fire when sparks from the kitchen stove smoldered in the crumbling plaster of the defective flue. All that was saved other than the night clothes we wore were my father's leather suitcase and my mother's gold watch. Even though we might have lost our lives in the fire, it did result in an almost immediate response to my mother's previous complaint about the three of us having to live in a one-bedroom house.

As was the custom at that time, if a farmer's barn burned down, dozens of relatives, neighbors, and friends for miles around would arrange among themselves to gather at the farm site at daybreak of a designated day. On such an occasion, with donations of lumber and nails and using their own saws, hammers, and other carpentry tools, and while wives and daughters cooked and served ham and potatoes from morning to night, the group of men would often in a single day's time complete a barn-raising. With this as a guide, within a week's time the church members had organized a similar project and called it a manse-raising.

There was no possibility of the manse-raising being completed in one day or even in two or three days since constructing walls and closets and ceilings required more than ordinary workmanship. More than that, the summer rainy season had started and there were days when no work could be done. Then in addition to wet weather, and due mainly to sprained backs caused by over-exertion, hammer-smashed thumbs, and similar on-site mishaps, there was a degree of absenteeism that hindered progress. However, even with delays, some necessary and others inexcusable, the building was finished in less than two weeks.

In the meantime, donated furniture and kitchenwares had been assembled. And on the final day of construction the chairs, beds, tables, and other furnishings were placed in the house for our use.

My parents and I had been rooming and boarding in the home of an elderly widow a few blocks away and we were able to move into our newly built home less than a month after the fire.

The house contained six rooms instead of four, much to my mother's satisfaction, and I had a room of my own. As for my father, after viewing the sap oozing from the unseasoned plank ceilings on the hot July afternoon, he said he wanted us to be on guard against the possibility that globules of pitch pine and resin would drop on our food at the dining table and at night always remember to cover our eyes in some manner before going to sleep at bedtime. My mother's only comment aside from approving of the larger size of our new home was that never again did she want to collect material objects that she might grow fond of and risk the heartbreak of another consuming fire.

$$= 2 =$$

By the time I was eight years old, I still had not attended school, public or private, and for many years thereafter it was my mother's contention that she was a better qualified and more concerned teacher for me than anyone else would be.

Whether or not my mother could have been cited for violating compulsory education laws was a matter that would not have given her the slightest worry for a single moment. Whenever I begged my parents for permission to attend the Prosperity public school, saying that I wanted to go where I would be in the company of other children, my mother always remained unmoved by my pleas. At a time like that, my father would go into a silent period as if to indicate that the decision had been made and I was expected to abide by it.

Undoubtedly, my mother did possess superior qualifications as a teacher and she had confidence in her ability to be an instructor for a person of any age. This was made evident by the numerous requests she received from parents and teachers to tutor high school students whose failing grades would otherwise prevent advancement or graduation.

As for my schooling at home, I endured the discipline of reading, writing, and arithmetic as best I could while always yearning for the companionship of boys and girls on the public school playground at recess. My solitary confinement as a home-taught student, however, was usually made bearable when routine study was put aside and my mother related an interesting incident in her life or recounted a fascinating storybook tale.

I had not forgotten hearing my father compare his unshaven appearance with that of Bluebeard and several times I told my mother I wanted to hear the story of the man with a beard so intensely black that it must have looked blue-black in color. I was always told that I would have a better understanding and appreciation of the legend if I waited until I was older and then read it myself in a book.

Being kept out of public school did not deprive me of having a playmate. A boy of my own age, who had curly yellow hair and whose name was S.J. Black, lived in a big white house only a block beyond our garden and peach orchard. When S.J. and I met for the first time, we began playing together by shooting marbles in my back yard. Later, we often spent considerable time batting and catching a baseball in his back yard.

Whenever we were playing at his house or mine, it was not easy to keep our clothes from becoming soiled. S.J.'s mother, like mine, was determined that he would be dressed at all times according to her strict dictates and I had seen her switch him with a small cane when he went home with specks of dirt on his clothes. My own mother did not hesitate to scold me for mischievous behavior but she never switched me.

There were several times when S.J. told me that he might run away from home if he had to keep on wearing the kind of clothes he disliked so much. Always appearing to be dressed for Sunday school or somebody's birthday party, what he wore was a blue serge jacket with short pants buckled above his knees. And with that he was always dressed in a white shirt, calf-length red stockings, and shiny-black patent-leather buckled slippers. He said his mother wanted him to be dressed in red, white, and blue like a patriotic American boy.

I could understand and sympathize with S.J.'s dislike for the kind of clothing his mother forced him to wear because my own situation was not much different. I had a similar attitude about the kind of clothing I was forced to wear, but I did not have any thoughts about running away from home. I may have been too fearful to go away alone and no doubt relied upon the hope that the time would soon come when I could wear ordinary clothing.

My mother had decided shortly after our coming to Prosperity that not only was I to be taught at home by her instead of being sent to public school but also, in order that utmost individuality could be attained, that she would design wearing apparel for me that would be unlike any of the commonplace styles of clothing worn by boys of my age. The outfit she created for me could best be called a Russian blouse with short pants.

The clothing I wore consisted of a white linen blouse or jacket that was so long it hung halfway to my knees and with that were knee-length, unbuckled pants of the same material. There was no necktie to be worn with the costume, but there was a wide, black, patent-leather belt with a brass buckle and that drooped downward over my stomach as far as my crotch. For a long time, there was no other style of clothing for me to wear and, since I was required to dress in clean garments every morning, surely there must have been a dozen or more of the Russian blouse and short pants costumes in existence.

Whatever may have been my father's thoughts and feelings during my ordeal of being forced to wear clothing of such extraordinary design, I could not remember hearing him make any comment about it in my presence. I did have the impression, though, that when he gazed at me wonderingly on several occasions he was perturbed not only about my unmanly clothing but also was concerned about the fact that my long reddish hair had not been cut in several years and hung in curls to my shoulders. In a later era, I probably would have been called a youthful hippie.

Long before another birthday, as it came to be, an extreme change in my life was to take place.

My mother's elder sister, who was a registered nurse, came to Prosperity from Richmond to visit us for a week during her vacation. Aunt Emma, accustomed to having absolute authority as supervisor in a hospital, did not hesitate to indicate with a determined shaking of her head and a pronounced frown the moment she saw me for the first time that she strongly disapproved of my appearance. Not a word about her unfavorable appraisal of me was uttered while I was present, but soon after her arrival from Richmond she and my father left the house and went for a long walk in the direction of the cemetery.

The next morning immediately after breakfast, and with careful procedure,

13

Aunt Emma opened her nurse's satchel and urged my mother to take a pill that would prevent her from suffering tension that might result from the excitement of their reunion after having been apart for several years. At first, my mother protested that she felt comfortably normal and needed no medication of any kind. In the end, though, she was persuaded to swallow the pill.

No more than a quarter of an hour later, saying she wanted to rest for a while, my mother went to her room to lie down. Soon after that, Aunt Emma and my father, after determining that my mother was breathing normally and could be left in the house alone, took me on the run downtown to the barbershop where the barber was waiting by prearrangement to cut off my long curly hair.

Very few words were spoken by anybody during the time the barber was at work. I sat on a stiff board atop the barberchair and watched the black porter sweep large bunches and strands of my hair from the floor into a dust pan and then dump it all into a large wastebasket with other hair cuttings.

On our way home from the barbershop, I had a glimpse of my strange-looking self in a store window and I wondered what my mother would say when she saw that I no longer had the long curls she had so often combed and brushed with expressions of pleasure. As for myself, I felt like a different person—so different that I wondered if I had mysteriously passed from one life and had entered another.

With each hand gripped tightly by Aunt Emma and my father, I was hurriedly taken into a merchandise store near the barbershop. After a pair of blue overalls and a bright yellow shirt had been selected, my father took me into a closet where my Russian blouse and short pants were replaced by the long overalls and yellow shirt.

It was almost noon when my mother woke up and asked for a drink of water. When I was taken into the room, the full glass of water fell on the bed from her hand and she cried out in a voice of anguish and despair as she stared at me.

"Who is that?" she said slowly after a moment. "What's he doing here? Get him out of this house! Where's Erskine?"

I could see Aunt Emma standing in the doorway with her nurse's satchel and watching my mother alertly.

"Carrie, that is Erskine," my father told her. "Don't be upset. Everything's going to be all right now."

Holding her hand tightly, he tried to calm her distress with soothing words while she continued to look at me with an unbelieving stare.

14

Presently, my father motioned for me to come closer to the side of the bed.

"Don't you come near me!" my mother said, thrusting the palms of her hands toward me. "Who cut off your hair? Who did it? Where are all those beautiful curls?"

Aunt Emma opened her satchel and took another pill to administer to my mother. After a few moments, completely overcome with tears, and with nothing more said, my mother meekly swallowed the pill with some of the water handed to her by my father. Gulping down a sob and closing her eyes to avoid the sight of me, she then slowly laid her head upon the pillow.

= 3 =

Several weeks after Aunt Emma had returned to Richmond, having given me a pair of gray corduroy knickerbockers that were long enough to be worn buckled below the knees, my father left on the train to attend a conference for several days at a church in Alabama. In his absence, not a word was said by my mother about my short hair and the overalls or knickerbockers I wore continuously.

At a later time, I decided she had pointedly avoided making any mention of hair or clothing because she realized that she had made a mistake in the beginning and that, for my own well-being, I should no longer be subjected to what Aunt Emma had called harmful and outlandish demands.

Although I had the good fortune to be relieved of the indignity of being compelled to wear the Russian blouse costume in public, as well as having to endure the taunting remarks of other children, my playmate S.J. Black was still being compelled by his mother to continue wearing a white shirt, a blue serge suit, and red stockings.

There had been several times when S.J. had come to my house to play and had begged me to let him take off his blue serge suit for a little while and wear a pair of my overalls and a yellow or blue shirt. When he did that, he took off his red stockings, too, and went barefooted until he had to go home. Neither his mother nor my mother ever discovered what was taking place and he always went home in a happy mood after changing from my overalls back to his required clothing.

It was during one of our afternoons of play that S.J. and I were told by two high school boys in the street in front of my house that we were too young to look at a photograph we begged to see. The two older boys were among several who were being tutored in English and mathematics by my mother and they came to our house during the week for an hour at a time. The two boys with the photograph, finally relented and said we could have one quick look at the picture if we promised never to tell anybody about it.

After promises were made, what we were permitted to see was the camera picture of a group of five high school boys standing on the bank of a creek with each of them holding a hand around his erected penis. The naked boys, all of them grinning pridefully, were members of a masturbation club that met from time to time to engage in an ejaculation contest.

As I was to find out later, the boy who could ejaculate the greatest distance with his penis was declared the winner of that day's contest and named president of the masturbation club until the next contest. At the time, I saw nothing unusual about the photograph other than that the naked boys were much more physically developed than I was at my age.

A few days later when I went to S.J.'s house to play in his back yard, he said he had not told his mother about the photograph we had seen in front of my house, because of the promise we had made, and neither had I told my mother or father. However, S.J. said he had told another playmate about the picture with the understanding that it would be kept a secret.

Whether the secret was kept or not, the other boy, who was a few years older than I, told S.J. that he knew all about the masturbation club and wanted to join it himself as soon as the members thought he was old enough to be one of them. He knew enough already to be able to describe to S.J. how the club members achieved erections for their ejaculation contests.

S.J. and I talked about all the reasons we could think of as to why a penis would become as enlarged as the ones we had seen in the photograph. After a while, S.J. said we could go to the outhouse in his back yard and try to find out more about what we wanted to know. When we went into the privy, and with pants unbuttoned and falling below our knees, we stood there looking at each other's penis and wondering what there was to be learned.

Suddenly, with no warning whatsoever, the privy door was thrown open and there stood S.J.'s mother staring at us in our almost complete nakedness with an expression of total shock on her face. With mouth agape and panting breathlessly, she leaned against the doorpost for support.

Presently, saying something indistinctly in a low tone of voice, she began looking back and forth from one of us to the other. Pointing directly at me in an accusing manner, she next was shaking her head with a threatening frown on her face. During all that time, S.J. and I were trying to pull up our pants and button them with trembling fingers.

Reaching forward, S.J.'s mother grasped him by his neck and jerked him roughly through the privy doorway. As I followed them outside, she suddenly turned and slapped my face with a stinging blow of her hand. As I tried to move backward and beyond her reach, she was ordering me never to come to play with S.J. again.

"You nasty boy!" she said, her voice rising shrilly. "Don't you dare ever set foot on this place again! You hear me! And I don't want you ever to speak to S.J. again, either. Now go home and stay there—you nasty thing!"

Before I would be slapped again, I turned and ran as fast as I could all the way home. When I got there, I did not say a word about what had happened while visiting S.J. Black and neither did I say anything about the photograph I had seen. I did not mention the picture of the naked boys because I was so afraid that my parents would become angry and upset and forbid me to play with S.J. or any of the other boys in the neighborhood.

Chapter Three

WE HAD LIVED IN PROSPERITY, South Carolina, for almost two years when my father was appointed secretary of the Board of Home Missions of the Associate Reformed Presbyterian Church.

The unexpected appointment was a pleasing event in my father's life because it offered frequent changes of pastorates and entailed extensive travel throughout the South. As I once overheard my mother say to him in a bantering moment—and which I always thought was an accurate description of my father—that if he had not chosen to be a minister he probably would have been just as happy and certainly more prosperous as a traveling salesman with a trunk full of sample shoes.

Due to an increase in salary, my father had been able to buy a new Model-T Ford convertible roadster—which like any automobile early in the century was a curiosity—and it was used for local travel and short trips within the state. We took longer trips on the train to such faraway destinations as Tampa, Florida, and Fayetteville, Arkansas.

As Home Missions secretary, his principal duty in the beginning was to reorganize financially troubled churches so that a pastor's salary could be provided. For that to be accomplished it was usually necessary to pacify quarreling factions within a congregation by finding ways to end disruptive feuds that often had divided family members to the extent that they were sitting on opposite sides of the aisle in the church and not speaking to each other.

These troublesome situations within a congregation usually resulted from such quixotic dissensions among members as to whether the church floor ought to remain bare for stomping feet or be carpeted, whether hymns should replace psalms, whether a piano should be substituted for the organ, or whether the elderly Negro sexton would be permitted to sit in the warmth of the auditorium during services in cold weather. It was not unusual for a newly ordained young minister to refuse to accept a call to become pastor of a congregation in turmoil until my father was able to find a way to bring about a change among feuding members and harmony was restored.

After Prosperity, our next place of residence for a year was at Timber Ridge, Virginia. Unlike the implication of its name, Timber Ridge was not a moonshiner's outpost in the Blue Ridge Mountains. Instead, it was a long-settled and respectable countryside community in the green hills and among the apple orchards of the Shenandoah Valley midway between the cities of Lexington and Staunton.

And, disappointed and depressed, for the first time in life I had no playmates.

In keeping with my mother's inflexible plan for my early training and education, she continued to instruct me at home in studies for my age instead of letting me attend the local school a quarter of a mile in walking distance from where we lived. As I had done before in South Carolina, I begged to no avail to go to public school in Virginia as all the other children of my age were permitted to do.

Sympathetic she was, and tenderly so, but nevertheless my mother remained unyielding in her decision that at home with her help I would have the benefit of being trained for life as an individual and not as a creature of uniformity. As explained to me, she wanted me to have better than ordinary advantages so that I would not be handicapped by the lack of vision and ambition. Over and over, she would say that anybody with two hands could dig ditches or wash dishes but only a person with a well-trained and discriminating mind is capable of directing his life to the best advantage.

Having no playmates and seeking something interesting to do when not confined at home by my studies, I found that a granite quarry not far from our house was the most engaging place in the entire neighborhood for observing any kind of activity. Thereafter, and almost daily for two or three hours at a time, I went to the quarry to sit on the edge of the open pit and watch the workmen drill and blast the blue-green rock below.

After several weeks, having been kept away only on rainy days, my visits to the quarry came to an abrupt end when two of the workmen who had been tamping dynamite into one of the deep drillings were blown to death accidently with a deafening blast while I was watching them at work. When I ran home to tell what had happened and how close to me a shoeless foot had fallen, I was told that it would be too dangerous for me ever to go back to the quarry again.

Being kept out of public school and having no playmates had been enough of a limitation of normal activity to bring about a personal calamity in the judgment of a young boy and then, in addition, being forbidden to go to the quarry brought about a deluge of overwhelming misery in my life.

When I could no longer keep from expressing my unhappiness and made my feelings known, my parents responded by saying they would try to find a way to provide recompense for some of the things I had been denied.

A few days later I was told that it had been arranged for me to go away for a week to visit my maternal grandmother in nearby Staunton. Every vestige of unhappiness and discontent vanished immediately. I had visited my grandmother in Staunton once before and I was elated by the prospect of going to stay again in her small white-painted cottage on a steep hillside street in the city.

When I arrived in Staunton, I soon found out that the boy of my own age with whom I had played during my previous visit still lived across the street directly in front of my grandmother's house. We met again and began playing that same afternoon at a vacant lot at the lower end of the block. It had been a warm summer day and long before nightfall my playmate's mother called him home for supper. I was left alone and I stayed to play longer at the vacant lot while waiting for my grandmother to call me.

I had been alone for only a short time when I looked up and saw a chubby man with tousled dark hair smiling down at me with a friendly nodding of his head. He said I could call him Benjy and asked me if I would like to see his new bicycle with a loud two-tone bell clamped to the handlebar. My grandmother had forbidden me to go more than a block away without permission and, since Benjy said he lived only as far as the upper end of the block, I did not think I was being disobedient when I went up the alley with him.

The bicycle was in an enclosed shed and its red color gleamed brightly in the lingering twilight. While I was admiring the bike, Benjy said I could go closer and ring the two-tone bell on the handlebar as much as I wished.

After ringing the bell several times, I turned around and saw Benjy standing there completely naked. He was holding his erected penis just the same way I remembered seeing how the five members of the masturbation club in South Carolina had posed for their photograph.

With his other hand, Benjy gripped my arm and pulled me across the shed to a blanket-covered bench. He sat down and, while twisting my arm painfully until I was forced to my knees, he said all he wanted me to do was play with him for a little while and then I could go home. When I made no move to obey him, he said he would give me a present if I promised never to tell anybody about being with him in the shed.

As if believing I would do as he demanded, he smiled and released the tight grip on my arm. When that happened, I sprang to my feet and reached the doorway before Benjy could get up from the bench and catch me. After I had reached the outside of the shed, and still hearing him yelling for me to come back, I ran as fast as I could down the dark alley.

I did not stop running until I was safely inside the brightly lighted kitchen of my grandmother's house. My grandmother, standing at the huge coal-burning range while cooking supper, looked at me in surprise when I burst into the room and slammed the door shut behind me.

When I was asked what had happened that made me run so hard that I was panting for breath, I said that I had been frightened in the dark. My grandmother put her arms around me, hugging me comfortingly until I stopped gasping for breath. After that, she told me that darkness was harmless and would not hurt anybody and that it was people who hurt other people.

= 2 =

In midyear 1912, near the end of which I was to be nine years old, we moved again and this time to Charlotte, North Carolina.

We first lived in one large room with billowing white lace curtains at a boardinghouse only a few blocks from the downtown business district and near a United States mint. Later we moved far away to the end of a streetcar line and there, where I had a room of my own, we lived in a rented row-house in a new housing development that covered an entire block.

Soon after arriving in Charlotte I was hired to work at a store for the first time in my life. That happened one afternoon when I was riding my bicycle on Trade Street and looking in the gutters for tin foil in discarded cigarette packs. The tin foil, which was similar to aluminum, could be rolled into the shape of a croquet ball and sold to a scrap-metal dealer for as much as ten cents.

I had stopped in front of a shoestore and Mr. Goldstein, whose name was lettered on the store window, asked me if I would like to go to work for him delivering shoes. I was to work every afternoon except Sunday and the pay would be two dollars a week. I agreed to the terms at once and was given directions for the delivery of the first pair and instructed to collect two dollars or bring the shoes back to the store.

All went well with the job for the next few days and at the end of the week I was eager to collect the first pay I had earned as a worker in the business world. But first, early Saturday afternoon, I was given two pairs of shoes in different sizes to be delivered to a woman who had agreed to return one pair and keep the best fitting pair for which two dollars would be given me to take to Mr. Goldstein.

I arrived with the shoes at the delivery address and found it to be a two-room shack near the city dump and surrounded by tall weeds and pools of stagnant water. The dilapidated shack looked as if it had been nailed together with tar-paper and other salvaged building materials from the dump.

The woman who had ordered the shoes lived there with her twin sons whose age was approximately the same as mine. While one boy was trying on shoes, the other twin and I went to the rear of the house to look at their playthings.

When I returned to the front door, I was given two dollars to pay for one pair of shoes and then handed the other pair to take back to the shoestore. The boy I had been with at the rear of the house looked enviously at the new shoes his brother was wearing and he asked me if he could try on the other pair. When he put on the shoes, the size was slightly too large for him but he was smiling through tears as he looked down at the shiny new shoes.

As I started back to the shoestore on my bicycle soon after that, I had two dollars for Mr. Goldstein but had left both pairs of shoes for the two boys to wear.

While trying to explain to Mr. Goldstein what had happened, he began waving his hands impatiently and said he had lived a long life and still could not understand how Christians and gentiles ever made a living in business and kept from going bankrupt. He told me that Jewish people were just as kind-hearted and sentimental as gentiles, but that Jews had learned from the past to earn and accumulate money first and then to contribute some of it to a worthy cause. He said he hoped I would keep that principle in mind if I expected to make a living in the world and keep out of bankruptcy courts.

It was closing time for the store and Mr. Goldstein turned off the lights. Just before locking the door, he said he owed me two dollars for a week's work, that I owed him two dollars for the pair of shoes I had given away, and consequently it would be a fair settlement for one debt to cancel the other.

After locking the door, he took a dollar from his pocket and handed it to me. First he said he did not know what had come over him and then he said he would feel a lot better if he contributed his share of the two dollars so that both boys would have shoes. Turning away then, he went slowly down the street talking aloud to himself.

That was the last time I saw Mr. Goldstein. On the following Monday, my parents and I moved from the boardinghouse to our new home in one of the row houses at the end of the streetcar line near the city limits. Some of the buildings were still under construction and, since only a few families were living there then, I could not find any boys of my age to be playmates.

However, there was a brown-haired girl living in one of the completed houses and she was only a year older than I and we were about the same height. I never knew her complete name but she said her first name was Doris. We soon found a favorite place to play in one of the unfinished buildings. Going there in late afternoon after the carpenters had finished work for the day, we would find piles of sawdust on the floor and curly wood shavings and a scattering of odd-shaped timber and shiny new nails of many sizes.

One afternoon while we were at play as usual, Doris said she wanted to play doctor-and-nurse. That was to be a new experience for me, never having played with a girl before, and I had no knowledge of the game and how it was to be played.

Doris was patient and helpful, though, carefully instructing me how to take the part of the doctor, and then she proceeded to take off the pink bloomers she wore under her dress. When I was slow to learn what to do as the doctor, Doris finally became impatient and said she would show me how to be the doctor and that I would be the nurse. Then she pulled down my pants and tossed them aside as quickly as she had taken off her pink bloomers.

It was only a few moments later when Doris' mother discovered us with a piercing shriek. The next thing to happen was when the angry woman picked up a small board from the floor and, with another loud yell, swatted me on the rump with a stinging blow before I could get out of her reach.

During all that time, not a word had been spoken and all I wanted to do was to get home as fast as I could. I grabbed my pants from the floor, shaking them loose from Doris' pink bloomers, and did not wait to put them on.

24

When I reached the doorway and looked back for an instant, I saw Doris putting on her bloomers. At the same time, her mother was lovingly stroking her long brown hair while glaring angrily at me.

= 3 =

Bradley, South Carolina, was a quiet little town in the red-clay farm lands of the western part of the state not far from the Savannah River. The population of slightly more than three hundred persons was divided almost equally between the whites and the blacks. It was said that a large family of Cherokee Indians lived in the swamp near the river but nobody would say he had actually seen even one of them.

There were two churches in Bradley for white people, the A.R.P. and the Baptist, and for the black people there was the Mt. Zion African Gospel Church. On the shady side of the unpaved main street facing the small yellow railway station there were two general merchandise stores, two grocery stores, and a farm and feed supply warehouse. Other than the stores, there was a cotton gin, a small brick bank, and an even smaller unpainted wooden structure housing the United States Post Office. Most of the other buildings in town, other than dwellings, were stables and cow sheds and chicken houses.

As for the dwellings, some painted and others unpainted, they were the bungalows and one-story homes of farmers and store owners and the few other businessmen in town. All the black people in Bradley lived, as required by custom, in plank or log cabins of one or two rooms in the Negro Quarter behind the cotton gin. Actually, for the most part, instead of being true black the Negroes were mulatto in color and often some of the children were lighter in color than their parents. Usually the maids and nurses employed by white families were quadroons or octoroons and the lightest in color of all.

There was little that a boy of my age could find to do in a place like Bradley and I soon became restless and depressed by the lack of activity. All the other children in town were at school from early morning until late afternoon. There was no park or playground where children could gather after school and on weekends. And on rainy days when I could not leave the house I became increasingly moody and, according to my parents, an irrational and irritating chronic complainer.

It soon became a habit of mine to go down the street to the yellow station in the middle of town to watch the three-car passenger trains on the Charleston and Western Carolina Railway arrive four times a day. Two trains daily traveled between Greenwood and Augusta in each direction north and south with a loud-whistling little steam engine coupled to the usual mail-express-baggage car and behind that was a separate coach for whites and another for blacks only.

Once a month shipments of gallon jugs of Tennessee and Kentucky bourbon arrived by express on southbound trains and were delivered to waiting customers who had obtained licenses to purchase whisky for personal use under the state's gallon-a-month law. The lure of the smoke-belching C. & W. C. trains, as fascinating as whistle-blowing steam engines never failed to be, was not to last very long when the monthly allotments of jugged whisky were so far apart. I had need of more interesting activity than that.

I was soon to discover that once a week I could have something interesting to do the whole day long. This was when I began ordering by mail five-cent packages of laundry blueing powder which I could sell to colored wash-women in the Quarter behind the cotton gin for ten cents each. After a few weeks I had a well-established route and was being welcomed with friendly waving of hands as I arrived with my laundry blueing to sell five cents cheaper than it could be bought in the local stores.

"Here comes Mr. Blueing Man!" was one of the frequent greetings I heard in the Quarter.

"I sure like your fine blueing," one of the washwomen would always say. "It always makes white look whiter than white."

I found out that Monday was the best day for my blueing route since it was the customary wash day in the Quarter. Later I selected Friday as being the best time for the delivery of *Grit*, the national weekly newspaper, to the twenty-two subscribers on my route since that was the day when my bundle of *Grit* arrived on the early morning train from Greenwood.

On one of the other days of the week, usually Wednesday, I collected old automobile tires and tubes and anything else made of rubber that I could find. Each collection was put into a burlap sack and shipped by express collect to a scrap dealer in Columbia. For this, sometimes I received as much as fifty cents a shipment. However, once to my great delight I received an even dollar from the dealer for a larger than ordinary shipment.

Eventually, following many weeks of prosperous business dealings, the market for laundry blueing became oversold, collecting money owed me for the delivery of *Grit* became too difficult, and I concluded that it was almost impossible to find another pound of old rubber anywhere in the whole town of Bradley.

While engaged in my various enterprises, I had called many times for mail and had often bought stamps at the post office. With that much experience in my favor, I was able to persuade the postmaster to let me help him with the sorting of mail and placing letters in the proper post-office boxes for patrons. In time, I became so proficient in the task of sorting mail, as well as selling and canceling stamps, that the genial postmaster was able to spend more time playing checkers at the nearby grocery store.

Engaged as I was in my new activity, I was fully occupied every day except Sunday for several weeks. In the end, however, my apprenticeship-without-pay as a postal-service clerk was abruptly terminated when a tall man with heavy black eyebrows who said he was a postal inspector from Washington came into the shanty-size post office one afternoon while the postmaster was at the grocery store playing checkers.

The stern-mannered inspector stared at me through the narrow wicket between the rows of mailboxes for a long time before gruffly ordering me to open the door to the mailroom. As soon as he entered, he told me to state my name and my age and the reason for my being there.

After several moments of severe questioning, the inspector ordered me to leave the post office premises with the command never again to enter the building and touch United States mail. Within a week, sad to say, the postmaster was relieved of his duties and a stranger arrived in town to take his place.

Chapter Four

WHEN MY THIRTEENTH BIRTHDAY came upon me, suddenly I was tall and lanky and realized that I was exceedingly awkward. After a lengthy pleasant and carefree childhood, it was embarrassing to know that without the slightest forewarning I had become an overgrown adolescent with no more than a minute comprehension of my place in life. For a long time, I was conscious of a desire to discover what my fate in life might possibly be but having no idea what direction to take in search of it.

My parents and I were living in a farming community near the small town of Atoka, Tennessee, which was not far from the Mississippi River and about thirty miles north of Memphis. My peripatetic father, his zest for life unabated, had become temporary pastor of the Salem A.R.P. Church and our home consisted of several rented rooms on the second floor of an unpainted farm house near the church building and the local public school.

In the late spring of 1917, following the entry of the United States into World War I, a YMCA executive secretary visited my father while on a fund-raising tour to solicit contributions for wartime YMCA activities at army posts. When I was brought into the secretary's presence, there were brief comments having to do with patriotism in time of war. Presently the secretary stated that he needed a driver for the YMCA Ford automobile at the Millington Army

Base near Memphis which then was a training field for aircraft pilots and gunners.

With patriotism in ascent, my parents, perhaps with some misgiving, finally consented to my enlistment in the YMCA's noble cause and by the end of that same day I was on my way with the pleasant-tempered executive secretary to the YMCA hut at Millington. Before leaving home, I had been informed that it was a military requirement that khaki clothing be worn on the base at all times. And so consequently I was able to conform to regulations by wearing parts of my Boy Scout uniform and buying other items at the post exchange with all military insignia removed.

As I was soon to find out, my only duty as the driver of the YMCA car was to be on call and readily available twenty-four hours a day. In the hut, I had the use of a small cot-size bedroom which originally had been a windowless janitor's closet. All my meals were paid for me by the YMCA at one of the enlisted men's mess halls. And my salary amounted to a dollar a day, paid weekly, and which was sufficient to cover costs of several pint bottles of milk and candy bars by the handful every day at the post exchange.

On Friday afternoon of my first week at Millington, I had been called upon to take the executive secretary to Memphis on leave for a few days and instructed to return for him the following Sunday night. He had taken a small suitcase and a large camera with him to the Peabody Hotel.

In time to follow, a trip to Memphis became a routine assignment as various YMCA staff members left the post on weekend leave. And always without fail, the destination would be the Peabody Hotel. The Peabody was a large, new, luxurious hotel with several ducks swimming in the pool at the base of the lobby fountain and in size and reputation it was also the city's paramount landmark. It was widely known at the time, too, for being an ideal gathering place for informal interviews involving receptive young women and inquiring men of all ages.

I would not have become so well acquainted with the Peabody Hotel at my youthful age if I had not been directed on one occasion to spend the night there. This event was arranged for the convenience and at the expense of one of the younger members of the YMCA staff. This particular secretary had not received leave of absence but nevertheless had had an overwhelming desire to go to Memphis for the night regardless of consequences. I was told before we left Millington not to let anybody know I was going on an unauthorized trip overnight and I was asked to promise never to mention the matter to anyone in the future.

After arriving in Memphis that evening and about an hour before midnight I was walking down the hallway to my room in the hotel when I came face-to-face with a young girl who appeared to be not much older than I. She was dark-haired and girlishly slender and she was wearing high-heeled slippers that made her look much taller than she actually could be.

The girl and I talked hesitantly about some trivial matter for several minutes and then I, feeling uncomfortable in the engaging presence of the strange girl, began backing down the hall toward my room. She followed me step by step and as soon as I unlocked the door, she pushed it open and was the first to enter.

The girl with the becoming smile said I could call her Susie and that she had arranged to have an all-night date with a man who claimed to be a staff member of the YMCA at Millington Army Base. Saying she had already been with him for more than an hour, and had promised to go back to his room at midnight, Susie began pouting with a displeased tossing of her head. Presently, in a manner of youthful complaint, she said he was the kind of man who wanted to talk about things she did not understand and were of no interest to her.

After a while, Susie proposed that if I would leave my door unlocked she would come back and spend the remainder of the night with me as soon as the YMCA secretary went to sleep. I agreed to leave the door unlocked when she left the room and I was soon too sleepy to stay awake any longer.

When I woke up early the next morning, Susie was sleeping soundly beside me in the bed. I got up and dressed as quickly and as quietly as I could and then tiptoed from the room without waking her.

On our way back to the YMCA hut at Millington, very few words were spoken. The young secretary did urge me several times to drive faster so he could get to his desk before the chief or anybody else on the staff might suspect that he had been away from the hut during the night on unauthorized leave.

Just before we got out of the car at the hut, the secretary nudged me with his elbow while a friendly grin was spreading over his face. Then he said that in appreciation for my having taken him to Memphis for the night he wanted to tell me something for my own good and which he had learned by bitter experience. What he told me then was that there were women in the world who would promise anything in order to gain what they wanted and then walk out and leave a man hanging high and dry like an old sock on a clothesline with the breeze blowing through big holes in toe and heel.

It never became known to the executive secretary that I had taken the young man to Memphis to spend the night and consequently neither of us received reprimands or threats of dismissals. However, I was not so fortunate following one of my trips taken a few weeks later to Memphis and the Peabody Hotel.

On that particular occasion, I was taking another young member of the YMCA staff to Memphis for his authorized weekend leave. After driving away from the hut and passing through the sentry gate, I was told to stop the car when we had gone about fifty yards from the base.

At the place where we stopped by the roadside there were several hand-waving young mulatto girls dressed in bright-colored clothing and wearing flashy beads and bracelets. It was not an unusual scene. Day and night, week after week, there were always a few of them at the roadside trying to attract the attention of airmen leaving the base on their way to Memphis.

My passenger knew two of the girls by name and they promptly came to the car when he called to them. Following a brief conversation, the girls opened the rear door of the sedan and rode with us, with much laughter and giggling, all the way to Memphis. We reached the Peabody Hotel just as the city lights were gradually appearing for the night and I expected the two mulatto girls to leave the car and walk the rest of the way to their destination.

Instead, I was instructed by the secretary to take the two girls to their homes or anywhere else they wished to go. For the next half-hour or longer, with street addresses and directions constantly being changed by the carefree girls on the back seat, we toured a large area of the city like three joy-riding juveniles driving somebody's car without permission.

Finally, saying they would meet me later in the night if that was what I wanted to do, the girls then asked to be taken to an address on Beale Street in the Negro Quarter. With no further mention of our meeting later, they got out of the car in front of what had the appearance of being the brightest-lighted cafe and juke parlor along the entire length of Beale Street.

Several days later when I was asked by the executive secretary why I had kept the staff car out so late at night on an authorized trip to Memphis, I told him about the two mulatto girls we had picked up outside the sentry gate and who wanted to keep on riding for a long time after getting to Memphis.

The chief was upset and angry and did not say anything immediately. Then presently, with a severe expression coming to his face, and in a husky tone of voice, he said that never again should I stop outside the sentry gate and permit any of the prostitutes to enter the YMCA sedan.

Not long after giving me the explicit instructions not to accommodate prostitutes in any way, the chief was transferred to another YMCA wartime location. It was then that I was promptly relieved of my duties and sent home.

= 2 =

The abrupt termination of a long and tireless period of almost continuous activity and excitement during the time I had been separated from family for the first time left me with the feeling that my new-found world had vanished completely and with no trace of my recent existence left behind. I was restless and moody and could find no interest, day after day, in the familiar scenes of fields and woods of home.

Gradually, though, I began to realize that I was searching for a way to bring back what to me had been the spirit and essence of my experiences in a strange world still vivid and haunting. I had no desire to talk to anyone, not even to my parents, about my experiences of the past several weeks in a momentous summer. I wanted to keep my private life in isolation and at the same time I felt a compelling need to express myself in some manner without prying curiosity by another person. Whatever was to happen, I still did not want anybody looking over my shoulder and inhibiting the expression of my innermost feelings.

So with pencil and paper I began writing a novel.

In my innocence, I did not have the slightest idea how to go about writing a novel. And certainly I had no knowledge of the requirements of storytelling. In fact, I had never read a full-length novel. I was familiar with the word novel itself only because during years of being tutored by my mother that particular term for a class of fiction was frequently used by her when referring to certain legends and classical writings. There was a period when I thought all novels had been written either by Victor Hugo or by Sir Walter Scott.

As for my own undertaking, I considered myself as being well-qualified to write a novel because for a long time I had been reading short stories in magazines passed along to me by my mother. She was an eager reader of *The Saturday Evening Post*, a weekly, and monthly *Cosmopolitan* and *Redbook* magazines. There may have been religious literature, other than the Bible, in our home but I have no recollection of having been given anything of the kind to read. As long as we lived in Tennessee, my father was a subscriber to a Memphis daily and Sunday newspaper and I was a constant reader of baseball news.

Over a period of many days, always behind the locked door of my room, I wrote on blue-ruled tablet paper as rapidly as I could the story of a young boy who ran away from his home in the country to escape from the harsh tyranny of cruel parents.

I did not consider that I was attributing to my parents unjust reflection after having been nurtured by them with loving care all my life. Instead, feeling it was justified by the freedom of expression and the gift of imagination in the writing of fiction, it was my intention to exaggerate for the purpose of making use of fantasy and conceptions which, my mother had often said, were among the basic elements of fiction. Combined with acquired knowledge, judicious mixtures of such elements, I was told, should enable a person with some degree of talent to achieve success preferably as a major novelist or at least as a popular storyteller.

After the opening chapter, my novel continued with the arrival of the runaway boy hungry and friendless in the big city. The action that took place alternated between Beale Street, the home of two young mulatto girls whose names were Betty and Hetty, and a young white girl who lived in the Peabody Hotel and whose name was Susie.

The inherent conflict in the story line involved both white people and black people who angrily disagreed when replying to the young boy's plea for help in finding the way to the house where his uncle lived. Whenever there was a hostile encounter between the two races, there was always the possibility of unrestrained violence being inflicted by both sides.

When the two young mulatto girls, Betty and Hetty, offered to help the boy find his uncle's house, they were threatened with whippings with leather straps if they made any effort to help the runaway white boy. After that, when Susie said she would help him find his uncle's house, she was told she would not be allowed to live in the Peabody Hotel any longer if she did such a thing.

When the novel was finished, it was composed of seven chapters and covered a total of twenty-two pencil-scrawled pages. The title selected for it was "A Boy's Own Story of City Life."

When my first work of fiction was proudly shown to my mother and father, their reaction was swift and uncompromising. I was soon to hear in no uncertain terms that my spelling, punctuation, and handwriting needed drastic improvement. There were other unfavorable comments, too, but not a word was said about my accomplishment as a writer of fiction. Disappointed as I was to have the novel ignored as being unworthy of mention, I decided that from that day forward I would rather hear adverse criticism of a story of mine than to have it completely disregarded.

My ill-fated attempt to write a novel, however, was not a total disaster. My parents were quick to decide that, in view of my inability to spell common words and to write legibly, I was to begin attending public school without delay.

= 3 =

The principal of the nearby public school decided that I should be enrolled in the seventh grade because of my age, which soon would be fourteen years. Although he was probably influenced to some extent by my mother's insistence that consideration should be given to the fact that she had tutored me extensively in the past when I might have been in school.

By the time I had completed the eighth grade a year and a half later I had earned, with my mother's help, passing grades in all my studies. Moreover, and without assistance, I had been the lone survivor of an elimination quiz conducted by the teacher of geography. The reward I received was a copy of *The Rise and Fall of the Roman Empire,* by Edward Gibbon. What was so captivating about the book—which had a price of 50¢ marked on the flyleaf—was that it was my first possession of the kind and I kept it on a table in my room where I could see it at all times.

After entering the public school, I soon became so occupied by various interests that it was not often that I recalled any of my experiences as driver of the YMCA staff car at Millington Army Base. And since no athletic program and no athletic facilities of any kind existed at the school, I had ample time to devote myself to several interesting diversions.

One of the activities I engaged in soon after the belated beginning of my school days was the building of wooden gums to trap rabbits for their hides. The gums, which were elongated and enclosed box-like troughs, were made with pieces of boards and any scrap of timber that could be found. At one end was a trap door that would be tripped by gray field rabbits lured inside by slices of apples or garden vegetables. Once I had as many as six gums at various locations in surrounding fields and hedgerows.

After skinning the trapped rabbits, their hides were nailed to the sunny side of a shed or barn and when sufficiently cured they were sold for ten cents each to a hide and scrap dealer in Atoka. With the money I earned every week or two, I always bought a pack of Camel cigarettes—without my parents suspecting that I was experimenting with cigarette smoking—

which cost ten cents a pack under-the-counter in a poolroom next door to the Atoka post office.

I never knew if the under-the-counter procedure was due to my youthful age or if open sale would be illegal and a violation of state or local laws. The owner of the poolroom was always quick to shake his head when I asked questions and would motion for me to hurry and leave the building. As it was, the furtive manner of obtaining the cigarettes was always as intriguing as the colorful picture of a camel on the package.

A few weeks after entering school I became proficient enough as a mechanic to be able to dissemble the engine of my father's Ford touring car and scrape off the crusted carbon that was continually accumulating on the cylinder heads and spark plugs. As a reward for my labor, I sometimes was permitted to go off alone and drive the car along the back roads of the countryside for an hour or longer.

The granting of the privilege to have limited use of the automobile coincided with the sudden and disturbing emergence of my sexuality. I had often wondered how I would be able to recognize the first signs of active masculinity and how soon the signs would become evident. The unexpected swelling and insuppressible throbbing of the penis was as thrilling as it was mysterious.

Relatively little time had passed since, without actual physical contact, I had slept through the entire night in the same bed with Susie, the fifteen-year-old Memphis prostitute. And now I was suddenly attracted by the manifest femininity of girls for the first time and I knew without the slightest doubt that it was caused by the irresistible lure of female sex.

There were several attractive girls of my age or slightly older who lived within my territory. And two of them in particular interested me to the extent that I became bold enough to ask for a date from time to time. There were no night or after dark dates in prospect since there was no place to go or no attraction to attend except for the improbability of escorting a girl to Wednesday night prayer meeting at one of the churches in the community.

Another reason for my avoiding dates other than those in broad daylight, and the most important one of all to me, was because I could not yet bring myself to be alone with a girl in her parlor or on a porch swing. Instead, I would ask her to ride with me in my father's car up and down the road for an hour or more in the afternoon. Even then there would be no hugging and kissing—and certainly no sexual intercourse—although often there would be both planned and unplanned opportunities for a few minutes of the excitement of hand-holding.

As I became more and more interested in one of the girls, I devised a way to attract her attention by guiding the car into ruts in the road in front of her home and then sitting at ease in the rear seat while from time to time leaning forward to blow the horn of the driverless car or then sitting on the floor out of sight. It was necessary to be alert, too, because there was always the possibility that another car would come down the road and the result would be a head-on collision.

Precisely at the important juncture in my life when I had come to believe with youthful optimism that I was at the verge of attaining an orderly and purposeful existence, being deeply concerned as I was with my studies in school and having a keen interest in helping to excavate an Indian burial mound in search of artifacts and, of equal importance, there being the likelihood of extended companionship with one of the attractive girls I had come to know intimately enough to engage in a satisfactory degree of hugging and kissing—well, that was the turning point at which I became downcast and heartbroken with the fear that life was passing me by and leaving me to an unmerciful fate.

All this was brought on when I was informed in a casual manner by my parents, as if it would be of little importance to me, that they had decided we would move immediately from Tennessee to a small town in Georgia on the opposite side of the state from my birthplace. It was the first time that I was not eager to leave one place and move to another.

Nevertheless, move we did and without delay.

A few days later when ready to leave for Georgia with possessions stacked solidly on the floor and rear seat of the five-passenger Ford, it was realized that no provision had been made to take our huge crossbred collie and bird dog named Shag with us. Since there was not enough space on the back seat for both Shag and me, my father suggested that he might ride on the front seat between him and my mother. In a few words, my mother declared that she was not going to permit that to be a possibility.

During a brief discussion, my parents decided to give Shag to a friendly neighbor who often had said Shag could be trained to become a good guard dog to protect his ducks and chickens from raids by roving foxes. My father tied a rope around Shag's neck and, following prolonged farewells when even my mother wiped a few tears from her cheeks, our shaggy dog was led across the pasture to the neighbor's house.

After our delayed start, it was late in midmorning when we finally began our long trip from western Tennessee to eastern Georgia. At twilight, we had reached a small town in northern Mississippi, having traveled about sixty miles that day, where we spent the night in a house that had a sign at the gate offering to rent rooms overnight to tourists.

The next morning when we were ready to leave, there was our dog Shag sleeping peacefully under our car. When the engine was started, it took Shag only an instant to become wide awake. Then with an eager wagging of his tail, he leaped to the space between the wide runningboard and the fender on my father's side of the car.

After leaving the tourist home, Shag balanced himself so well that even when we would go around street corners and sharp curves of the road he never once fell to the ground. During the remainder of our trip through Mississippi and Alabama to Georgia, he never lost sight of us during the day and always at night he slept under the automobile as though afraid we might drive away and leave him behind again.

Chapter Five

OUR NEW HOME IN THE small town of Wrens in eastern Georgia was the paint-flaked, rusting tin-roofed manse of the Associate Reformed Presbyterian Church. The five-room dwelling, together with a detached wood shed and a chicken house, was situated on a narrow lot under tall weeping-willow trees. Where we lived was on a sandy byway close to the center of town and the Augusta Southern Railroad station.

Bordered on three sides by trellises of morning-glory vines, there was a small plot of ground at the rear of the house that was used for a vegetable garden. The gloomy-looking clapboard building had been constructed with unseasoned pine lumber many years in the past and the surface was beaded with amber-colored globules of rosin that in earlier years had oozed through the once-white paint.

There were not many houses in the town that were any more imposing than the A.R.P. manse while many of the places in which people lived were white, yellow, or brown tin-roofed bungalows. As for the people themselves, the larger number of them were black field hands and mill workers and house servants. Other than a few doctors, mail carriers, schoolteachers, and chain-gang guards, the whites were merchants and clerks and farmers and their families who had moved to town.

The fertile farming land surrounding Wrens was ideal for growing cotton and the owners of sharecropping plantations had become wealthy during World War I. Likewise, the owners of forest lands and lumber mills were among the wealthiest citizens and owned the most expensive automobiles.

However, the region was situated not far from the barren sand hills and the depleted soil of the tobacco lands between Wrens and Augusta. The impoverished people from the sand hills and tobacco roads, hungry and ragged, were frequently in town begging from house to house for handouts of food and clothing and a little money with which to buy cure-all medicine. There always seemed to be one or more feebly crying, sickly looking babes-in-arms among the begging families.

The most persistent mendicants had perfected the technique of sitting on the doorsteps of a house and, for hours at a time, alternating knocking loudly and moaning in a distressed voice to gain the sympathy of a householder. As a result, the destitute people came to be known as the Weepers.

Soon after we had arrived in Wrens from Tennessee, there was the occasion when my mother became so provoked that she jabbed the tufted end of a broom at a small group of Weepers who had remained on our porch and continued their pathetic moaning long after my father had given them a large sack of sweet potatoes and several cans of pork-and-beans.

"I know they are hungry and they are deserving people and I feel sorry for them," my mother said after the Weepers had been prodded into leaving our porch and had gone to another house on the street, "but something had to be done. We need food ourselves, too, and there's not always enough of it. From now on, there's going to be a limit to how kindhearted we can be at this house."

I came to know more about the Weepers after I began driving a country doctor's car for him after school on weekday afternoons and every Saturday from early morning until late at night. The young doctor was a compassionate man and probably treated just as many Weepers without charge as he attended patients who were able to pay his fees. Once he said with a solemn shaking of his head that he had not been out of medical college long enough to have tightened the fibers of his compassion with apathy but too long to be able to treat an unfortunate patient with the indifference of a medical student dissecting a cadaver.

There were some cases where extreme poverty existed and the young doctor would suggest that I could be able to understand how needy some human beings were if I looked inside one of the hovels of a seriously ill person.

In such instances, where sometimes as many as four or five persons of different ages lived, it was likely that there would be little more in a one-room or two-room cabin than a corn-shuck mattress on the floor and a soot-blackened fireplace used the year around for cooking hoecake.

When school ended for the summer, I was offered a full-time job as driver for an older doctor who made house calls and attended patients over a wide area of the county. His practice was confined almost exclusively to families of wealthy farmers and lumbermen and at no time while I was employed by him did he call at the home of a black person or one of the Weepers.

By that time, I had become so familiar with the activities of a country doctor that I seriously thought of studying medicine for a career. However, this budding ambition vanished completely one day when I drove the doctor on what I thought was going to be merely another routine house call.

What happened was that the doctor was seriously wounded by a farmer with a double-barrel shotgun who had come home from the field for midday dinner an hour earlier than expected by his wife. The doctor was able to stanch the flow of blood from his shoulder while lying down on the back seat of the car and from there he urged me to drive the car faster and faster to get to Wrens where there would be another doctor to attend to his shotgun wound.

"Hurry, Erskine," he called to me several times.

"Yes, sir," I said, trying cautiously to steer the automobile down the middle of the narrow unpaved road.

"Hurry and go as fast as you can," he urged me. "Be careful—but hurry! I need help!"

Bouncing and jouncing on the rutted dirt road, I drove the car with all the speed I thought would be safe for the distance of about four miles back to Wrens and the other doctor.

"What's wrong with me?" I could hear being said behind me. "God knows I ought to know better. And here I am bleeding to death. Good God, how could I be so foolish? I never thought I'd let myself get into this kind of trouble over a woman."

= 2 =

When I entered Wrens High School in the previous autumn of 1918, I was to be fifteen years old three months later and should have been enrolled in the freshman class due to the lack of middle-school credits. Instead, I found myself placed by the principal, Professor McCollum, in the junior class.

41

The probable reason for my being put into an advanced class was that I stood six feet tall and was husky in appearance. Under the circumstances, not unlike it had been in Tennessee when I attended public school for the first time, undoubtedly I would have disrupted classroom study among younger and smaller students because of my relatively large size.

I was an indifferent student and had little difficulty in finding adequate excuses to skip study periods and sometimes to be absent from classes for entire days. On two occasions, another student and I had left our classroom without permission and had gone downtown to pass the time at the drugstore soda fountain. Professor McCollum was informed of our absence by our teacher and he found us and sent us back to school on the run with the threat of expulsion if we did such a thing for the third time.

I suppose one reason for my indifference to formal schooling was because in my early years I had not been subjected to the discipline of required study and attendance. As the consequence of that dispensation in the beginning, no doubt later I was prone to be far more interested in the activities of people in daily life than I was in the slow and tedious process of acquiring a textbook education.

My interest in finding a gratifying activity that was not within the high-school curriculum had led me in the middle of my first year in Wrens to apply for a part-time job at a cottonseed-oil mill. I earned a dollar a night shoveling cottonseed into conveyor troughs at the mill only a few blocks from home. All this had been carefully planned and for a while it was accomplished without the knowledge of my parents.

The split-shift at the mill lasted, as I recall, from midnight to six o'clock in the morning and the workpeople other than me were young mulattoes and blacks who sometimes had jobs as houseboys or yardmen for white families.

What I came to know about some of the white citizens of Wrens by working at night in the oil mill several nights a week for almost a month was an enlightening revelation of life. Or it just as well might be described as having been a seminar devoted to the theory and practice of male and female aberrant relationships in an American small town.

In the close confines of the cottonseed storage shed, and especially when accompanied by the sound of raindrops falling on the tin roof, it was an enthralling experience to overhear the houseboys tell of incidents involving white people—some scandalous, some tragic, others humorous, and all of them related with unrestrained fervor. It was always as if no white person would be present to hear what was being said. All the time, too, the tales being told about white people by the blacks were startling with insight and implications that revealed the inherent anxiety of black people living in the shadow of white people.

Near the end of the shift in early morning, and as a befitting conclusion of a night of hard labor, the colored workpeople would often engage in sarcastic and lighthearted banter directed not at white people but at their own race. This usually became a scatological recital in language profane and obscene that described all possible as well as all improbable instances of sexual aberrations involving family members from the cradle to the grave. With no white person permitted to participate, it was an exclusive pastime for black males and known to them as "playing the dozens."

And as for me, all this came to an abrupt conclusion when I fell asleep at the breakfast table one morning after working at the oil mill on the midnight shift. That was when I had to confess to my parents and tell them what I had been doing during the past month while they slept soundly through the night. Shortly afterward, my father said that perhaps no great harm had been done but that it would have been better for me to be older before being exposed to anything like playing the dozens.

= 3 =

Following my close association with the young mulatto houseboys and yardmen at the oil mill, it was probably inevitable that I would have taken more than casual interest in the young colored housemaids who worked for many of the white families in the town. My own mother employed an attractive young girl with mulatto coloring. Bessie was her name and, since I spent most of the daylight hours at school or driving for a doctor, there had been little opportunity to become acquainted with her.

When I finally did find myself in the presence of Bessie other than at home, it was late on a Saturday night and I had gone with several classmates to an area near the Negro Quarter where there were several warehouses and storage sheds fronting on a dark alley. When my friends and I walked past one of the warehouses, we could hear subdued voices that were little more than loud whispers. Not a face could be seen in the dim starlight.

The boys I was with had been there before on Saturday nights and they knew the names of some of the girls. Each time one of them answered the call of her name there was the sound of suppressed laughter and sometimes the movements of a shadowy figure could be detected. Presently, one of the girls in the darkness, evidently having recognized me, called out in a tentative tone of voice.

"Bessie is here," the unseen girl said. In a few moments, in a bolder manner, she spoke again. "Here's Bessie."

Embarrassed and disconcerted, not having the slightest notion that my mother's housemaid would be among the girls in the alley, I whispered to one of my friends that I had to go home and could not stay another minute. He gripped my arm and tried to stop me but I pulled free and ran out of the alley toward home.

Shortly before the incident in the alley took place, there had been a series of small books in the category of What-a-Young-Man-Ought-to-Know placed on the table beside my bed. Each time I found one of the books, which I decided had been purchased for my youthful guidance, I read it in eager interest from cover to cover without pause.

By the time I had finished reading the third and last book in the series, I was so thoroughly apprehensive and fearful of the probability of being infected with syphilis and gonorrhea that time after time, as the author had advised, I searched parts of my body for telltale evidence that I had caught the diseases. More than that, and for many days, I carefully washed my own plate as well as knife and fork before beginning a meal even though my mother insisted that what I was doing was unnecessary because Bessie had been instructed always to scald the diningwear.

Since the day following my Saturday night visit with friends to the warehouse alley was Sunday, it was not until Monday when the drugstore was open that I could overcome my timidity enough to ask the pharmacist in a tremulous voice if I could buy a condom for a friend. The pharmacist smiled at me with an assenting nod of his head.

"I'll be glad to do that, Erskine," he said as he reached under the counter. "And if you're doing this for a friend, then your friend ought to buy the same for you."

When I was handed the small, round, tin container, I was quick to thrust it into my pocket out of sight. The cost of fifty cents was paid with nickels and dimes.

"Don't forget to tell your friend you'd like him to do the same for you," the man behind the counter said.

All the way home I tried to think what I was going to do with the condoms and when they would be used for protection against syphilis and gonorrhea. I had been deeply impressed by the advice of the author of the sexual

44

guide for young men and I intended to take the necessary precautions to keep from becoming infected.

Since moving to Wrens, I had not become seriously interested in any of the girls I had observed at high school and had had merely casual words with a few of the ones I considered the most attractive. By that time, I no longer had any lingering regrets for having left behind the girls I had been fond of in Tennessee and I felt no urgency to make new friends to take their place in my life.

The one time that I was on the verge of becoming sexually involved to the extent of having intercourse with a girl in Wrens occurred without the slightest instigation on my part. This took place about a year after our moving to Georgia when one of my classmates asked me to come to her house one night and sit on the front porch to entertain one of her friends from a nearby town who was visiting her over the weekend. This was long before I had acquired the condoms and, anyway, I was too completely stunned by the strange girl's explicit proposal to be able to perform.

The visiting girl who was a year older than I boldly put her arm around my neck while we were sitting in the porch swing and said she wanted to engage in love play. Surprised and speechless, never having faced such an experience before, I could not think what to say in reply. Becoming more insistent the longer I was silent, the girl said intercourse was a lot better than merely hugging and kissing. When I still did not respond, she said with a teasing intimacy that there was nothing to be afraid of because we were all alone on the porch and nobody would know what we were doing.

Perhaps it was a show of her own willingness, or it may have been to incite me to action, but whatever her intention was she opened her blouse and pulled up her dress to reveal almost total nakedness. Once before I had seen the bare breasts of a girl in Tennessee while she was changing into a bathing suit at a swimming party. However, this was the first time I had ever seen the exposure of the pubic region of a young woman.

I was so startled by what the girl had done, in addition to being unable to make any response, that in my state of nervousness I knocked over a large jardiniere that stood at my end of the swing and it fell to the floor with a resounding crash. The jarring fall evidently had been heard throughout the house, because almost immediately there were loud footsteps in the hallway.

With an exasperated gesture, the displeased girl jerked her dress downward over her legs and knees. With a glance I could see that her blouse was only partly closed.

Leaving the porch as quickly as I could, neither waiting to replace the jardiniere in its upright position nor with a word of apology for my behavior. I reached the street just as somebody turned on the porch light. After that, I ran all the way home with my footsteps echoing in the quiet of the night.

= 4 =

At the beginning of my second summer in Wrens, I was able to get a job turning the hand press in the plant of the local weekly newspaper, the *Jefferson Reporter*, which was owned and edited by Charley Stephens. A short time later I was given the additional task of setting type by hand. With that start as a newspaperman, I was soon permitted to write notes about engagements and marriages for the society page and write other news items about happenings of local interest.

Following several weeks of apprenticeship, I was left in charge of the newspaper when Charley Stephens decided to leave town and go on a lengthy fishing trip on the Georgia coast. This meant that in addition to writing copy for the sheet, two pages of which were boiler-plated, it was my responsibility to handset the type, print the newspaper, fold it, and deliver six hundred copies to the post office for subscribers. The only thing I did not have to do in the owner's absence was to try to sell advertising and try to collect money for subscriptions.

When Charley returned to town, the first thing I said to him was that I thought I should be paid for the several weeks I had worked on the *Jefferson Reporter*. He looked surprised to hear what I had said about wages, and I, too, was surprised that I had brought forth enough courage to mention the matter.

"Now look here, Erskine," Charley said gravely with a frown. "You came in here of your own free will and said you wanted to come to work on the paper. Not a single, solitary word was said about paying you to learn newspapering. That's the honest truth, isn't it?"

I told him I thought he would want to pay me something and that I had been paid a dollar a night for working at the cottonseed oil mill.

"Boy, let me tell you something," he said, darting a finger at my face. "You'd better hurry back down there to that mill and try to get your old job back again if money's the only thing in life you're after."

"But, Mr. Stephens, couldn't you pay me just fifty cents a day?" I asked hopefully.

"No," he stated, shaking his head emphatically.

I thought about the matter for a week and then in the end I asked Charley if he had any objections to my quitting the job. He looked at me sternly for a moment and then said that I would probably live to be sorry if I did but that I could quit if that was what I wished to do.

I quit.

It was depressing to be isolated in a small town such as Wrens was in those days without being able to find some activity to relieve a spiritless existence that threatened to inflict a young person with a harmful wayward-ness. But being wayward in Wrens was not easy. There were not enough juvenile delinquents to form a gang and the chief of police enforced a strict curfew on the streets from dusk to dawn. Otherwise, the only activity of any interest to a person of my age was to go to the drugstore soda fountain and stand there with merchants and traveling salesmen drinking Coca-Cola with a squirt of ammonia in every glass.

Unemployed and restless by reason of the lack of anything else of absorb-ing interest, and along with many men and boys in Wrens that summer, I began going to baseball games played two or three times a week between the local semi-pro team and teams in other eastern Georgia towns. The club manager was no doubt worried by more important matters, one of which was undoubtedly financial, and he probably gave me permission to keep box scores of the games so I would stop bothering him.

After scoring several games with the help of one of the pitchers on the team, I was able to do a fairly credible job and was eventually appointed, without salary, official scorekeeper for the club. Even more than that, I was given a pass to all home games, a baseball cap to wear, permission to sit in the dugout with the players, and sometimes I was allowed to go on a road trip with the team to another town.

In the course of time, with the help of friendly players on the team, I acquired enough proficiency to be able to use my own judgment in record-ing hits, errors, assists, batting averages, and prepare statistics with acceptable accuracy.

Making use of my experience as official scorekeeper for the Wrens semi-pro baseball club, and undoubtedly with some degree of presumptuousness on my part, I mailed several reports of baseball games to the sports editor of the *Augusta Chronicle*.

Within a week, my dispatches were being published in the newspaper together with complete box scores. Next, I began receiving bundles of stamped and addressed envelopes for future mailings. Instructions were sent to me, also, advising me how to prepare paste-up columns of my published reports to be mailed to the sports department and for which I would be paid two dollars for every column of my dispatches in print.

I was so pleased and elated to know that I had become an accredited sports correspondent for a daily newspaper with a large circulation that I was not only ready to forgive Charley Stephens but, more than that, I would have willingly told him how appreciative I was of his refusal to pay me fifty cents a day to keep me in bondage as a printer's devil. Whatever Charley's attitude toward me may have been after seeing some of the dispatches in the *Augusta Chronicle* with my by-line, he avoided any opportunity to speak to me when we passed on the street by steadfastly gazing beyond me into the distance.

This was an exciting moment in my life. It was a time that I knew would always be remembered. And it was an occasion for a celebration of some kind. But the only thing I wanted to do about it was to go down to the drugstore soda fountain, put a nickel on the marble-top counter, and call for a Coca-Cola with a squirt of ammonia to drink while standing there with the merchants and traveling salesmen.

Chapter Six

ON A RAINY DAY IN May, 1920, which was the occasion of the graduation exercises of my class at Wrens High School, I had been the only student among the twenty-six boys and girls on the stage of the auditorium who did not receive a diploma.

I was fully aware that I had not earned the required number of credits or units for graduation, having previously been informed in private of my failed efforts by the kindly Professor McCollum, and in place of a diploma I was prepared to accept a glaringly blank scroll. What I had not anticipated was the moment when I myself received the customary applause from the people in the audience as each student was presented with a scroll.

At that time, in full view of an audience of as many as two hundred persons, all of whom were probably well aware of my plight, I had no feeling of embarrassment or humiliation for what I had brought upon myself. Being in the midst of my classmates and in full view of the onlookers, I did have moments of feeling out of place, but nevertheless I was not to be shamed into a state of regret and remorse for my predicament.

In fact, even more than beyond being stoical in such a situation, I felt that I had achieved a measure of superior experience and practical knowledge for use in the future that could not have been gained in a dutiful adherence to scholarly studies alone.

Feeling comfortable with such an attitude, I even then came to appreciate my mother's desire to give me personal guidance early in life rather than turn me over to apathetic instructors who did not possess her ability and dedication as a teacher. Likewise, I was grateful for my father's quiet insistence that I should avoid follow-the-leader conformity and instead grow up to be independent in thought and judgment in matters social, religious, and political.

With the less than glorious end to my public school days, I was more anxious than ever to be able to go away to college. I was determined to take myself away from Wrens and not let myself be coerced by a heartless fate to remain there to the end of my life. College was my goal in the immediate future and I did not intend to let anything keep me from attaining it.

The small town of Wrens had become an important part of my life for the time being and to no less an extent than had been the brief periods of living in Prosperity, Charlotte, and elsewhere. However, I had become too accustomed to transitory living to let myself become anchored so early in life to be like a rusting ship no longer seaworthy.

For the matter at hand, the time had come to decide upon possible colleges and universities to consider for application for enrollment. As expected of my mother's allegiance to her native state, the University of Virginia was first proposed to be the destiny for my higher education. That was followed by the naming of the University of Georgia and Georgia Tech for consideration.

After that initial surge of enthusiasm, such lofty aspirations were quick to be dismissed. There simply was not sufficient money available. Next, I came to realize in the harsh light of reality, and with all exalted expectations suddenly shattered, that my being able to be accepted by any college or university without the required standard entrance units would be doubtful if not impossible.

This gloomy prospect for my future was a continuous concern until the day in early summer when my father returned home from what he described as having been a brief trip to attend to some affairs in South Carolina. His advice to me was that I should continue working as a string correspondent for daily newspapers during the summer and at the end of that time the matter of my entering college somewhere would be settled. That was all he would say, but he did not appear to be worried about the final outcome.

With my experience as sports correspondent for the *Augusta Chronicle*, I already had presumed to consider myself capable of acting as general news correspondent in Wrens for some of the other daily newspapers in the state. The results did not come anywhere close to my expectations. My lengthy dispatches of several hundred words rarely appeared in print in the *Savannah News* or the *Atlanta Constitution* and even the *Augusta Chronicle* usually blue-penciled my general news items down to a measly two- or three-inch length. It took a long time to have enough printed matter to be able to paste up a twenty-two inch column for a payment of two dollars.

The advice given me by the state news editor of the *Macon Telegraph*, Mark Ethridge, was helpful and appreciated although little more than an inch or two of my dispatches from Wrens ever appeared in that newspaper.

Mark Ethridge, who was the first authentic newsman I had ever spoken to in person, encouraged me to continue my writing and working for the *Macon Telegraph* by saying I should consider my string correspondence as being ideal training for future writing of any kind and that it could be as valuable as a year of instruction in a school of journalism.

Newly inspired, and in the absence of a fire at a cotton gin or sawmill or an occasional murder in the community, I went to work to extend my interests beyond baseball by interviewing tourists on their way to Florida who stopped at filling stations for gasoline and by speaking to traveling evangelists and carnival performers arriving in Wrens for engagements. Publication of any part of the interviews was a rarity.

= 2 =

In the following September, three months before my seventeenth birthday, I entered Erskine College in Due West, South Carolina. My enrollment had been arranged by my father and the understanding was that I would strive to eliminate my deficiencies and meet the requirements by taking special courses.

Erskine College, which was a small four-year institution maintained by the Associate Reformed Presbyterian Church, had been named in honor of Ebenezer Erskine, a Scottish theologian, who had founded the sect with other dissidents and transferred its operation from Scotland to the southern states of America. My father was a graduate of the college and, after serving in the United States Army in Cuba during the Spanish-American War, had returned to study at the Theological Seminary of the college and be ordained as an A.R.P. minister. It was at that time that he met my mother who was a teacher of English and Latin at the nearby Womens College of Due West. I came by my name in deferential regard for the theologian, not necessarily the college.

I was pleased and elated to have been able to leave home and enter any college. However, what I found in Due West was not to my liking. I was far from being impressed by the sight of the trash-littered campus of the college and the alternately dusty and muddy main street of the town. And I had not envisioned attending a college with an enrollment less than that of Wrens High School.

As an entering student, I found that certain rules and regulations were not only prescribed but gleefully enforced by a few sadistic members of the upper classes. From the beginning, I decided not to be one of those freshmen who would meekly submit to abusive physical hazing, unbuckling my pants and being swatted at will on my bare buttocks with a paddle.

I had decided to try to play football for the first time in my life, and I stated emphatically that I would have no time for such horseplay or for anything other than football and my studies. Perhaps due to my towering six feet of height and my summoning up of an authoritative depth of voice, I was granted a partial exemption. However, in no uncertain terms, it was indicated that, as an alternative, I would be designated a smuggler.

Instead of being swatted with paddles and boards, I was directed to smuggle food and snacks from the dining hall at each of the three daily meals and to deliver these purloined edibles to a dormitory room with a secret entrance where a poker game ran almost without interruption most of the day and night.

Like myself, some of the other freshmen chose the option of being on call to go for cigarettes, carry laundry, shine shoes, and perform similar menial tasks rather than submit to paddling. There were usually as many as four or six upper-classmen seated at the large round table in the remote dormitory room and some of them were always hungry. There was no certainty about it, but it did seem to me that some of the surly-tempered, thick-necked football players were mercenaries who had been recruited for purposes other than educational and were accorded special privileges.

My assignment to smuggle food from the dining hall became difficult to perform whenever there was a scarcity of biscuits or sausage or fried chicken to be gleaned from the tables after hungry students had departed. Excuses made to players in the poker game for the shortage of snacks were not accepted in good humor. On more than one occasion, I was ordered to produce—or else bring the paddle. The tone of voice of some of the hungry poker players was intimidating enough to send me without argument to the kitchen pantry after midnight to break-and-enter for the purpose of gathering a laundry sack full of chocolate cookies, Boston baked beans, and canned pineapple.

At the close of the football season in my first year at Erskine College, I was relieved of my duties as designated food smuggler for the poker players. Following that, and in search of some activity other than attending morning chapel services and daily Bible classes, I discovered that it was possible and not at all difficult to travel long distances at no cost by riding freight trains.

The usual way to get on board a train was to wait for darkness in a railway yard where freight cars were being shunted and coupled. Then when the train began moving, I could climb into a gondola car if no open-door boxcars were available.

I never attempted to ride anywhere on a passenger train without a ticket. A friendly hobo had advised me during my first trip on a freight never to ride a blind-baggage car on a passenger train because the car might be carrying United States mail in addition to express and baggage and I would be taking the risk of being arrested and jailed.

During the remainder of the college year, I usually spent weekends traveling on freight trains to some selected designation in South Carolina and came to be a frequent visitor to Greenville, Anderson, Spartanburg, Greenwood, and Columbia. Only once did I go as far as Charleston and return on a weekend. As for something to eat while away from Due West, the money for that had been carefully allotted after having saved monthly board money instead of paying all of it to the college dining hall.

When the college term ended in June, I went to Calhoun, Georgia, a small town in the Blue Ridge Piedmont fifty miles south of Chattanooga, Tennessee, where I had obtained a job as a stonemason's helper. There the two of us worked on a project, which was the construction of a granite-wall church, all summer long. Constantly carrying a heavy hod of mortar on my shoulder up a ladder to a scaffolding or hefting a block of solid granite from the ground to the top of the wall came to be the hardest work I had ever undertaken.

At the end of summer, though, when the four granite walls had been erected to roof-top level, I knew I was in the best of physical condition for football. When I returned to Due West, the coach selected me for the varsity team at the conclusion of the first week of practice.

I played center, or ball snapper, without missing a single game that season. That was unusual in those days when soft leather helmets provided little protection against injury and face masks did not exist. For that reason, college football players frequently suffered concussions and fractures that were so serious they could not play all the games during the season.

At the end of my first year as a varsity player, the athletic department of the college announced that a banquet for the football players would be presented as a reward for a better-than-usual winning season. The banquet, for which the football players were explicitly directed to be as well-dressed as possible by wearing suit coats and neckties and not sweaters and sneakers, was scheduled for a week after Thanksgiving. Moreover, and to the dismay of many, it was announced that, since it was a social event, a young woman of suitable age and character should be invited to accompany each football player to the banquet.

I was at a loss to know what to do about the edict, inasmuch as it was not a coeducational college and I did not know any girls in town. But fortunately a classmate, Froggy, said he could arrange everything for both of us.

As Froggy explained his plan, he said his older brother was a senior at Furman University in nearby Greenville and was well acquainted with two girls who often were invited to similar functions at colleges elsewhere in the state. When I asked for more information about the two girls from Greenville, Froggy said they were former students at a school for girls and were only a few years older than he and I.

Moreover, my classmate said the two girls had the reputation of being sophisticated and always at ease in the company of football players. And the only cost to us, I was assured, would be the few dollars we would pay for their room at the local two-story hotel since their sole interest as visitors was in having a good time.

On the evening of the banquet, Froggy and I escorted the two girls from the hotel to the college dining hall. The four of us were seated at our table and had begun the main course when I realized I did not know the name of the blonde girl seated beside me and who was my date for the night. Apologetically, I asked her what was her name.

"Are you sure you really want to know?" she said with a quick tossing of her head.

"Yes, and I wish I'd known sooner," I said seriously.

She leaned closer to me until I felt the touch of her shoulder. Her perfume was like orange blossoms.

"Agnes or Mabel or Becky," she said slowly and distinctly. "Which do you prefer?"

"How can that be—three names?" I asked at once.

"Don't you really know, Erskine?"

At first, I shook my head. A moment later, I was nodding slowly in reply. In wonderment after that, I tried to think how the girl could have suspected that it was my habit to carry in my pocket at all times the small container holding the three original condoms and on each of which was printed the name of Agnes, Mabel, or Becky.

All through the rest of the banquet, and then while the football coach talked about the glory of the past season and the glowing prospects for the following year, I gave scant attention to what was being said. Instead, I was trying to decide if the provocative blonde girl from Greenville who gave me the choice of three names to call her was actually aware that the same names were printed in large letters on the Merry Widow brand of condoms.

At the conclusion of the banquet, it had been proposed by Froggy that the four of us take a walk in the pale moonlight down the street to the football field. The playing field was still grassy and green before the coming of the first frost of winter and Froggy and the other girl left us and went out of sight beyond the goal posts at the far end of the field.

It was not until late morning of the following day that I was able to reassure myself that the blonde girl who had given me the choice of three familiar names to call her was undoubtedly as sophisticated and worldly-wise as proclaimed by Froggy and his older brother. When I went back to the football field that morning, the castoff prophylactic was exactly where I thought it would be. And I could see that the name on it in the light of day was Agnes.

= 3 =

During the fall term in college and for a while beyond the end of the football season, my grades had improved and I had eagerly attended all my classes and completed all assignments satisfactorily.

As a much changed person, I even asked one of the professors to advise me how I could plan a schedule of study that would enable me to overcome my deficiencies and be assured of graduation after two more years of college.

A few days after returning to Due West from Wrens at the end of the Christmas and New Year's holidays, however, I woke up one morning with the realization that I had reverted to my previous state of complete dissatisfaction with Erskine College and once again resented its religious impositions. My renewed dislike and hostility were overwhelming. I was downright miserable.

What offended me most of all at that time was the requirement to participate in prayer meetings and to attend classes teaching the doctrine of divine creation. I had no intention of allowing myself to be compelled to pray aloud in public and to recant my belief in evolution as taught to me by my mother.

I was sure my father would be sympathetic and not critical of my attitude, because as far in the past as I could remember he had made it clear that I should be independent in thought and law-abiding in conduct. And, as he said, Christian religion was a matter for me to reject, if that was my choice, and replace it with a philosophy that had a more rational appeal to me. In keeping with the principles he advocated, I had neither been asked to join the church nor even to attend a service to hear one of his sermons. Freed of any obligation or restriction, it had been my decision to be an agnostic.

Deprived of football at the end of the season as a consuming interest, and with a waning interest in my studies, I soon began spending more and more time away from the campus riding freight trains as far away as Gastonia and Charlotte in North Carolina. Surprises were frequent inasmuch as destinations could not be foretold with any accuracy since, unlike passenger trains, freight trains operated in a mysterious manner of their own without making published timetables available.

And as it was, even when not traveling, I was avoiding classes and often failing to execute assignments. This resulted in my being warned by professors that I would surely fail my courses if I did not greatly improve my grades and, equally as important, stop cutting classes.

In desperation, with my unhappiness in the restrictive environment of Erskine College increasing in intensity each day, I not only continued my antipathy toward what to me had become an unacceptable way of life but I also tried to find ways to provoke the college administration to be compelled to expel me. Although I should have been expelled for some of my overt provocations, being as serious as they were, nothing of the kind that I undertook to do succeeded in my favor.

Finally, long before the end of the term—late March or early April—I took matters into my own hands. The result was that I packed my suitcase and boarded a passenger train to New Orleans, Louisiana.

I had no feeling of regret or loss for leaving the college. Not for a moment did I think I was making a mistake. Instead, it was an invigorating feeling of relief to know that I finally was escaping from a fanatic domination that might have made a subdued captive of me to the end of my days.

I had saved some of my room and board money by working for meals and I left Due West with enough money for railroad fare and, hopefully, some for living expenses until I could find a job. After many days of unemployment in Louisiana following shortlived jobs as a deck hand on a cargo ship and a stable boy at a racetrack, I was hired as a member of a crew of magazine-subscription salesmen. The sales manager and crew of eight boys and men of various ages boarded a train in New Orleans late one night and arrived in the lumber mill town of Bogalusa, Louisiana, in the predawn darkness of a drizzly morning.

The crew of salesmen was divided into pairs and each group was instructed to enter one of the lumber mills or wood-working plants and sell subscriptions to a hunting and fishing magazine to workmen at a price of one dollar for twelve monthly issues. We were told that each dollar collected would be divided for the crew manager to receive twenty-five cents, for the magazine publisher to receive fifty cents, and for the salesman obtaining and collecting for the subscription to receive the remaining twenty-five cents. At the end of three days, the crew manager disappeared and so did all the money we had collected.

A day later, I was the only one of the stranded salesmen left in Bogalusa. My search for some other job to provide something to eat came to an abrupt end a day later when two policemen cordially invited me to ride in their patrol car. It was a short ride of only three blocks to the Bogalusa city jail where I was swiftly booked as a vagrant and put into a large cell block with an elderly black man who had white hair and an upper row of bright gold teeth.

My friendly cellmate, expressing concern for my welfare, especially since it was my first time in jail, said that even a white boy like me might be kept imprisoned for a month or more without trial no matter how minor the charge might be. When I asked about himself, he said his name was Bojo and that he had already been in jail for nearly two months awaiting trial on a charge that he had failed to prevent his two rabbit hounds from barking at night and disturbing the peace.

A few days later, after twice a day having been handed a wooden spoon and a tin pail of boiled turnip greens and fat-back, I had become fearful that I would be kept in jail month after month as Bojo had forewarned me. I had a life to live—and not as an inmate of a Louisiana jail.

I succeeded in begging the jailer for an envelope and a sheet of paper. Immediately, I wrote a letter to my father and told him where I was and how I came to be there. The only money I had for postage was a twenty-five-cent coin and the friendly Bojo warned me not to trust the jailer to put a stamp on the letter and mail it. Climbing to the top of the cell where there was a small iron-barred window, I waited hopefully for many hours to see somebody on the outside whom I thought I could trust to mail the letter for me.

In late afternoon, a barefoot boy with tan skin and close-cropped hair, and who looked about ten years old, stopped in the weed-grown lot by the side of the jail when I called to him. The boy hesitated to come any closer at first and he stood there gazing dubiously at me behind the iron bars for a long time. But finally he did come closer and I was able to get him to promise to mail the letter for me. The quarter was dropped from the window first and then the letter was dropped.

The colored boy picked up the money and then the letter and then quickly turned and ran until he reached the far side of the vacant lot. There he stopped and looked back with a brief wave of his hand before running down the street until he was out of sight. After that there were tears in my eyes and all I could do was hope that the waving of the boy's hand was a reassuring gesture.

Exactly five days later the secretary of the Bogalusa YMCA came into the cell room with the burly jailer and told me that I had been released and could leave for home on the evening train.

When I said good-by to Bojo, he smiled with a blinking of his eyes and a flashing of his gold teeth. He said then that he would miss me in the cell block but was glad I could leave and go home. I wanted to thank Bojo for his good advice about not trusting the jailer to mail the letter to my father but I did not know what to say in the jailer's presence. What I did do was to take my Wrens High School gold ring from my finger and hand it to my surprised friend and benefactor. After that, on the way to the YMCA to take a shower after the solid week in the Bogalusa jail, I was told that my father had sent money by telegraph for my railroad fare to Georgia.

I arrived home the next afternoon and my father was at the depot when I got off the train. He came up to me and shook hands and smiled without a trace of displeasure. I was glad to see him, too.

I can recall only one thing that was said as we walked along the sandy tree-shaded street toward our house.

"What did you think of Louisiana, son?" my father asked. "It's a much different part of the world, isn't it?"

Chapter Seven

IT WAS WITHIN A FEW days after coming home from my misadventures in the state of Louisiana that I put a new ribbon on my typewriter and returned to work as a string correspondent for morning newspapers in Augusta, Atlanta, and Macon.

Gratifying it was to find that my dispatches reporting fires, accidents, and other newsworthy calamities were published at greater length after less bluepenciling than had been the case in previous years.

However, I soon realized that I missed the absorbing interest I had found in college life and I set myself to make it possible to experience it the next time in keeping with the ideal concept of campus existence I had established in my mind. This attitude was a selfish one, of course, but I looked upon it as being the only satisfactory way for me to take if I expected to succeed in being my own man.

I still anticipated being closely questioned—as well as severely scolded—by my father concerning my reason for leaving college in South Carolina. But other than asking what I had discovered about life in the lowlands of Louisiana nothing more was said.

I concluded that my father was well aware of my dissatisfaction with an uninspiring environment as well as why I could no longer endure being confined by restraining religious precepts. Furthermore, I was sure he would not have been overly critical of what I had done if I had told him of my discovery that the college administration in do-gooding zeal had arranged for saltpeter to be put into dining hall food and why that did nothing to enhance my overall respect and admiration for the institution.

During the long train rides to and from Louisiana, to which was added the hour after hour of meditation in my cell at the Bogalusa jail, there had been considerable time for valuable thoughts and reflections about life in the past, the present, and, most important of all, in the future. Ever since my first attempt to write a fictional story based on my experiences as a YMCA chauffeur in Tennessee I had carefully nourished in private and held in readiness for the future the desire and determination to become a writer of short stories and novels. I realized what I lacked, at that stage in my life, was the ability and the confidence to proceed.

My interest in writing for newspapers as a string correspondent was that of a student of English who considered journalism as being an ideal training ground for a writer of fiction. From their common origin, I considered divergent journalism to be the relating of facts, fiction as the realization of the imagination.

It was during the course of learning the essential difference between fact and fiction that I learned that it was necessary to make a distinct separation between creation and imitation. I could not have had a better practical lesson in distinguishing between the honesty of creation and the dishonesty of imitation or plagiarism. This was the result of an incident that occurred during my first year at Erskine College and involved flagrant theft and use of another person's writings.

What happened at that time was that a senior wrote a short story for publication in the college annual. First, the student was immediately praised by faculty members as being an accomplished writer with a brilliant future assured. Next, it was discovered by a fellow student that the story was almost a word-for-word plagiarism of a short story by a well-known author published six months earlier in the *Saturday Evening Post*. Neither the guilty student nor the college administration considered the theft of another writer's work to have been reprehensible and he was graduated with honors in English composition.

The impression left upon me was so deep and meaningful that I resolved to avoid any possibility of being tempted, knowingly or unknowingly, to copy the work of another writer. With this ideal in mind, I put myself to the task of trying my best to initiate and develop my own style of writing and steadfastly to avoid imitating the style of another person. With such zealousness rampant, it was necessary for me to keep from being influenced by the admirable fiction of an already established author. Inevitably, I then was faced with the possibility of not letting myself read anything at all.

Having previously concluded that the world should be divided with writers on one hand and readers on the other, and of course placing myself among the writers, I came to realize that a compromise would have to be made in order to accommodate a limited amount of reading. Since I had so much writing of my own to try to accomplish, I could not bring myself to devote valuable time to reading the heralded masters of the past. Instead, I decided to select one book by a contemporary author as being representative of his work.

The result of this plan was that I would be able to read and become acquainted with the writings of a few selected authors without the likelihood of a single book influencing the style I hoped to establish as my own. Thereafter, I intended to maintain the habit of reading a book by a contemporary author whenever I could find the time between the endings and the beginnings of my own writings. In making the decision to read only a few selected books and devoting most of the time to writing my own fiction, I was fully aware that the time would come when I would have to admit I had never read a page of such writers of the past as Nathaniel Hawthorne, Jack London, or Mark Twain.

Reading, however, held little interest for me at this time in my life. My consuming interest was to be able to delineate the joy and sorrow, the humor and tragedy of people among whom I lived and, at the age of nineteen years, I had come to view the way of the world as being the primary source of the material on which to base short stories and novels. Being limited in experience and knowledge, I was in search of a strange new world.

The world I knew was composed of small towns and farming communities and my vision did not extend beyond the boundary of the horizon. I was anxious to explore the unseen and the unknown and become a part of the exciting life that existed somewhere—and I knew it did exist somewhere because I had heard my parents describe it in detail from the books they had read. Even so, there was practical knowledge to be acquired, too.

As an example, I had come to believe the world was round even though a neighbor in Atoka, Tennessee, had argued with such strong conviction that I might have been convinced that it was flat if I had not relied upon the wisdom of my parents. And it was the word of my parents, too, that contradicted the statement of a faith-healing evangelist in Bradley, South Carolina, who said that prayer, and prayer alone, would cure cancer.

The intensity of life around me seemed to increase day by day as I waited hopefully and impatiently for the opportunity to escape from the small world in which I was confined. I believed what I needed was to be able to find a distant point from which I could have an ideal perspective of the life about which I wished to write. Even though I lived in the midst of the people and scenes I was to write about, I knew I would never be able to accept and tolerate the existing poverty and ignorance and cruelty that was commonplace in the area and even to a greater extent on the nearby sandhills and tobacco roads.

Having no desire to change the world, nevertheless I was motivated by the urge to write about the economic and social plight of the disadvantaged in such a way that readers would be moved to react with sympathy and eventual assistance for the creatures of a subhuman world.

The lynching of an elderly black man accused of molesting a white woman was an unusual event but once was more than enough. The midnight torching of the cabin of an undesirable white family and the ensuing death of two small children occurred only once but again once was an uncivilized act. The display of inhumanity by a white chain-gang guard beating a manacled black convict with a bull whip until blood dripped from his face and neck to vanish in the yellow dust of the public road may not have been repeated a second time. But once...

And along with all this material for a writer, sensational religious manifestations flourished with all the unbounded vigor of an untrampled kudzu vine.

I never fully understood what was my father's reason for purposely exposing me to various forms of primitive religious excesses although later I assumed that what he had in mind was to discourage me from being captivated by such exhibitions. But expose me he did even though he never once proposed that I attend his own church services.

Instead, my father often suggested that I might be interested in going with him to remote parts of Jefferson, Burke, and Richmond counties to witness foot-washing services, a clay-eating communion ritual, a coming-through orgy, a snake-handling performance, or an emotion-charged glossolalia and unknown-tongue spectacle. It was my assumption on many occasions that my father hoped that my reaction would result in my being spared, at some time in the future, the indignity of indulging in the absurd.

= 2 =

With no desire to return to work at the *Jefferson Reporter* as a non-profit employee, since I was anxious to earn all the money possible as a string correspondent, my aim in life was to be able to find ways and means to enter the University of Virginia.

Soon after returning to Georgia from Louisiana I had, with the encouragement of my mother, written to the University of Virginia for catalogues and bulletins and all other pertinent materials available to a prospective student. Among the items I received, and which I had requested in particular, there was a bulletin describing all the scholarships offered at the university.

It had been quite a shock to learn that the yearly tuition fee charged non-Virginians amounted to several hundred dollars. And the least expensive room and board I could obtain in Charlottesville was twice as much as I had paid in Due West. Including tuition, and calculating other costs closely, the expense of attending the University of Virginia at that time amounted to at least twelve hundred dollars a year. My father said the limit he would be able to let me have would be a third of that sum.

My future as a student at the university was indeed bleak and depressing in outlook. Even if in some mysterious manner the financial obstacle could be eliminated, there was still the almost certainty that I would be unable to qualify for a scholarship based on my deplorable records in high school and at Erskine College.

Unpromising as the future may have been in the spring of the year 1922, nevertheless I was in no mood to allow myself to be discouraged. I remained determined to find a way to become a student at the University of Virginia.

Diligently combing and scanning and rereading all the university materials I could obtain, I was elated to discover late one night in the month of May that I might be able to qualify for and perhaps be granted a tuition-paid scholarship. The particular scholarship had not been used during an interval of several years although it was listed and described as being an active one. It was the only scholarship of its kind listed among scores of others and, remarkably, it was offered neither on the basis of merit nor need. And the grant provided the full amount of tuition for a period of four years.

The only requirement of the applying student was that he would attest that he was a lineal descendant of a soldier in the Confederate Army during the Civil War—or, in other terms, the War Between the States. The Civil War had been over a long time and evidently the scholarship had remained in a dormant state for many years. However, I had no hesitancy whatsoever in reviving the use of the grant and, if necessary, even the controversy on which it was based.

The scholarship of long standing had been established by the United Daughters of the Confederacy and evidently the organization was surprised to learn that it was still being offered. In fact, when I received notification of the grant to me, there was a brief note saying the members of the UDC committee were happy to be able to assist me although few of them were aware that the scholarship was still being offered until my application was received.

It is to be presumed that the admission committee of the University of Virginia likewise was at least mildly surprised when it was realized that a student with a transcript as deficient in scholastic units as mine had been able to enroll in any college or university. My explanation would be that probably my transcript dropped to the floor during the committee meeting on a rainy day and somebody inadvertently stepped on it with a muddy shoe and the resulting blur provided a providential improvement over the original.

I began my first year at the university with an off-campus room at Miss Yeager's, the least expensive rooming and boarding house I could find, and it was my good fortune to get a job in the same neighborhood.

My working hours were from six o'clock in the evening to midnight in a poolroom and the duties were those of a cashier and janitor with the additional assignment to rack the pool balls in the triangle after each game played on the six tables. Also, the owner asked me to glue and clamp new tips on the cue sticks in my spare time. The salary of a dollar a night for six nights a week, together with the money supplied by my parents, enabled me to pay for room, board, class supplies, and some clothing.

Late at night, after most of the students had left the poolroom, I usually found time enough to do some of the writing that was always calling to me. Sometimes this would be in the form of jokes which were slipped under the door of the *Virginia Reel*, the university humor magazine, and that was done stealthily after hours so that I would not be recognized as a would-be contributor. From time to time one of my jokes would appear in print anonymously.

My contributions to the *Reel* did not amount to anything more than a beginner's exercise in the practice of authorship as likewise were the few jokes that were accepted for publication by the nationally-circulated *College Humor*. My abiding interest remained firmly fixed in the creation of fiction and I was fortunate to find inspiration for what I wished to accomplish when I accidently discovered an out-of-the-way alcove in the college library. The secluded recess was a reading area devoted entirely to the display of unassuming little magazines of very small circulation that published experimental poetry and fiction together with essays that were caustic and stimulating.

The names of the little magazines, some of which were only two or three dozen pages in extent, were as unfamiliar to me as were the names of the authors themselves. There was not a single copy to be seen of well-known magazines such as *Collier's* and *Cosmopolitan*. Instead, the magazines on display had such titles as *This Quarter*, *transition*, and *The Prairie Schooner*. I was so impressed by my discovery that I quickly made up my mind to become a part of this new world of writing. And for many years I bravely submitted every short story I wrote to one after another of the little magazines.

It was my keen interest in the work of writers published in the little magazines that led me to discover, in book form, Theodore Dreiser's *Sister Carrie*, Ernest Hemingway's *In Our Time*, and Sherwood Anderson's *Winesburg, Ohio*. After that, I had the comforting feeling that the writing of fiction was to be the work of my lifetime.

= 3 =

With the coming of the spring of 1923 in the undulating foothills of the Blue Ridge Mountains, bringing with it the delicate breezes from the green countryside, I had the feeling of having become completely integrated in the life and environment I had yearned for since my high school days.

I had chosen not to be a candidate for the football team, I had not been tapped by a fraternity, and I had not offered my services as a reporter for *College Topics*, the student newspaper. However, I did try to conform to the prevailing customs and styles and I may have succeeded in acquiring the appearance of being a typical University of Virginia undergraduate. As a willing conformist, I wore a Cape Cod fisherman's yellow slicker in rainy weather, soiled off-white corduroy pants with cuffs dragging behind my heels in fair weather and foul, and I was never without a necktie from the time I dressed in the morning until I went to bed at night.

After finishing my first year at the university, and then returning after a summer at home in Georgia where again I took up the work of a string correspondent and scorekeeper for the Wrens semi-pro baseball team, I began my second year by registering for multiple courses in sociology, economics, and English. These three were the subjects that interested me most of all and I gradually excluded physics, chemistry, and Spanish from my life. From the beginning, I was unconcerned about grades and academic standing and gave little thought as to whether I was passing or failing a course. To me, all that mattered was the intensity of feeling that a subject could impart.

Not limiting myself to undergraduate courses alone, I took the liberty of attending graduate classes in sociology and English. I found these two subjects to be ideally compatible and after field trips from Charlottesville to state hospitals and insane asylums and similar institutions I began writing about what I had observed and the impressions I had received.

At first I wrote strictly factual reports, much like the newspaper correspondence I had done, but then gradually I began using my observations and impressions for sketches and brief fiction. Soon I was more interested in my own reactions than I was in composing theme papers for such English course assignments as "What Wordsworth Means To Me" and "Humanity As Exemplified by the Lake Poets."

Other than being absorbed in my desire to become a writer of fiction depicting the reality of life, and being interested in only a few selected courses of study, I was curious to find out for the first time in my life what the sensation would be and what effect the drinking of a quantity of intoxicating liquor would have on me. Once while a high-school student in Georgia, I had tasted red whisky but it was so small in amount that I had derived no sensation whatever from it.

In the era that was a full decade preceding the repeal of Prohibition, the favorite intoxicant among university students was corn liquor distilled by moonshiners in the nearby Blue Ridge foothills. Moonshining was a highly-profitable occupation among a large number of mountaineers and newspapers often published photographs and lengthy accounts of raids on stills by government agents.

My roommate at Miss Yeager's, Louis Ballou, a student of architecture, and I decided that we should be adventurous and go to the source of supply for a quart-size glass jar of corn liquor instead of buying it from a campus bootlegger. Louis said he was on friendly terms with a student of nursing in training at the University Hospital who had said she would be glad to help us get what we wanted. The girl, whose name was Roberta, told Louis that she had been born and until recently had lived with her family in the moonshining region and could give us explicit directions to find a place about fifteen miles away where corn liquor was distilled and sold for three dollars in quart-size fruit and vegetable canning jars.

With a borrowed car, Louis and I left for the location in the foothills as soon as it was dark on a Sunday night. We easily found the white frame house by the side of the road as directed by Roberta and boldly knocked on the front door.

Louis had the money in hand when the door was opened by a tall black-bearded man of middle age.

"What do you want?" the man said, speaking roughly in an annoyed tone of voice.

"A quart of corn," Louis told him. "Here's three dollars."

"Is that so?" the man said. "Who are you?"

"We're university students—a nurse at the hospital—"

"Well, here's who I am," he told us, reaching into his pocket and showing us the shiny silver badge of a government revenue agent. "How about that?"

"Well, I don't know—exactly—" Louis was able to say.

"Then I'll tell you," he said. "You boys had better go back and have a row with that nurse. That's Roberta and she's my niece. This is not the first time she's sent students out here." His voice had become pleasant and friendly. "Roberta really gave you a turn, didn't she?"

We hurried back to Charlottesville and there we bought the corn liquor in a glass jar from one of the campus bootleggers. Not to be deprived of the experience of becoming totally drunk, and not inclined to waste the time uselessly berating the nurse who had misled us, Louis and I went straight to the back yard of Miss Yeager's boarding house.

There in the quiet of the night we shared the quart of corn liquor to the last drop. Almost immediately, as it seemed, we were reeling, sopping, maudlin drunk and happily engaged in a prolonged and boisterous rough and tumble tussle. I had not had such a satisfying experience since the early days when Bisco and I wrestled endlessly on the white Georgia sand. After fighting like enemies, Louis and I earnestly assured each other that we were friends for life.

A few days after my roommate and I had engaged in the drunken brawl, I spoke to Roberta with the intention of scolding her for having directed us to her uncle's house to buy corn liquor. Roberta pleaded with me to forgive her, saying she was sorry, and indicated that I would be warmly welcomed at the home of her parents if I wished to visit her during a weekend. It was agreed that I would come to see her a few days later.

With a borrowed car, I drove to the same neighborhood where Louis and I had gone to buy corn liquor. I arrived at sunset and knocked on the front door of a house where Roberta had said she would be expecting me.

A burly young mountaineer opened the door and confronted me with a glowering countenance. "What you want here?" he said in a rough manner.

"I came to see Roberta," I answered.

"Like hell you will. Get yourself away from here."

"Why?" I asked in surprise.

"Because I said so."

"Who are you?"

"I'm her brother."

"Why can't I see Roberta? She said—"

"Because she don't see no men. That's why."

"But she said I could come to see her tonight."

"She's said that before. But nobody's going to fool around with her."

"What do you mean?" I asked. "I don't understand—"

"It's none of your business," he told me, shoving me backward across the porch. "And don't come here or nowhere else after her again. She's different. Only part of her is female and the other part ain't. Now get the hell away from here."

When I got back to my room at Miss Yeager's, the first thing I did was to look up the meaning of hermaphrodite in my dictionary. The definition was exactly what I thought it would be.

Chapter Eight

AT THE END OF MY second year at the University of Virginia, in the flowering spring in the rounded foothills of the Blue Ridge Mountains, I had no desire to return to Georgia for the summer and resume the life of a string correspondent and baseball scorekeeper.

By that time, having associated with students from many regions of the United States, I was well aware that I would never be content until I could put myself beyond the confines of the South so that my vision of life would be that of an American and not solely that of a Southerner.

Resolutely, and with no thought of what hazards might be in store for me, I went to Philadelphia on the train and entered the summer session of the Wharton School at the University of Pennsylvania for the study of advanced economics. I had become convinced that, other than acquiring proficiency in writing in the English language, economics and sociology were basic elements necessary for the achievement of reality in interpretive and imaginative storytelling.

I did not have the benefit of another scholarship and I knew without asking that my parents could not afford to pay tuition and my room and board in Philadelphia. And whether my parents approved or disapproved of what I was undertaking remained something I did not pause to ponder.

Foremost in my mind was the need on my part to be totally free to follow my inclinations regardless of how ruthless and harmful my actions might be to friends and family members. Kindness and consideration were admirable characteristics but I felt that first of all as a writer I was obligated to be true to my objectives in life. Anyway, the silence of my parents probably indicated better than words that they did not object to my venture and it may well have been that it was an indication they hoped and believed I would survive in Philadelphia without their help.

And survive in Philadelphia I did.

A newspaper help-wanted advertisement led me to an immediate job as a night-shift counterman in a fast-food cubbyhole on lower Market Street. The hours of work were familiar to me, being from six in the evening to midnight, and the pay was considerably more than I had earned racking pool balls in Charlottesville. Besides, I was permitted to eat all the hot dogs and drink all the orange-colored water I could consume.

With mornings devoted to courses in economics and evenings spent downtown selling hot dogs and excessively-diluted orange juice mostly to men on their way to and from a nearby burlesque theater, my afternoons were free until I came to know a Chinese student in one of my classes at the Wharton School.

Following a friendly conversation after class one morning, I was easily persuaded by Wu Hsi-shan, a young man of my age, who was the English-speaking son of a Shanghai merchant, to act as his guide and protector when he wanted to go downtown to a motion picture theater or to buy clothing at Wanamaker's department store.

Not only was my salary much more than I had ever been paid before for any work, it was also an interesting experience to act as a bodyguard and accompany the young student to a Chinese restaurant for a lengthy exotic meal after we had visited Wanamaker's or had seen an exciting western film. Wu Hsi-shan's favorite actors were Tom Mix and William S. Hart and, when none of their films were being shown, he was always content to be taken to see any motion picture that featured cowboys, outlaws, cattle rustlers, buffalo stampedes, or shoot-outs in frontier saloons.

While successfully protecting Hsi-shan from all harm as I was paid to do, I foolishly let myself be victimized by a streetwalker. This took place on a cold and rainy night about half an hour before midnight closing time at my stand-up, eat-and-drink place of work. An aging young woman in rain-damp clothing and with water-soaked black hair came in from the street and stood shivering forlornly in the bright light at the counter. She was Rosie, a timeworn streetwalker many years older in appearance than in actual age, who several times previously had stopped to say a few casual words while hopefully waiting for somebody to approach her.

On this particular night, Rosie said she was tired and sleepy and rain-soaked and wanted to get out of the miserable weather for the remainder of the night. When I asked her why she did not go home, I could not hear the reply she made in a mumbling of words. But a moment later she began clearly pleading with me to let her sleep where I lived in a student rooming house. She was so insistent that I agreed to let her go home with me.

My single bed was no wider than a cot and I let Rosie use that while I slept on the floor with a pillow and a blanket. When I woke up the next morning to go to my class at the Wharton School, Rosie was no longer there and neither was my biscuit-size Ingersoll one-dollar pocket watch nor the nearly three dollars in change that I had carefully placed on my study table before going to sleep on the floor. However, the savings in my pocketbook which I kept hidden under the mattress had not been touched. When I told Hsishan what had happened, he frowned sympathetically while slowly shaking his head but made no comment about my ineptitude.

I was fully aware at the conclusion of the Wharton School's summer term that classes would soon begin at the University of Virginia. Nevertheless, I had become deeply engrossed in textbook economics to such an extent that I had exciting visions of arbitrage, commodity futures, due bills, free ports, and demurrage that gave me the feeling of a compelling need to enhance my knowledge of economics with practical experience in the field.

Naturally, in order to acquire such necessary knowledge, I was led to search for job-training in retail merchandising. And for the second time a newspaper help-wanted advertisement provided the opportunity for me to go to work immediately in my next endeavor.

The result was that a few hours later I was taking my suitcase with me on the night train to Wilkes-Barre, Pennsylvania, and carrying instructions from the district manager to report at seven o'clock the next morning to the foreman in the basement stockroom of the Kresge variety store.

$$= 2 =$$

My first assignment as a Kresge employee was to open huge wooden hogsheads of straw-packed glasswear from Czechoslovakia, bales of cotton bibs

71

and aprons from Hong Kong, and large crates of toy cuckoo clocks made in Germany. After the merchandise had been inspected for damage and then placed in storage bins, the stockroom foreman then gave me a list of items in quantity to be taken from the basement to the sales counters on the street-level floor and placed on display.

The candy counter and the phonograph record counter were the two most active and constantly patronized areas in the store and required restocking with merchandise several times a day. The salesgirls at those stations, for whatever reason there may have been, invariably appeared to be the most attractive, vivacious, and flirtatious of all the female employees. They were the girls that the floor manager was frequently scolding and reprimanding for spending too much of the company's time on combing their hair and buffing their fingernails instead of being in readiness to serve customers and move merchandise. When warnings were ignored, there had been instances when combs, mirrors, and other cosmetic aids were confiscated.

Provocative and appealing as were some of the salesgirls, there was no opportunity to engage in social mingling with them after store hours. The manager had let it be known that it was a strict company policy not to tolerate dating of Kresge salesgirls by male employees. With this warning in mind, together with the knowledge that a young man prior to my coming had been fired from his stockroom job for defying regulations, I was careful to protect my job by avoiding entanglements with any of the Kresge salesgirls.

In the absence of any social intercourse under the circumstances, one of the assistant managers said that since my evenings were free it would be to my advantage in pursuit of advancement in the Kresge organization to learn the art of dressing street-front windows after the closing of the store at six o'clock. I declined, saying I was engaged in a project of my own at night.

I was content with my job in the stockroom, knowing full well that it was only a temporary interlude in my life, and I had no ambition to advance to the position of store manager or assistant in the Kresge chain. I intended to learn to be a writer and become an author by profession. That was all. As it had been for many years, any other activies were to be used for whatever value they could contribute to help me reach the ultimate goal of being an accomplished storyteller in the written word.

After my first full month on the job, several of the earnest young men in training for advancement invited me to go with them on Sundays in a rented automobile to inspect window displays in Scranton and other nearby cities. I always declined the invitations with thanks, using whatever excuse I could bring to mind, while knowing to myself that I had already gained all the practical experience I needed in stockroom management and window-display arrangement. It was only a few weeks later when I was ready to give up my job and seek something else to do.

Leaving the underground job in the Kresge store and returning to above-ground life, I had the persistence to gain a try-out for the Wilkes-Barre team in the Anthracite Football League. Everybody else at the try-outs looked as if he had been a hard-rock coal miner all his life before deciding to become a hard-nosed football player.

I was assigned to the scrimage squad in the beginning and instructed to get my muscles beefed up as quickly as possible. This was not an easy thing for me to do inasmuch as I was six feet tall and weighed little more than a hundred and fifty pounds.

When the bushy-haired coach, who himself had the bulging muscles of a coal miner, asked me what position I had played at college, I told him the ball-snapping center.

"Not on this team you won't," he said at once. "Centers in this league weigh two hundred pounds or better or else they don't get home for supper very often. Weighing less than that, they'd be taking their meals in the hospital. What else can you play?"

"I never played any other position," I told him.

"So that's all you ever learned at college, huh?"

"I suppose so, but—"

I was silenced by a wave of his hand.

"Never mind," the coach said. "You look skinny enough to be fast on your feet. Maybe you can play at end and catch passes. Since you're a college boy, you ought to be able to learn quick. We'll see. Now get going."

After weeks of scrimmage and three games, I was dropped from the squad when the coach noticed that my bloody nose had been tilted to one side at an odd angle.

Properly sympathetic was the coach, who pointed proudly at his own squashed nose, but moments later I was told that no medical treatment was available for a player with a broken nose who had been dismissed. He did say, though, that perhaps someday better protection would be provided for football players when helmets were made more solid and perhaps face masks of some kind would be attached to headgear to guard against broken noses and damaged teeth.

It was November then and too late to return to Charlottesville for the fall term at the University of Virginia. I could feel the familiar tingling sensation that always accompanied the urge to write something, preferably fiction, but every attempt to write with a pen or pencil instead of using a typewriter was so unsatisfactory that I became too angered and frustrated to continue. I might have rented a typewriter if I could have found one that was not excessively large and cumbersome. Actually, I probably had come to a stage in life where thereafter I was to be overly particular about the size and weight of the yellow paper I preferred for writing as well as insisting on having use of the precise brand and model of typewriter of my choice.

With savings from previous jobs almost exhausted, I searched the Wilkes-Barre and Scranton newspapers for several days before finding a likely help-wanted offering. Acting quickly, I found the job still available when I applied. And I went to work that same night as the short-order chef, waiter, cashier, and janitor on the graveyard shift in the twenty-four-hour restaurant at the Wilkes-Barre Union Railroad Station. It was a comforting feeling after a week of meager meals resulting from dwindling savings to walk into the warmth of the Union Station on a snowy night and immediately find I had the privilege of having a sizzling ham steak and a steaming cup of coffee.

Not only was the restaurant salary substantial, but also I had the privilege of eating all the ham steak, sausage and eggs, apple sauce, cole slaw, Danish pastry, chocolate pie, and glazed doughnuts I could consume between eleven o'clock in the evening and seven o'clock the next morning. After two weeks, my broken nose began to heal, although still slightly tilted, and I had gained almost ten pounds that would have been helpful to a would-be professional football player in a league heavily weighted with anthracite coal miners.

With no restaurant experience other than the serving of hot dogs, I did manage, with one notable exception, to serve the late night and early morning customers without conspicuous fault. To be sure, there were minor complaints about burnt toast and empty water glasses and failure to keep coffee cups full. But what did become a frequent embarrassing early morning event was my failed attempt to serve a regular customer a perfectly timed two-and-a-half-minute boiled egg in an egg cup.

I had not replaced the Ingersoll watch that had been taken by Rosie in Philadelphia, there was no egg timer in the kitchen, and I could not see the minute hand of the station clock distinctly enough to be able to time a boiling egg correctly. The customer who wanted his early morning egg boiled no more and no less than two-and-a-half minutes and served in the unbroken shell in a traditional china egg cup was a middle-aged brakeman who came

74

into the station restaurant every morning, except Sunday, at five o'clock on his way to work in the railroad switchyard.

"What's the matter with you, kid?" the complaining brakeman said many times in his surly manner after breaking the end of the shell with a spoon and testing the consistency of the egg I had boiled for him. "Can't you never do nothing right?"

"I'm sorry," I would say. "I'll try again."

"Quit your trying and do it like I want it," he would say.

I might have asked the brakeman to let me use his railroad watch with the prominent second hand to time his egg. But I was always too intimidated by his gruff manner to make such a suggestion. The only thing I could do was to go back to the kitchen each time and boil egg after egg until one of them was found to be acceptable when the shell was opened.

= 3 =

On the snowy, wind-blown New Year's Day of 1925, I was on my way to Charlottesville in the rickety, engine-knocking, third- or fourth-hand Ford roadster I had bought with the savings sequestered from my earnings at the Wilkes-Barre Union Railroad Station restaurant. The only stopping along the way was intended to be for food for me and gasoline for the automobile. And the only delay occurred when I became lost in Baltimore for nearly two hours and had to ask numerous persons for directions before one citizen could tell me how to go from there to Washington.

A few days later I had registered for a new term at the University of Virginia and had been able to return to the nightly routine of racking balls and replacing cue tips at the poolroom. And I had moved into a small apartment with Louis Ballou.

I was pleased with all of the classes I was taking while the most satisfying one of all was a graduate course conducted by Professor Atchison Hench. My appreciation began immediately with the first meeting of the class when there was no formality whatever imposed upon the twenty students seated at the large and imposing roundtable.

It was then in a casual manner that the tall, soft-spoken, friendly Professor Hench proposed that all of us should feel free to address one another by first name only. Furthermore, he asked us to remember to call him by the name he preferred—Atch.

Even if there might have been any doubt in my mind about my full appreciation of the course of study, it vanished at once when Atch responded to a question by one of the twenty students seated at the roundtable. The outspoken student demanded to know why such an advanced graduate course was listed in the catalogue as English Composition when listing it as Creative Writing would be more academically appropriate. The student then commented that English Composition sounded like an elementary high school course of study and that even some junior colleges had courses listed as Creative Writing.

Atch probably had been asked the same question many times before and this time his pleasant smile and gentle reply indicated that he had fully anticipated such a query. And evident it was that he was pleased to have the opportunity to offer a few comments concerning the academic pomposity of any educational institution that would lead a student to assume that learning the art of writing was as simple a procedure as memorizing the multiplication table or, at the most, being able to recite from memory the sonnets of Shakespeare.

As if undecided how frank he should be in reply to the complaining student, Atch walked the length of the conference room with the appearance of being in deep thought. It was not until he had come back to his chair at the roundtable that he gazed at the gathering of students with a sweeping smile coming to his face.

It was then that Atch Hench made the suggestion that any student who intended to enter the teaching profession might be better off transferring at once to some other college or university that offered courses described as Creative Writing. In that case, he continued, such a person would be well qualified as a professor to contribute to the perpetuation of the illusion that there was an assured way to become a master in the field of writing.

There was a period of silence at the roundtable. Then in a few words Atch let it be inferred that the students who elected to remain in the class and who applied their talents to the basic principles of learning to write acceptable essays and short stories for class projects would profit from the advantages offered by English Composition while letting the others wallow in the slough of Creative Writing.

There were nodding heads and various degrees of smiles at the conclusion of Atch's remarks and not one of the twenty students made a move to leave the room for what might be in prospect elsewhere.

It was during this period that I came to realize that I had acquired an unexpected interest in life that was strictly personal and sentimental and nowise academic. Leaving Atch's class one afternoon, I inattentively walked headlong into an attractive, blonde, startled, graduate student whose name I was to discover was Helen Lannigan and whose age was the same as mine. The immediate result of our accidental meeting was the beginning of a close friendship.

I am sure there were many reasons for my being attracted to Helen in addition to the usual physical desire for coupling. With my battered remains of the Ford roadster still somewhat serviceable, Helen was easily induced to be my companion, on long drives into the countryside in the honeysuckle-perfumed Virginia nights. And when we were not together, I had a yearning for her presence if only for a brief moment while changing classes or meeting on the steps of the library.

Even though Helen was a graduate student at the university and majoring in French after having graduated from the College of William and Mary, I had the belief that we possessed comparable intellects. And in addition to having similar interests, and many likes and dislikes in common, we had a mutually understood attitude toward reading and writing.

Perhaps it was due to the latter circumstance that Helen was sympathetic and understanding and did not hesitate to urge me to follow whatever guiding light that came within my vision. But not only was I encouraged by her to strive to perfect my writing, I was fascinated by her long and silky blonde hair, too.

Before the end of the term, Helen and I went early one morning on the train from Charlottesville to Washington to be married. With the eager help of a jolly-mannered ingratiating taxi driver, who said his name was Jerry and whose cab we took at the railroad station in Washington, we obtained a marriage license and were married that afternoon in the parlor of the taxi driver's pastor.

Immediately after the ceremony, which was witnessed by the minister's weeping wife and smiling Jerry, we went to a Western Union telegraph office. It was then that I sent identically-worded telegrams to Sara in Georgia, Elise in Tennessee, and Maude in South Carolina.

As I recall, the text of the three telegrams was as follows:

MARRIED HELEN LANNIGAN IN WASHINGTON DISTRICT COLUMBIA TODAY STOP THOUGHT YOU WOULD LIKE TO KNOW RIGHT AWAY STOP VERY SORRY DID NOT LET YOU KNOW ABOUT IT SOONER STOP KIND REGARDS AND BEST WISHES ERSKINE

After reading the telegram, Helen's only comment was to the effect that she was surprised I had so quickly forgotten the names of the other young women in Alabama, Florida, North Carolina, and elsewhere with whom I had been intimate and who surely would have appreciated receiving a message of condolence from me.

The taxi driver, smilingly and approvingly, slowly read the telegram aloud to himself. With enthusiastic gestures, he shook hands first with me and then with Helen.

"I always like to help out college students who come to Washington to get married the first time," Jerry said then.

"What do you mean by that—the first time?" I asked him.

"Well, it's somehow like this," he said uneasily. "What I mean is it seems like it happens that college people are always getting married over and over again. While people like me who work at my kind of job somehow usually manage to get married just once and for all."

Chapter Nine

HELEN AND I SPENT OUR honeymoon, and brief it was, on the night train from Washington back to Charlottesville. The reason for our hasty return to the university was because neither of us wished to stay away from our classes any longer than necessary.

The lack of sufficient money being the cause for our not having the privacy of a berth in a sleeping car, our seats for the nightlong trip home were midway in the brightly-lighted Southern Railway passenger coach. This placed us in full view of dozens of curious onlookers who seemingly took fiendish delight in staring at Helen and me as though we were there purposely to provide them with a night of vicarious pleasure. When we boarded the train, the conductor remarked that we looked like a newly married couple, which we readily admitted, and he had lost little time in spreading the word through the coaches.

During the first hour on the train, sinking deeply into our prickly pile seats, we were content to hold hands while talking about our afternoon marriage in Washington and discussing some of our expectations for the future. After a while, lulled by the swaying rhythm of our coach and the pulsating sound of the steam engine's wailing whistle, there were long moments of whispered intimacies and exchanges of endearments, and yet even that soon became far from adequate for such a momentous occasion. For a long time, we wondered what could be done about such a frustrating situation.

Helen and I had often been sexually intimate during a period of many weeks until the time came when we realized that we were so much in love that marriage was not only desirable but inevitable. Now with the ceremony performed, and legally made husband and wife, the realization of actually being married came to be so overwhelming that all restraint gradually began to vanish as though we were alone on the train and not in full view of strangers watching every move we made.

Presently, we could distinctly hear unsuppressed snickers from nearby observers. This was something that could not be ignored and immediately we felt embarrassed to realize we were making a public spectacle of ourselves.

In whispers, and not to be deterred, Helen was quick to propose that when the prying passengers stopped watching us so closely she would go to the lavatory for women at the rear of the coach and wait at the doorway. After that, I was to follow her and we would go inside and lock the lavatory door for privacy.

When Helen left our seat as planned, no one among the passengers took particular notice and shortly afterward I followed her without attracting attention.

Safely behind the locked doors of the lavatory, and not concerned about the possibility of other women passengers trying to enter, Helen and I, swaying with the rhythmical motion of the train, clung together with uninhibited ardor. In the cramped space of the lavatory, there was no way we could make love in the usual manner. However, while there was urgent knocking and rapping on the lavatory door, we ignored the annoying sounds and, hastily improvising under the circumstances, soon consummated our marriage.

During all the time we were in the lavatory, we were lulled by the *click-clack* of the train's wheels on the track and now and then could be heard long and lonely love-calls of the engine's whistle sounding as if calling to its lost mate.

When the lavatory door was opened, we were confronted by two elderly women who had astonished expressions on their faces at the sight of me. And later, after Helen and I had returned to our seats, the conductor stopped and stared at me accusingly with a lifting of his abundant thick eyebrows.

In the dawn of day when we left the train in Charlottesville along with several other passengers, the unsmiling conductor was standing on the station platform. Whether or not he was actually speaking to me, I thought

I could hear him saying that he hoped I would never again ride on his train and inflict distress on female passengers. After leaving the station and looking backward, I could still see the conductor watching me with disdain until Helen and I boarded a streetcar to take us to the university and the morning's classes.

= 2 =

It had been early in March of 1925 when Helen and I were married in Washington and not long after the middle of the same month I again was on a train in the night but this time traveling alone to Atlanta tense with the fervent hope of being able by some act of fortune to get a job as a newspaper reporter.

My decision to withdraw from the University of Virginia before graduation had not been a pleasant action to take after a prolonged and arduous struggle to gain admittance in the beginning. Nevertheless, while disappointment could be endured, ruthless necessity was in complete command of my life.

After two blissful and carefree weeks of married life, I had come to realize with a startling awakening in the harsh light of financial need that my UDC scholarship and meager earnings of a dollar a night in the poolroom did not furnish adequate support for a married couple.

Leaving the university brought additional sadness when, in order to buy the train ticket to Atlanta, I had to sell for as little as it would bring in a forced sale the pitiful but beloved wreck of the first automobile I had ever owned.

It was difficult not to be sentimental deep in the night while the Atlanta-bound train roared and whistled forlornly through the network of flickering lights in the factory towns of North Carolina. With hands tightly gripped, I was able to console myself with the reminder that I would be parted from Helen for only a short time before being reunited somewhere. However, try as I did, I could not keep from feeling dejected and depressed with the sorrowing thought that I was leaving behind forever my car and my university. It was helpful, though, to say to myself from time to time during the remainder of the night that the future was of more importance than the past.

When I left the train at the Union Station in Atlanta in the cool mist of early morning, I was much less confident of the future than I had been during the night but my hope and expectation for the immediate present urged me to walk faster toward the awesome brick building of the *Atlanta Journal* on Forsyth Street.

After walking around the block several times, the purpose being to try to rid myself of as much nervousness as possible, at last I entered the newspaper building and found my way to the newsroom on an upper floor.

The city editor, Hunter Bell, was a gruff-voiced newspaper veteran who spoke a formidable southern Georgia dialect with a drawl that was sure to challenge a listener to try to guess what was being said. As a native of Albany in southwest Georgia, Hunter's pronunciations were best described as being authentically typical of the Allbinny Drawl.

More youthful in years than in appearance for a man in his early thirties, Hunter that morning was wearing a tightly-fitted shirt with brilliant lavender stripes and he had the sleeves rolled above his elbows. Evidently he had shaved earlier that morning but already his face was swarthy with his emerging black beard. All the while his bristling black hair tossed back and forth over his head as if fearful of the consequences of not following his commands.

While I waited for an opportunity to speak to the city editor, he sat hunched over a knife-scarred desk and slashed repeatedly at a sheet of copy paper with broad strokes of his heavy black pencil. The large newsroom was in a din with the noisy clatter of many typewriters and the strident sounds of telephone conversations of reporters in the adjoining sports department.

Finally, Hunter shoved the edited sheet of copy paper aside and at the same time glared at me with an unyielding look as if I had purposely affronted him in some manner.

"Who are you and what do you want?" he said, speaking in a single breath without pause.

I told him my name as quickly as I could and said I wanted to apply for a job on the newspaper.

"Do what on a newspaper—housebreak a lovable little puppy doggy?" Hunter said in another single breath.

Gripping my hands and shoving my clenched fists out of sight in my pockets, I told him in haste that I wanted to work as a reporter, that I had been a student at the University of Virginia, and that I had to leave to find a job. The reason I gave for coming to Atlanta to apply for a newspaper job was that I had been born in Georgia and wanted to work on the best-known newspaper in my native state. I hurriedly finished by telling him that I had majored in English and had studied sociology and economics and had written jokes that had been published in *College Humor* magazine.

Hunter leaned back in his chair with a weary sigh. Jabbing at the top of his desk with the blade of his pocketknife, he said he would never expect to know why supposedly intelligent people did not stay in college and get a worthwhile education instead of thinking they could go to work on a newspaper and have no more worries in life. He was silent for several moments before turning his head to look at me with a slight smile.

"Look here," Hunter said then in his drawling manner. "Listen to me. Forget about those college-boy jokes of yours. We're putting out a newspaper here—not a joke book. And I think by looking at you that maybe you can handle things. I've got two empty desks in this newsroom. And I need help. Go down to the business office on the first floor and find Mr. Brice. That's the name. Brice. Tell him what qualifications you think you've got and your age and what-not. Answer his questions but don't mention college-boy jokes—he's a serious-minded businessman. After he's done with you, go around the corner to a soda fountain and treat yourself to a nice cold Coca-Cola. That's the thing to do in this town. Then you can come back up here in half an hour and I'll let you know one thing or another."

The business manager of the newspaper was an elderly, pleasant, ruddy-faced man with a stout chest and searching gray eyes. He was wearing a black suit, a thin black necktie, a starched white shirt with a high-standing stiff collar, and he had the appearance of being a solemn church deacon who was trusted to deposit every penny of the Sunday offering in the bank on Monday morning. After making careful notations of the information asked of me, Mr. Brice dismissed me with a wave of his hand and turned away abruptly with the loud squeaking of his swivel chair.

I gulped down the Coca-Cola at the soda fountain in all haste and then after delaying as long as I could I went up to the newsroom to find out what Hunter Bell's fateful decision would be. As soon as I entered the newsroom, I could see Hunter beckoning to me with his upraised hand. I hurried to his desk.

"I'm taking you on, Caldwell," he said immediately. "And not because you wrote some jokes for a magazine. Anybody can make up jokes—I've even done that myself. But Mr. Brice passed you along to me and I think you want to make it on this sheet and I need somebody on a typewriter in a hurry. You'll be paid the starting rate. Twenty dollars a week."

Before I could say how pleased I was, he leaned forward and pointed at a vacant chair behind a desk and typewriter.

"That's your station, Caldwell," Hunter was saying, still pointing at the chair with a jabbing of his finger. "And you can start right away. You'll be doing obituaries. That's what I need you for now. People are dying day and night all over town—and complaining like hell about not getting their names in the paper. How do I know dead people are complaining? I've got ears, boy. I've got ears. Now get busy and wind up that typewriter and phone all the undertakers in the city and take in the fresh obits. I don't care how short your obit sticks are just so you fill up two columns of space every day. Now, that's it, boy!"

I could then thank Hunter gratefully for giving me the job and I told him I would be back in three or four days to go to work. I was halfway across the newsroom before he recovered enough to shout at me to come back to his desk.

"What's this about coming to work three or four days from now?" he asked in a tone of voice that was like a confidential whisper. "Is that what I thought I heard you say?"

I told him I wanted to go back to Charlottesville and pack my things to bring to Atlanta.

"Things?" he said said with a slight tilting of his head. "What things?"

"Well, I've got some books and a few other—"

"Books! Books!" Hunter yelled at me. "If I'd known you think more of your bologna-stuffed books than you do about a newspaper job, I'd never have hired you. I want a hard-assed reporter—not a soft-assed bookworm."

"All right, Mr. Bell," I said at once with a submissive smile. "I'll stay here now and go to work. My wife can pack the books for me and bring them down when she comes. I'm sure she won't mind—"

"Good God!" Hunter exclaimed in a loud outburst. "Wife! Is that what you said? You mean you're married?"

All I could do was nod my head while a fearful feeling came over me. There was some consolation, though, in having the thought that while I was on the verge of losing the cherished job at least my application had received favorable treatment in the beginning. This led me to wonder if I could succeed in getting a job as reporter on the *Atlanta Georgian* which was the competing afternoon newspaper. My thoughts were abruptly shattered when Hunter slammed his fist on his desk.

"Look here, Caldwell," he said with a compassionate shaking of his head. "If I'd known that—Holy Jesus! But being married and with that kind of pay—twenty dollars a week—I don't see how—but I'd hate to take back your job after—"

"Please don't do that, Mr. Bell," I begged. "Let me keep the job. My wife and I can manage somehow. Helen will do all she can to help. We talked about not having much money to live on before I left the university."

Hunter slowly leaned back in his chair and gazed across the newsroom as if he were observing a strange object at a great distance.

"Look here, Caldwell," he said presently. "I think I understand how you feel. It's like what happened to me when I was younger and newly married—well, not exactly the same thing but similar—my wife and I—"

Jabbing his finger at the vacant chair behind the desk and typewriter, Hunter said not another word while I hurried to my assigned station to become a reporter for the *Atlanta Journal*.

= 3 =

Free Lunch—After several weeks as a reporter, I had acquired an ability to compose to Hunter Bell's satisfaction three- and four-inch "farewell items" for the daily obituary columns. This achievement led to being assigned to cover the proceedings at the weekly luncheons of Kiwanis, Lions, Rotary, Chamber of Commerce, Convention Bureau, and other businessmen's clubs at the Biltmore, Ansley, and other large hotels.

It was the policy of all the service clubs to provide the press with complimentary meals in return for anticipated favorable mention in the city's three daily newspapers. And it was presumed that Hunter was concerned about the meager income Helen and I had for food and rent and that he was making it possible for me to have numerous free lunches as additional compensation.

At the end of my first week on the luncheon circuit, I had become uncomfortable in the presence of the well-dressed businessmen and would have returned to my desk in the newsroom to resume writing obituaries if Helen had not protested. As the result of her persistent urging, I used part of a week's pay to buy a derby hat and a walking stick. From that moment, dressed as usual in my brown tweed coat with the threadbare cuffs and wearing the baggy-kneed gray trousers, the derby and cane invigorated my psyche to a greater degree than a new made-to-measure three-piece suit could ever have done.

Initiation—My induction into the society of working journalists came about as the result of my having written a highly-embellished encomium describing the accomplishments of the executive secretary of the Atlanta Convention and Tourist Bureau. I had been thoroughly brainwashed by the jolly secretary during a lunch at the Ansley Hotel that consisted of lavish servings of chicken *a la king* and ambrosia *supreme*.

My article that resulted from the sumptuous meal was published in a half-page spread with my by-line. And it was without doubt the prominent spread with by-line that brought about the initiation proceedings by fellow reporters.

The initiation ordeal took place when I was the only reporter on duty on Saturday night watch in the newsroom and, while waiting for the final Sunday edition of the _Journal_ to be put to press, that was when my desk phone rang the first time. The call was from a reporter who said he happened to be at Fort McPherson, an army base in the Atlanta suburb, and I was told that a race riot was in progress with both white soldiers and black soldiers in possession of machine guns and unlimited supplies of live ammunition.

When the reporter who said he was on the scene began dictating his excited account of the race riot for the front page, there were frequent interruptions by _rat-tat-tat_ sounds of machine gun fire in the background. By the time the reporter, supposedly on the scene, had finished dictating, I had made over the entire front page of the Sunday final edition. With that completed, I hastily got up from my desk to take the copy to the printers in the composing room.

Doors were suddenly flung open and there stood the several conspiring reporters shouting exultantly and tapping pencils on the woodwork to simulate the sound of machine guns. It was only a moment until I realized that I had been thoroughly initiated, chagrined, and exhausted by the hour-long ordeal. And it was a long time thereafter until I wanted to see my by-line in a newspaper again.

Book Reviewing—Before the end of my first year as a _Journal_ reporter, I wrote to several newspapers from Richmond to New Orleans saying I would like to write book reviews for their literary sections. Only one reply was received. This response was prompt and enthusiastic and it came in a letter from Cora Harris, the editor of the Sunday book-review page of the _Charlotte Observer._ I was told that she would be glad to send me some books for review and in fact was mailing me half a dozen that same day. While expressing regret for not being able to offer payment, she did say I could keep all the books I received for review.

It was not long until I was receiving many review copies every week. As the result of hasty reading and keeping late hours, I was able to write three or four reviews several times a week. The following morning on my way to work I would sell several of the books for twenty-five cents a copy at a second-hand bookshop. The books I did not sell were packed in large cartons and stored in our flat for some undetermined use in the future. I took care to keep the dust jackets from being torn or smudged so that they would keep the books looking new and unread.

Not long after beginning to write reviews for the North Carolina news-paper I was informed by Cora Harris that my columns were appearing weekly in the *Houston Post* in addition to the *Charlotte Observer.*

While I still was not offered payment, even when my reviews were being syndicated, I hesitated to ask to be paid inasmuch as I was receiving larger bundles of new books, and more often, than I had in the beginning. Conse-quently, I could sell many more books as well as stockpiling large numbers of them in cartons for later use. I had no idea at the time what I might be able to do with hundreds—perhaps even thousands—of copies of new books. That was something I was willing to wait to determine in time to come.

Short Stories—Almost every night, after completing a minimum number of book reviews, I devoted as much time as possible, which was usually as long as I could stay awake, to writing and almost endlessly rewriting a short story. By this time in my life, I had written dozens of short stories and only after long intervals had I persuaded myself to stop rewriting a story and sub-mit it to a large commercial magazine with the hope of finding acceptance and publication. So far, every story had been promptly returned with a blandly-worded rejection slip.

The writing of fiction—the short story and the novel—was to be my sole objective in life. Journalism, book reviewing, or any other gainful activity was a makeshift to be abandoned as soon as I was able to attain my ultimate goal as a writer.

My Mother's New Hat—During my brief career on the *Atlanta Journal*, the only time I ever asked for press passes was when I wanted to see a foot-ball game to be played in Atlanta on Thanksgiving Day between the University of Georgia Bulldogs and the Georgia Tech Yellowjackets. Asking the sports editor for two tickets for Helen and me, to my surprise I was handed four tickets for stadium seats on the fifty-yard line.

I wrote at once to my parents in Wrens and invited them to come to Atlanta to see the game with Helen and me. Several days later my father wrote that they would like to come but that my mother said she did not have a new hat and fall clothes to wear in the city.

What came to mind immediately was the recollection of the time when I was very young and heard my mother tell my father she could not attend a picnic with him because she did not have a new hat to wear. I had felt so sorry for my mother that I told her when I grew up I was going to buy her a pretty hat with long streamers hanging down the back.

On this occasion, Helen wrote to my mother and told her that we were buying her a fashionable fall hat to wear at the football game and described it as having long green ribbons hanging down the back to compliment her auburn hair.

My parents arrived from Wrens in ample time before the game for my mother to try on her new hat in a leisurely manner and decide what would be the most becoming angle for it to be worn.

Chapter Ten

IN 1928, LESS THAN THREE years after Helen and I were married, we were the parents of two sons, Pix and Dabney, and were living on the eastern slope of a round hill in Mount Vernon, Maine.

The gabled, three-story, ten-room, eighteenth-century, wooden dwelling which was to be our home for many years was originally a farmhouse and was surrounded by distant views of crisscrossing rock walls and palisades of white birch. Now painted in subdued shades of gray, the house had been converted in the present century into a summerplace with airy verandas but with only a single fireplace remaining for wintertime heating.

We had come to live in the quiet countryside of Central Maine after I had resigned from my newspaper job even though my salary had been increased to twenty-five dollars a week.

At the time of leaving Atlanta in our aged but sturdy Ford car, I had no thought that our move was a reckless undertaking. Likewise, at no time thereafter did I regret what we had done. There had been discussions for weeks before finally deciding what we were going to do and both Helen and I were convinced we would be able to live at ease regardless of hardships that would surely come upon us.

I am certain that one reason for leaving my job at the Atlanta newspaper was that I felt the need, as in the past, to experience life in some other region of the United States. This habitual inclination to move ever onward might have been caused by the fear of possible confinement in a Louisiana jail or an Erskine College. In addition to any such fear, I was aware of a compulsive desire to devote full time to the practice of storytelling and the invention of credible characters for my way of writing fiction. And to that end, I was determined not to consider a half-way or part-time compromise to be acceptable.

I still had not succeeded in getting even one brief story accepted for publication in a magazine or anthology—either with or without payment. Nevertheless, blindly stubborn or egotistically willful or just plain foolish, I was not to be deterred from trying at any cost to improve my ability to write fiction of my own conception and not to let myself be discouraged by early failures.

With all my might, I intended to work and wait and work some more regardless of whether it would take another year or seven long years to be published. And I was willing to wait those seven years or even longer to produce a publishable novel, whereas in the meantime I was increasingly impatient to get a short story into print.

In this beginning, shortly after our arrival in Mount Vernon, I began experimenting to find out what hours of the day and night were best suited and most productive for me as a writer. I came to find out that there was little noticeable difference in results whether I wrote in the daytime or through the night; consequently, my times of writing day or night came to be as irregular as the tides of the ocean.

What did become a favored routine, however, was the alternating of days for writing and for physical labor. Cutting wood one day and revising a story the next day became so physically and mentally invigorating that any forced change or interruption of the schedule was likely to result in my feeling some degree of resentment.

One of the principal reasons for favoring the state of Maine as a suitable place to live for several years was that I felt the need to go as far away as possible in order to gain a revealing perspective of the scenes and circumstances of life in the South. Other than obvious differences in social customs and economic traditions, there were certain to be more subtle contrasts to be found in family life and public activity. Whatever I was to discover in the North, whether it would be of a startling nature or merely a tedious repetition of the commonplace, I was confident I could make good use of my findings.

Another reason, and it was an important one, for the decision to leave Georgia for Maine was the offer made to me to become the custodian and caretaker of the farm and buildings in Mount Vernon where, for our own use, I would be able to grow potatoes and rutabagas for food and to cut wood for warmth. At the time, being able to live free of rent and grow our own food was a highly opportune event in our lives when our only source of income was from the sale of a review copy of a book for twenty-five cents.

This timely design for living came about when Helen's parents were informed of our intention to move to Northern New England. What was proposed by them was that we occupy their vacation house which they visited only one or two months in summer. Thus it came about that we went to live in Maine, instead of in Vermont or New Hampshire, where for my part I would be expected to help prevent any vandalism from occurring on the property, to help harvest blocks of ice from the frozen lake to be kept in sawdust storage for use in summer, and to make several barrels of cider with the apple press to store in the celler in autumn where it would be kept to ferment to the proper alcoholic degree. At the time, anticipating long months of snowy winter in a large, drafty, bare-floored building with only a wood-burning fireplace for warmth, it seemed to be proper that lighting at night would be provided by kerosene lamps and not by electricity.

Even though I expected to fulfill my obligation as caretaker in good faith, I did intend to devote the greater part of my time in Mount Vernon to writing short stories, novelettes, and full-length novels. And writing book reviews, too.

I was receiving weekly from Cora Harris as many as fifty copies of new books of fiction and non-fiction for review in the *Charlotte Observer* and the *Houston Post*. And still limiting my Sunday reviews to eight or ten in number. As usual, too, I was stockpiling the new books by the hundreds and storing them in cartons stacked to the ceiling in one of the large spare bedrooms.

There was the possibility that the books with a high cover price would be saleable for much more than a quarter of a dollar. However, I preferred to maintain the policy of selling every book for the basic price of twenty-five cents rather than have the dealer reject some of the titles arbitrarily and make it necessary for me to take them back home.

At intervals, which would vary between once and twice a month depending upon when we were in need of items of groceries from the nearest

A & P store, I would take a large load of new books to Portland in our car and sell them at a secondhand bookshop.

Each time I went book peddling with fifty or a hundred copies and received twelve-fifty or twenty-five dollars in cash, I would recall with a nostalgic quiver of remembrance the times in Tennessee when I would be able to accumulate four or five pelts of cottontails I had trapped in rabbit gums and could sell for ten cents each.

= 2 =

In early summer, deep in the silent damp forests of inland Maine, the countryside was an enchanting world of softly unfolding shades of green. The gently undulating hills were dark green islands of spruce and fir, the new-bright green-leafed maple and birch waved a proud plumage in the mild breeze, the lush meadows bordering the meandering streams were verdant carpets, and the placid waters of the lakes were endlessly blue-green in color.

To a newcomer from the Deep South, who had imagined the region of Northern New England to be a panorama of stony fields and jagged hills, the countryside was serene and unhurried, and the aches and pains of civilization were distantly remote. One could surely write to his heart's content in such a place, a voice was heard to say, if writing could ever be done.

Summertime in Maine, though, I was soon to learn, was a brief season during which an unwary newcomer could easily become the prey of the harsh elements of winter. Summer, then, was the allotted season of a few weeks granted by the mercy of nature for the sole purpose of husbanding for winter. Fleeting and urgent, this was the time to seek and acquire at any cost, for nine months of unyielding cold, the essential creature comforts of fuel and food. Food meant potatoes, and I planted potatoes. Fuel meant wood, and I cut wood.

Having little conception of the quantity of wood needed to heat a large house, I asked my next-door neighbor, a farmer named Arthur Dolloff, how many cords of wood did he think I would need for heating from September to May. Walking part of the distance of half a mile between our two houses, Arthur stood by the side of the road and contemplated the gray-painted dwelling on the hillside with a fixed frown on his weathered face. Several times his head moved slightly from side to side while he remained unhurried in comment.

Arthur was a lifetime resident of Maine and had constructed almost single-handedly with native foresight his five-room, story-and-a-half salt-box house. The walls and attic of his gleaming white home were thickly insulated, the rooms were small and low-ceilinged, and he kept the outside foundations permanently banked with sawdust for protection against ground frost. Arthur's attached woodshed, the largest room in the house, was stacked rooftop-high the year around with well-seasoned hardwood for the kitchen and room stoves. Once he and his wife, Erma, had left the state of Maine for a brief interval. That occurred when they went on the train to Florida to spend the month of January but had returned home after only five days in Orlando with the complaint that they could not endure what Arthur called the prickly heat of the tropics.

"Well, Mr. Dolloff," I spoke up presently, "how much heating wood do you think I'll need for the winter?"

"The newcomers never do learn to know better," he said as if I were the one who had changed the subject. "I'd favor making a God-given law against it."

"Against what?" I asked, curious about his remark.

"Painting a dwelling in the God-given State of Maine any color but white. It was Boston people who moved here and started doing it. First it was Swedes from Boston who bought a fine-painted white dwelling down the road from here and painted it as ugly yellow as anybody's old tom cat. Then it was that house where you live that was built to stay white and then was painted gray like a navy ship anchored in Portland Harbor. Anybody but Boston people knows that white is the only God-given color for a respectable Down East dwelling to be."

Arthur turned away from the sight of the gray house on the hill and started moving slowly toward home. Walking beside him, I waited only a few moments before again asking what amount of wood I should provide for the winter.

"Maybe eighteen-twenty cords," Arthur then said. "Unless the Old Boy has a mind to bring down upon us a cold winter. If that's to be, I'd want five-six more for tolerable comfort."

"How cold does it get in winter, Mr. Dolloff?" I asked.

"Twenty below nights, average. Be wise to provide for forty below and not be sorry."

"Well, then, Mr. Dolloff, how long do you think it would take me to cut twenty to twenty-five cords and store it in the woodshed?"

"Not having the benefit of outside assistance?"

"I'll be doing it alone."

"Guess from now to Groundhog Day, maybe a mite longer, if weather permitting."

I remarked that if that was the case then I should get started right away.

"Wouldn't doubt the wisdom of it," he agreed. "Frostbite is a villainous thing."

It was late in summer when I began felling birch trees with ax and saw in the woodlot and stacking the logs in the attached woodshed. The white and gray birch trees grew closer to the house than any other and the wood was lighter to carry than maple or beech. By the time of the first snowfall of autumn, I had cut and stored about ten cords of sap-soaked birch.

As a single-handed accomplishment, it looked like a great amount of ideal firewood to me. However, when Arthur Dolloff came to look at it, and after a brief glance at the stacks of wood, he backed away while shaking his head disapprovingly.

"What do you think of it, Mr. Dolloff?" I asked him.

"Cussed birch won't make heat when it's green and won't do nothing but make ashes when it's dry," he replied without hesitation. "Maybe next year you'll come to have a mind to cut and store the God-given rock maple and keep your family free of chillblains."

With the coming of winter, most of the ten cords of wood had been burned in the fireplace and snow was three feet deep in the woodlot. In order to conserve what wood was left, we kept a fire burning only in the kitchen stove. Daylight at that time of year came late in the morning and, after a few brief hours, it disappeared in the middle of the afternoon. Nights were always colder than zero Fahrenheit and frequently as much as forty below zero. The creaking of the ancient timbers of beams and studs in the cold darkness sounded like the hurried cracking of nuts by hungry squirrels.

Upstairs in my unheated workroom I wore a navy watch cap pulled down over the ears, a sweater, a leather jerkin, and a padded storm coat while seated at my typewriter. I kept a woolen blanket wrapped around my feet and ankles while warming my fingers occasionally in woolen mittens.

Outside the windows of the workroom, stretching eastward over the unending expanse of glistening knee-deep snow and windswept stony hummocks, the winter had put the earth at rest for a season. The only sign of life would sometimes be seen on clear days under pale blue skies when an antlered moose tramped laboriously through the deep snowdrifts.

Arthur Dolloff was so greatly provoked with me when he knocked on our front door during an afternoon snowstorm that at first he stood there saying not a word while stomping his boots on the stoop and scowling at me with obvious displeasure.

Finally, when Arthur did speak, his complaint was that the brown field rats that were in the habit of coming to live in the warmth of the cellar of our house in the depth of winter had moved down the road to the warmth of the Dolloff cellar where they were devouring Erma Dolloff's choice cooking apples and Arthur's state fair prize-winning seed potatoes kept for spring planting.

"I didn't know the rats would do anything like that, Mr. Dolloff," I said meekly. "I mean, I didn't know they would move from one house to another in wintertime."

"Well, now you know it," he said sharply. "Those brown field creatures can be smarter than some of the ordinary humans. And if you had enough heat in your house, those cussed rats would've stayed here where they have a lifetime habit of wintering."

Arthur gazed at me with a squinting of his eyes as if undecided whether to pity me for my ignorance or whether to rebuke me outright for being the cause of the invasion of the rats at his house.

"The whole cussed trouble," he said at last, "is that you newcomers from Boston or some other blighted locality don't abide by God-given customs like a Mount Vernon townsman rightfully does."

Turning away abruptly after that, and with not another word spoken by either of us, Arthur began trudging homeward through the swirling snow in the early darkness of a winter day.

That same night, and occasionally for nights afterward, there could be heard the muffled sound of shotgun blasts in Arthur's cellar as he fired away in an effort to rid his premises of the horde of warmth-seeking brown field rats and save his wife's cooking apples and his blue-ribbon seed potatoes.

= 3 =

I was living during a period of my life when possibly I could have been permanently discouraged and might never have recovered enough confidence to continue striving to attain some degree of success as a writer of fiction.

If I had measured my conception of success by the amount of money to be earned as a writer, rather than by a self-imposed standard of significant storytelling, I would have had good reason to abandon forever writing as an occupation. Somewhere along the way I had acquired the belief that it was best for me not to consider writing as a means of making money but instead to produce fiction that would be worthy of recompense.

It could be that this attitude was responsible for the fact that I was never of a mind to write a short story or novel with preconceived plot or ending. While writing, with people and situation established to my satisfaction, my engrossing interest then as a writer—and as I perceived the quest of a reader to be also—was to discover what was going to happen next in the story.

In storytelling, what I wanted to portray was a revelation of the human spirit in the agony of stress or the throb of ecstasy. And I believed this could be accomplished effectively only when characters and situations were invented by me and were not imitations of life but interpretations thereof. Consequently, I felt it was necessary for fiction to seem to be more real than life itself in order for it to be believable in the mind of the reader. True realism then was not the reality of life but a forceful illusion of it.

I suppose I was entitled at this time to ponder and to meditate concerning my future in philosophical terms since it did diminish the reality of the present. This reality was the consistent rejection of my stories by magazine editors and which resulted in the almost daily routine of waiting ever hopefully at our roadside mailbox for the delivery of mail by the R.F.D. carrier.

Waiting, ever waiting, was an ordeal I probably imposed upon myself so as to generate enough fortitude and stamina to be able to endure the consequences of trying to become a published writer. The officious mailman himself, becoming annoyingly sympathetic, was able to determine by the size and weight of arriving mail that my returned manuscripts precluded checks of acceptance from editors.

Well! After all that time, I was in no way prepared for the surprise of seeing my first short story in print.

What I had received in the mail on this day of days was an issue of *transition,* an English-language literary magazine published in France and with it in the large envelope was a letter from the editor inviting me to submit more of my stories. The letter also stated that the magazine was unable to offer payment for published material.

The brief story in *transition* appeared with the title of "July," which was one of several names I had used when it was submitted to several other publications. Later it was reprinted in collections and anthologies with the final title of "Midsummer Passion." The multiple titles for the same story resulted from a whimsical notion that each time it was rejected by a magazine under one title then a different name for it would perhaps make it acceptable by another magazine. I decided then that once was enough use of an artful wile and, with increasing doubts about it being an ethical procedure, I never again resorted to such legerdemain to try to get anything published.

It was not until much later after the flurry of excitement had subsided that I realized that "Midsummer Passion" was a story with state of Maine characters in a local setting and had been written in New England only a few months after we had moved there from the South.

Enthusiastic I was at the time, and temporarily putting aside my abiding involvement with Southern social and economic life as material for my writing, my new-found environment was an inspiring and irresistible source of material for storytelling. Several other stories with Mount Vernon scenes had been written during that same period, among them being "A Very Late Spring," "Over the Green Mountains," and "Country Full of Swedes."

The jubilation at our house on that day when the first story arrived in print was unrestrained.

The excitement lasted not just for one day but for many and in the end many changes in our lives had taken place.

First of all, I decided to stop reviewing books for Cora Harris and to devote all my time to the writing of fiction. There were to be no more long hours in the night reading books written by other persons. My time was to be my own in an exciting new era.

Next, it was proposed by Helen that, instead of continuing to sell books to dealers from the stock of review copies on hand for a quarter each, we should open a bookshop of our own and use the approximately three thousand accumulated copies to sell for the full cover prices that ranged from two dollars to ten dollars and more.

Finally, taking the few dollars remaining from the recent sale of review books, Helen and I took Pix and Dabney to the village store and the four of us gorged ourselves on walnut fudge ice cream.

Chapter Eleven

THE CELEBRATION OF THE FIRST publication of a work of fiction in a magazine came to a glorious climax with a magnificent bonfire in the mild breeze of a sunny day on the shore of the lake at the bottom of our hill.

To begin with, Helen and I had started the fire with the entire collection of rejection slips received from magazine editors over the years. The refusal notices of various sizes and wordings had been kept until then in several shoe boxes expressly for such an occasion.

Continuing the ceremony, I had not been satisfied until I had burned to ashes the dozens of short stories I myself wanted to reject then as being better unseen than kept any longer as a reminder of my early ineptitude.

And then finally, with self-criticism unrestrained, one by one I had put to fire the collection of poems that Louis Untermeyer had read and had kindly returned with the advice for me to seek my future in prose and not in poetry.

I was still as fully committed as I had ever been in the past to suffer from or to profit by the unpredictable fortunes of a writer of fiction although for the present there was the necessity to provide livelihood. This immediate need had taken me to Portland where I had rented a vacant store on Congress Street at Longfellow Square. The purpose of this being, as Helen had proposed, to stock a bookshop with our more than three thousand review copies to sell at the retail cover price of two dollars and two-fifty and upward.

While there were still more books to be transported from Mount Vernon to the store at Longfellow Square, and not yet having sold the first copy of those on hand, we had been advised by a pleasant-mannered young man with a trim mustache, who said he was the representative of a window-cleaning company, that it would be to our benefit for business purposes to contract for weekly service.

Otherwise, we were given to understand, there was the possibility that bookshop trade would be disrupted and our customers inconvenienced.

As an indication of what might take place, the affable salesman described in vivid detail the recent stink-bombing of the dry-cleaning establishment next door and stated that the owners had failed to take advantage of the opportunity to sign a contract with his window-cleaning company. I had declined to enter into an agreement by saying there was no money available for the service and that the street-front display window was so small that a few swipes with a damp towel would be sufficient.

Although the door was open, the bookshop was still not ready for business when the next proposal was received. This was an offer made by a slender young woman who appeared to be between twenty-five and thirty years old and who had long brown hair and an engagingly lingering smile. She indicated from the beginning that she had no interest in reading or buying books and had come into the store for the express purpose of getting permission to leave a large quantity of her business cards on display to be available for her prospective clients or customers.

After a lengthy conversation, I still was unable to find out anything about the persistent young woman other than that she was offering her services as a companion of an unspecified nature.

Whenever I questioned the young woman about her name, and the type of companionship she offered, the result was that she always pointed to the word "Companionship" on her business card. After she had placed a stack of her cards on a table and was turning to leave the bookshop, I asked her once more to let me know her name. What she did then was point at her telephone number on the card and leave with a smile on her face.

Like the first two persons who had visited the bookshop, the third visitor likewise was not to be a customer. The person this time was a pleasant young woman with almost imperceptible traces of graying in her dark hair and she introduced herself as being one of the librarians in the children's section of the Portland Public Library.

"Everybody calls me Eve," she had said with a toss of her head, "and I'm so glad they do. I like it because I detest my given name and think Eve is the most suitable name of all for my personality."

I did not ask then to be told her given name but later I found out that it was Alphonsine.

The object of the visit to the bookshop—Eve or Alphonsine—had quickly been made known. She was resigning from her position at the library and was planning to take a nun's vow of celibacy for admittance to a convent. The library staff was arranging a "farewell Moxie party" in honor of Eve and Helen and I were being invited as owners of a new bookshop in town. The party was to be held the next day in the basement of the city library where the children's section would be closed for the afternoon and where ice-cold Moxie and cookies made by librarians would be served to adults.

Long after Eve's invitation had been accepted, she still appeared to be reluctant to leave the bookshop. After several intervals of silence, she then said boldly that she needed to confide in somebody other than a member of the library staff or even a relative or close friend.

"What am I to do?" she said weakly with a helpless drooping of her head. She was silent for several moments as she looked down at the nervous entwining of her fingers. Presently she glanced up with a pleading expression. "Oh, what can I do?"

After that, little urging was needed to induce Eve to say what was so distressing. With a brightening of her countenance, she was soon revealing that she would feel unworthy of taking the vow of celibacy and entering a nunnery as planned if she did so when still a virgin. Evidently she believed that a woman could not be truly penitent as a nun if she had not committed adultery or fornication. Consequently, believing as she did, she was fearful she would never have peace of mind as a nun and would regret it for the rest of her life if she failed to leave her maidenhood behind her in the secular world.

When I suggested that it probably would be helpful if she talked to a Catholic priest about her trying situation, the distraught Eve immediately became tearful and ran crying from the bookshop and then out of sight around the corner.

The next afternoon at the farewell party for Eve in the public library, before we could speak to anyone else, Helen and I were introduced to a bright-eyed young woman with tumbling blonde hair who said she had come to the library party purposely to meet us because she had been told that we were opening a small bookshop at Longfellow Square.

To no extent reticent concerning her personal life, the assertive young woman said she did not want to return home to Brookline, Massachusetts, where she would be compelled to live a restricted existence with her possessive mother. Instead, she said, what she wanted more than anything else was to live in Portland in freedom from domination and, with her adequate monthly remittance, become a bookseller with us in our new store. Her name was Marge Morse. Marge was tall and blonde and attractively slender. It was soon disclosed that she was a recent graduate of Smith College in Massachusetts and had lived during the past year in Switzerland where her life had been made miserable by an unfulfilled love affair.

Soon after meeting the vivacious Marge Morse it seemed to me that she would be an ideal assistant in the bookshop and both Helen and I had been impressed by her friendly personality and quiet aggressiveness. I had no intention of devoting time of my own trying to sell books of other writers when I had my own ambition to foster and I intended to be relieved of any such obligation as soon as the Longfellow Square Bookshop could be completely stocked and opened for business. It appeared to me to be wise to let Helen and Marge Morse assume complete charge of the store. With all this in mind, an appointment was made for the three of us to meet the next day to talk at length about Marge coming to work with us.

We had been at the farewell party for almost an hour and were ready to leave when we saw Eve in the crowd standing at the Moxie-and-cookie table. Waving both hands, Eve ran to catch up with us before we could leave. She was breathless and excited.

"I want you to know," she said, lowering her voice and leaning forward to speak in confidence. "It's the most marvelous thing! You've just got to hear about it!"

The three of us went to a quiet corner of the library.

"Now, here's what happened," Eve said, her voice husky with excitement. "I didn't speak to a priest as you suggested. It would've been too embarrassing. It wouldn't be like going to confession at the cathedral. Instead, last night at a friend's house by sheer luck I met a young, unmarried, very handsome Unitarian minister—and I spoke to him. I really did. And he was so understanding and very anxious to help me. So the way it turned out— yes, indeed—everything was what I had hoped for. And the way it all happened—I was so fortunate—it happened before it was too late."

Below: Caroline Bell Caldwell, Erskine's mother (1901). Right: Ira Sylvester Caldwell, EC's father (1895).

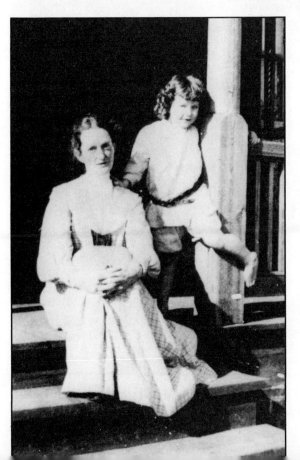

Above: Ira Caldwell (1930). Left: Young Erskine with his mother in Prosperity, South Carolina (1908).

"Our new home in the small town of Wrens in eastern Georgia was the paint-flaked, rusting tin-roofed manse of the Associate Reformed Presbyterian Church. The five-room dwelling, together with a detached wood shed and a chicken house, was situated on a narrow lot under tall weeping-willow trees."

Erskine Caldwell (left) and Helen Caldwell (far right) with a neighbor and sons Dee (Dabney) and Pix in Mount Vernon, Maine (1931).

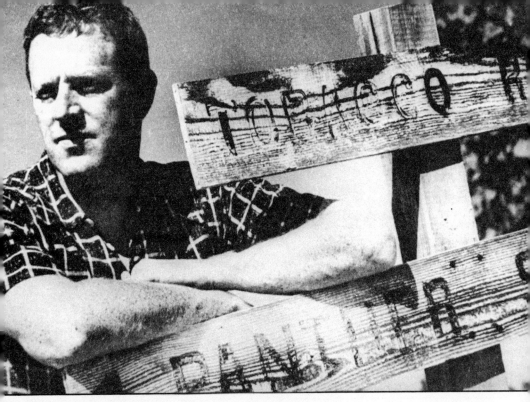

Erskine Caldwell on Tobacco Road near Augusta, Georgia. Photo by Margaret Bourke-White (1936).

Left: Helen Caldwell in Hollywood, Florida (1939). Above: EC's daughter Janet Caldwell (1943).

Erskine and Margaret Bourke-White on board a British wartime convoy ship in the Barents Sea (1941).

Left: Erskine broadcasting from Moscow during the German-Russian War (1941). Above: Third wife June Caldwell (1951).

= 2 =

Elated by the new freedom to devote all my time to the pursuit of author-ship, no longer being obligated to spend hours and hours reading books for review and with the Longfellow Square Bookshop open for business in charge of Helen and Marge, I was anxious to take a night bus as soon as possible to New York with a suitcase full of manuscripts. And I would not fail to take my Corona portable typewiter and Target cigarette-making machine with me.

Sales at the bookshop after the first week had amounted to only a few dollars and probably not enough to pay the bill for electricity. There were no profits for me to draw upon and so I took one of the few remaining loads of review copies from the storage room in Mount Vernon and sold them to a Portland secondhand dealer for the usual twenty-five cents each.

In the morning of my first day in New York, having rented a hall bedroom with cot for three dollars a week, I selected at random the name of one of the several literary agents listed in the telephone directory. After having made an appointment for the same afternoon, I went to the address on Madison Avenue with my suitcase full of short stories, novelettes, and fragments of novels in various stages of completion.

The literary agent took a long, interested look at the pile of manuscripts I placed on his desk. Presently he said there was such a great amount of material to be inspected that I would have to leave everything for him to read at a later date. I had no intention of leaving a lifetime accumulation of manuscripts in New York with a stranger and I quickly made excuses not to do so.

As I was leaving the office, the agent said I would be welcome to bring back the manuscripts at any time and leave them for a reading and evalua-tion. And then in parting, he said with a smile and a firm handshake that my name was suitable for literary purposes and that we would not have to change it to something else.

Among the papers in my collection of pieces of fiction was a letter I had received previously from Alfred Kreymborg, who together with Lewis Mumford and Paul Rosenfeld edited the *New American Caravan*. The let-ter had informed me that a short story I had submitted would be published in the forthcoming issue of the anthology. The story was the same one that had been published in *transition* earlier with one of the multiple titles I had used in order to gain acceptance by an editor.

I was unable to speak to Alfred Kreymborg on the phone, but somebody at his address promised to deliver my message to him. The following day I received a telephone call from a person who spoke so rapidly with a distinctive German accent that for a while what he was saying was completely unintelligible to me. When I did not respond, the caller then began speaking more slowly and distinctly.

What I heard then was that the caller's name was Erich Posselt, that he had been talking to Alfred Kreymborg, and that he wanted to publish a book of mine. When I told him that I had an unpublished novelette with me in New York, he asked me at once to bring it with me and meet him exactly in one hour on the curb at the northwest corner of Madison Avenue at 44th Street.

I was at the designated meeting place at least a quarter of an hour early. Nervous and waiting expectantly on the curb beside my large tan leather suitcase, I wondered why a publisher would want me to meet him on a New York sidewalk rather than at his office. The only reason I could think of was that he might be so busy with his publishing activities that he could only find enough time to speak to me in passing while hurrying from one appointment to the next.

The sidewalk was crowded with people walking briskly in both directions and during that time not one person had given the slightest indication that he might be in search of me. Glancing anxiously at my watch, I could see that it was exactly ten minutes past the time for our meeting at the curb. When I looked again, the time was almost fifteen minutes past the hour.

Suddenly there was a sharp blast of a taxi horn behind me in the street and I looked around at that moment just as the rear door of the taxi was flung open. Inside, somebody was beckoning to me with urgent motions of his hand.

"Here I am—Erich Posselt—you're Caldwell," I was told in the same strange-sounding accent I had heard over the phone. The dark-haired, lean-faced man did not appear to be more than thirty years old and was not stout and full-faced as I had imagined him to be. "Yes, I'm Erich Posselt. Hop in and we'll get acquainted. We don't like to waste time, do we? It's a great life but a damn short one, huh? That's what people here in your country like to say. Yes?"

As for his qualifications as a publisher, Erich said he had had wide experience and considerable success as a literary agent and, while that career had served its purpose, he now fully expected to be far more successful financially as a publisher. The more he talked about himself, the more enthusiastic he became, while less became my concern about his abilities as a publisher and a trustworthy person. Probably by prearrangement with the taxi driver, we had already gone uptown as far as Harlem and were returning down Park Avenue.

Erich did not ask to see the manuscript of the novelette until the taxi stopped in front of the brownstone dwelling on West 49th where I was staying in a hall bedroom on the top floor. The location was in the area where noisy poundings and drillings were being made continuously day and night with all the attendant sounds prior to the actual construction of Rockefeller Center. Due to the jarring vibrations and disquieting sounds, the rents charged at the soon-to-be demolished brownstone rooming houses were the lowest in the city.

The taxi driver put fingers in both ears to deaden the sounds in the street while I was opening the suitcase and getting the untitled manuscript for Erich. It had been arranged that Erich would read the novelette while riding in the taxi for the next hour and, it being a more quiet area, he would then meet me on the curb of the southwest corner of Fifth Avenue and 47th Street.

Before leaving in the taxi, Erich promised he would make a quick decision about publishing the novelette and assured me there would no quibbling on his part over reasonable terms of publication. By then, I was so excited by the prospect of having my first book published that, if Erich had made the request, I probably would have signed over to him all rights to the suitcase full of manuscripts.

Less than an hour later, I was standing at the curb on Fifth Avenue at 47th Street waiting nervously for the taxi to arrive with Erich Posselt. Over and over, I was repeating the spoken hope that my book would be accepted and published.

Within only a few minutes of the time agreed upon, I was seated beside Erich in the taxi and he was shaking my hand with a firm clasp. Then with an assenting nod he quickly withdrew his hand and opened his large briefcase. He did not speak until he had taken out a set of documents that appeared to be the contract for publication of the novelette.

"We are in business, Caldwell," Erich said with a pleased smile, speaking slowly and distinctly. "You've written a fine book and I'm proud to be your publisher. Now, you sign and I sign. Soon there will be a beautiful book and both of us will be very happy about it. That makes the good life for both the author and the publisher, huh?"

Without hesitation, I signed two copies of the contract without having read a single word of it. We had traveled then as far as Greenwich Village when the driver turned the taxi around to take us back uptown.

Along the way, I was handed my copy of the contract with The Heron Press which had been signed by the president and editor, Erich Posselt, and with it a check for the amount of two hundred and fifty dollars. It was the first money I had ever received for my writings and was such a large sum that all I could do was stare with glazed eyes at the check in my hand.

We had reached 49th Street by that time and, as I was leaving the taxi, I heard Erich saying that the untitled manuscript would have to have a name for publication and for that he had chosen the title of *The Bastard*. I was not certain that I liked the title Erich had given my novelette without first consulting me but in my distracted condition I could not bring myself to argue about it.

As I stood on the sidewalk and watched the taxi and Erich Posselt disappear around the corner, I found myself not thinking about the title of my book but wondering if Erich actually had an office of any kind or if he always conducted his publishing business as it had been that day on the back seat of a New York taxicab.

= 3 =

I returned to Maine much sooner than I had planned. It was having the contract for the publication of my first book that had impelled me to go home and write and revise and write some more. And it had been even more inspiring when, after being at home only a few days, I received a briefly-worded note from Maxwell Perkins who was editor-in-chief of Charles Scribner's Sons.

The surprising letter from Maxwell stated that he had read several of my short stories in little magazines and that he hoped I would let *Scribner's Magazine* see some of my unpublished stories. Without delay, I began sending Max Perkins a story a day for a week. And each story was promptly returned. But I was in no mood to accept discouragement. Thereafter I sent him two stories a week for a month.

Finally, feeling morose and restless as the result of no favorable action by Max Perkins, and at the same time knowing that Helen and Marge Morse were selling enough review copies to keep the Longfellow Square Bookshop in business, I decided to travel rather than wait for what might be of no consequence in the end. By that time I had begun to wonder if Max Perkins would ever accept a story of mine for magazine publication.

Since moving to Maine from Georgia, except for a very few trips by bus to Boston or New York, I had been confined at home and unable to travel widely as I had in the past. The destination that appealed to me then most of all was the Pacific Coast and, since I had never been farther west than Arkansas, I knew I would never be satisfied with my life until I took that transcontinental journey.

I spent many days trying to convince myself that I could travel across the United States on a bus and have enough money left for living expenses when I arrived. Helen was in favor of my taking the long trip that meant so much to me although she tried to persuade me to wait until more money would be available.

Then suddenly all worry vanished. Max Perkins not only accepted for publication in *Scribner's Magazine* two short stories, he also proposed the publication of a collection of my stories in a volume which later I decided to call *American Earth*. I immediately had three hundred and fifty dollars in addition to the advanced royalty given me by Erich Posselt and in a few days I began the trip that was to take me to Los Angeles. I took with me the tan leather suitcase, my Target cigarette-making machine, and my Corona portable typewriter.

In my eagerness to reach the Pacific Coast, except for a one-night stop-over in Kansas City, Missouri, my living and sleeping took place on a Greyhound bus for five days and five nights between New York and Los Angeles. After arriving at the end of the bus trip, I took a streetcar to Hollywood in search of an inexpensive hotel or lodging house. I had been told at the bus station that there were several small hotels in the vicinity of Vine Street and Hollywood Boulevard.

When I left the streetcar and had walked a short distance, the first hotel I saw was a small, three-story, white-stucco building with the name Mark Twain over its entrance. Inside, when I asked about the cost of a room, the rate quoted by the clerk was much more than I could afford to pay. The clerk then said he could offer something cheaper if I paid a week in advance.

When I told him I had baggage and should not have to pay in advance, pointing at my suitcase and typewriter, the clerk turned away with a wave of his hand.

"That's a typewriter you've got there," he said accusingly. "You'll have to go somewhere else for a room. I have nothing for you in the Mark Twain. We've had nothing but trouble with writers with typewriters. They come in here from all over the country with big notions and run up big bills. Then they skip out in the middle of the night and all we ever find left behind is an empty suitcase. They always somehow manage to get away with their typewriters."

Lugging my suitcase and typewriter, I went down the street toward Sunset Boulevard and entered the first hotel I reached. It was the Warwick Hotel, only two stories in height and much smaller than the Mark Twain, and its lobby was comfortably furnished for lounging. A woman with a pleasant smile and ringlets of blonde curls, appearing to be about thirty-five years old, asked me in a deeply-accented Southern voice if I wished to rent a room by the day or by the week. When I was told that the weekly rate was seven dollars, I promptly signed the register with my name and address. I was not asked to pay in advance.

On the way to my room, the curly-haired woman asked me if I actually lived in Maine as indicated when I registered. When I assured her that I did, she said she would have to believe me but it was plainly evident that I had spent enough time somewhere in the South to acquire an authentic Southern accent.

When I reached my room, I locked the door and closed the curtains over the window. I knew I was going to fall asleep any moment after days and nights of lost sleep on the bus and I could barely keep my eyes open any longer. But first I wanted to roll a cigarette with my Target machine. Then lighting the cigarette, I took a long and satisfying draught of tobacco smoke and immediately fell forward on the wide bed.

I remembered nothing after that until I was partly awakened from a deep sleep hours later by a noisy commotion in the hall outside my door. Drowsy as I was, and annoyed to be waked up, I was wondering why any hotel would tolerate such a disturbance and permit guests to go on a shouting rampage in the middle of the night.

At the height of the din, I opened my eyes wide enough to see a helmeted fireman, after he had splintered the wooden door with an ax, enter the room with the sweeping beam of a spotlight.

It was then for the first time that I was aware of the unmistakable odor of burning cotton in the room. After that, I could see a haze of grayish smoke hovering over me.

I finally realized what had happened when two of the firemen lifted me roughly from the bed and two other firemen doused the smouldering mattress with fire extinguishers. It was then that I stood beside the bed and saw that at least half of the mattress had been burned completely and left only the metal bedsprings to be seen.

"The poor guy doesn't know how lucky he is," one of the firemen said after inspecting my body for any evidence of burns. "They're not all that lucky—smoking in bed. And another half-hour—maybe an hour—and he'd been burned dead for sure."

The chief of the fire squad asked the curly-haired owner of the hotel if she intended to call the police and have me arrested for smoking in bed and setting the mattress on fire with my cigarette.

"No," she said firmly. "I'm going to move him to another room and let him get some sleep. He traveled all the way across the country on a bus and I feel sorry for him. No, I don't want him arrested. He talks just like anybody in Georgia—and I'm from Georgia, too. No, I don't want him taken away. I'm going to keep him right here."

Chapter Twelve

AFTER ALMOST TWO WEEKS devoted to days and nights of writing in my room at the Warwick Hotel in Hollywood, I suddenly had become so dissatisfied with the results of my work that when I woke up on a foggy morning I immediately began making plans to leave. I soon had my clothes and papers packed in the suitcase and realized that I had the same feeling about the numerous short stories I had been writing and revising that I always experienced when I concluded that a certain story had reached the limits of refinement and was not to be subjected to another moment of close scrutiny.

What I was well aware of was that I realized the time had come for me to put short stories aside for a while and begin working on a full-length novel. The novel was vague in concept but little by little it was becoming discernible in my consciousness. And I was not being deluded by the belief that I had mastered the short story as a form of fiction, because I was convinced that in its perfection it represented the sum and substance of all imaginative writing.

With little forethought but motivated by recollections of the past, I set myself to return to the bleak surroundings of the tenant farmers and sharecropping families existing in the wasteland of a vanished agricultural empire. Happy with my decision to leave Hollywood, I took the first bus leaving for the long trip back to a familiar land.

I had been away from East Georgia in the vicinity of the Savannah River for a long time and I went back to find that there were new school buildings, that some of the weather-grayed churches had been painted, and that a few of the sand-and-clay roads had been paved. The landless and the sickly and the poverty-stricken families, though, both black and white, were still existing in their bare hovels on sand hills and tobacco roads.

These were the pathetic people, most of them being illiterate and in ill-health for the length of their days, who existed in timeless agony without hope on earth but clinging to the belief that their pains and hunger would miraculously disappear when they were born again as so glibly promised by every passing evangelist. Their tragic lot was to have come into the world before the conscience of their fellow men rose to provide assistance and welfare for the unfortunate. I often recalled my father's way of expressing compassion for their predicament when he would say "those people are as God-forsaken as a toad in a post hole."

One day after another in the wintry weather of East Georgia I went into the remote countryside of a triangle formed by parts of Jefferson, Burke, and Richmond counties and always found it difficult to put down on paper a satisfactory realistic image and interpretation of degredation as I had observed it. The difficulty I was having with my writing then was made even less bearable by the landlady from whom I had rented a furnished room on Telfair Street in downtown Augusta.

My room was in a dilapidated, three-story lodging house with sagging portico and weather-grayed walls. In earlier times it had been the elegant mansion of a wealthy cotton broker and now was a dismal sight in a weed-grown garden behind a rusting iron fence.

The climate of Augusta and the surrounding sand hills of Richmond County at that time of year was usually mild and balmy. And my visit would not have been so uncomfortable if the weather had not turned unseasonably damp and cold with frosty nights and sunless days. There were no means whatsoever to provide my room with the "cozy warmth" so often mentioned by the ingratiating, frizzly-haired, heavy-breasted, fifty-year-old landlady with the smiling snuff-stained lips.

It was a morning several days after I had moved into the lodging house with my suitcase and typewriter when I woke up shivering in the cold draft of damp air. That was when I realized that the several pipes of various sizes in a corner of the room were merely exposed bathroom pipes and that not a single one of them was there to provide gas or steam to heat my room.

As soon as I could dress and find the landlady, I told her that I wanted to move to another room that provided the cozy warmth she had promised. With a nervous chewing on the snuffstick in the corner of her mouth, she said all the other rooms in the house were occupied but that I could come to her room and enjoy the warmth of her electric heater whenever I felt chilly.

"Look here, Mrs. Henderson," I told her right away, "I want the privacy of a heated room of my own. I'm a writer and that's why I'm here and it's what I need in order to do my work. You shouldn't have rented me a room that was not going to have heat in this kind of weather."

The landlady, with her eyes blinking mistily, looked hurt and offended. Lowering her head, she wiped her cheeks with the wad of a small handkerchief. Presently, and with quivering lips, she pressed the palms of her hands against her cheeks.

"I'm just a poor, childless woman all alone in the world," she said forlornly as a single tear rolled down her cheek. "My husband died twelve years ago leaving me this house and thinking I'd be safe and sound to the end of my days. But something's always going wrong that has to be fixed and I'll never have enough money to buy an electric heater for every room in this house."

"I'm sorry to hear that, Mrs. Henderson," I said. "And I wouldn't complain about the lack of heat if it hadn't been for this cold weather these frosty nights—"

The landlady reached out and clutched my arm with a desperate grip. More tears were trickling down her flushed cheeks.

"Please don't make me give you back the rent money you paid in advance—please don't go somewhere else and rent a room—please stay here—I'll—I'll—"

My thought was that the perturbed Mrs. Henderson was going to offer— even insist—that I take her electric heater to my room and I was wondering if I would want to accept such a favor and leave her without heat. With a pathetic quivering of her lips, she tightened the grip on my arm.

"I'm going to leave you now and go to my room," she said in a calm voice as the lines on her face softened with a smile. In another moment, she had relaxed her grip on my arm and was moving backward. "Yes, I'm going to my room now. And when I get there, I'm going to kneel down and begin praying long and earnest for a change in the weather. God always listens to me when I'm humble and serious and pray for something important in deep earnest. This time I'll be so earnest that God will want to hurry and make this cold spell of weather go away and not let it last another night."

When I woke up the next morning, the day was sunny and warm. More than that, sitting up in bed, I found that I had been sleeping in the warmth of a thick, silky down-filled comforter that had been spread over me during the night.

= 2 =

I had not been at ease in the lodging house on Telfair Street in Augusta after the incident involving the lack of heat in my room and at the end of the week I left on a bus for New York.

At the time, I probably was seeking an excuse of any kind so I could pack my belongings and leave town. What had happened was that while my impressions of life among the people in the nearby sand hills and tobacco roads were clear and distinct in my mind, and I felt that my interpretations were justified, nevertheless I was having difficulty in transforming into reality with the austere meanings of written words the mental images and emotional perceptions of humanity.

My state of mind was not unusual. I had been in such quandaries before when I was uncertain about what direction I should allow a story to take. And regardless whether I needed an excuse of any kind, I knew it was necessary for me to go away in order to be able to look back at the scene with perspective vision.

When I arrived in New York in the cold and rainy twilight of a winter day, I went downtown in search of a room instead of returning to the raucous din of West 49th Street. Leaving the subway, I walked along Sixth Street in the dimly-lighted neighborhood of Second Avenue in Greenwich Village. This was a familiar scene of three-story-and-basement brownstones, narrow sidewalks, piles of rubbish in the gutters, and small groups of silent people huddled in the dampness of sheltered doorways. I had looked for a room to rent on the same street during my previous visit in New York but, depressed by the sights and sounds, I had then decided to look elsewhere.

This time, seeking quietude in the Village, I soon found a sign offering a room for rent in one of the dimly-lighted brownstone dwellings. Mrs. Brook, the fleshy, heavy-jowled, middle-aged landlady, took me up the steep stairways to a small room on the top floor. As she unlocked the door and handed me the key, she was gasping and wheezing from the exertion of climbing the stairs.

Presently, with a fluttering of her hands as she fanned her face, Mrs. Brook said she expected me to pay the rent in advance every week and

114

not to disturb any of the other roomers on the floor. While she was speaking, a personable young woman who looked more like an efficient secretary than any of the many prostitutes to be seen on the streets in the neighborhood left the room next to mine and went down the stairway.

"That's my niece," Mrs. Brook said. "She's living here with me temporarily and I don't want her annoyed and disturbed in any way. If you'll remember that and don't do it, me and you won't have no trouble at all."

During the remainder of the week, while I was at work with my noisy typewriter in the day and usually far into the night, I did not see the young woman again and there was no sound at all from her in the adjoining room. At the end of the week, since she had not brought any noisy visitors to her room to create a disturbance, I wanted to stay another week and perhaps longer. However, when I went to Mrs. Brook's office door with money in hand to pay another week's rent, the landlady shook her head and refused to take the money.

"No," she said firmly. "You can't stay here any longer. You'll have to leave and find yourself a room somewhere else."

"Why can't I stay?" I asked. "What have I done?"

"You make noise day and night with that typewriter of yours and it keeps my niece awake and gives her bad headaches. And to make it worse, when she found out you're a writer, she began having terrible nightmares. She ran away from her husband and both you and him are writers. That's what. She don't like being in the same house with anybody who's a writer. Now you know why you can't stay here. I've got to protect my niece."

It was plainly evident that Mrs. Brook was not going to change her mind and let me stay so I went upstairs for my suitcase and typewriter. On my way out, I saw Mrs. Brook standing at her doorway. She nodded to me with a friendly smile.

"I want you to know one thing," she said earnestly. "It's not because of anything personal that you have to leave. It's because my niece is a young thing and got upset when she found out you're a writer. Being so young and all, I've got to look after her and treat her like family. Her husband did hit her some and she's so inexperienced that she ran away from him because she don't know how to take that from a man. I'm an older woman myself, though, and maybe wiser, too. That's why I don't believe all writers are cruel and abusive to women."

I found another hall bedroom in a cold-water flat only a block away and the rent was seven dollars a week. I settled down in the new location right away as though there had been no interruption in my work. It was the kind of neighborhood where I had the choice of eating a meal of thick lentil soup and gray bread for twenty-five cents in one of the small restaurants on Second Avenue or making several meals of a loaf of rye bread and daisy cheese for the same cost to eat in my room. Also, I could re-ink my typewriter ribbon over and over again and there was a shop on Second Avenue where a water-stained ream of yellow second-sheets could be bought for a quarter.

I had thought about it ever since arriving in New York from Augusta and was still undecided about telephoning or going to see Max Perkins at Scribner's. The reason for being uncertain was that I did not want to talk to anybody about the full-length novel until I had written at least the first-draft of it and I had not made much progress with the preliminary sketches for the theme I had in mind.

However, I did call the number given me for The Heron Press and left a message for Erich Posselt. I did not expect to find Erich in a conventional office, remembering his way of conducting business in a taxicab, and several days passed before the manager of the lodging house handed me a slip of paper with a number for me to call. The number was not the same as that of The Heron Press.

When I finally was able to speak to Erich on the phone, he was no less voluble than he had been the first time but his fast-talking, German-accented manner of speaking was much more understandable. First of all, Erich said *The Bastard* was with the printers and would soon go to the bindery.

"Believe me, Caldwell," he said enthusiastically, "we've got a handsome product for the market. You just wait till you see the illustrations—you'll stand up and say you're proud of it. And it'll make a lot of people stand up and take notice when we put it on the showboat and sail it down the river. I guess you've heard that expression all your life, huh?"

Before I could ask when I would receive an author's copy of the book and if I could buy extra copies at a discount to sell at the Longfellow Square Bookshop in Portland, Erich said he was very anxious to know whether I had another completed manuscript of a novelette for publication.

He was told that not only did I have one for publication but that it, unlike the previous one, already had a title.

"And what's the name of it?"

"*Poor Fool.*"

"What does that mean, Caldwell?" he asked rapidly. "Is that a common

American expression?"

"It means only what it says."

"That's great. It's really great. It's just what the doctor ordered. You know that expression, huh?"

Without waiting to hear anything else I might have said, Erich said he wanted me to send him the *Poor Fool* manuscript and that he would pass it along to one of his several partners for publication. He explained that he was so busy with his many literary projects that another publisher, Alex Hillman, would bring it out in a limited and illustrated edition with the imprint of The Rariora Press.

No mention was made of an advance payment of royalty, or even the matter of a contract, and when I began asking questions, Erich said all the details would be handled by The Rariora Press. The fact that my second book was to be published by a person unknown to me was disturbing enough to make me wonder if the wise thing for me to do would be to find a trustworthy literary agent to represent me in all future negotiations with publishers.

= 3 =

Enclosed in one of the letters I had received from Helen was an invitation from The Macaulay Company, publishers of the *New American Caravan,* to attend a gathering of contributors to the anthology. The cocktail party, which was the first of the kind I had ever attended, was in a combined office and warehouse building closer to the garment district than to the usual literary haunts of Madison Avenue.

There were two memorable attractions at the party. One of them was a plentiful buffet service that provided the only full meal I had had in many weeks and the other attraction was Mae West. Fully fed and introduced to Mae West, I was then able to attain the experience of meeting Laurence Stallings, Mike Gold, Edwin Seaver, Georges Schreiber, Dawn Powell, Louis Mumford, John Chamberlain, Georgia O'Keeffe, and Edmund Wilson.

I had crossed the crowded room and was ready to leave when a dark-haired man with a prominent mustache put his hand on my arm. He was of medium height and appeared to be no more than thirty years old.

"Please allow me to introduce myself," he said, reaching out to shake hands. "My name is Maxim Lieber and I am an authors' representative. I was told you are Caldwell and a contributor to the *Caravan*."

Nodding, I asked, "Are you the same as a literary agent?"

Maxim Lieber smiled slightly. "Well, now," he said, "do you think this is a suitable occasion to engage in a discussion of semantics?"

"Maybe not now or ever," I said, moving toward the door.

He quickly placed his hand on my arm again.

"Just one more question before you leave, Caldwell," he said. "Do you have a representative?"

"No," I told him, "I don't have a literary agent."

He placed his business card in my hand.

"This could be a very fortunate meeting for both of us," he said, pointing at the card he had given me. "Very fortunate, indeed. I'll be waiting to hear from you."

I lay awake for a long time in the darkness of my room that night while recalling the excitement of having been in the company of so many writers and others in the literary field. With such thoughts in mind, I decided that before returning home in Maine I did want to see Max Perkins and be guided by his advice. My last thought before falling asleep was that I would call him on the telephone the first thing the next morning and try to arrange to see him as soon as possible.

As I had hoped, it was soon arranged that Max Perkins and I would meet in his office at Scribner's before the end of the week. At first, Max proposed that we should meet at eight or eight-thirty in the morning, saying that nobody should go to work any later than that, but after a few moments he said noon would be more suitable so we could go out for a light lunch.

The meeting in the office of Max Perkins was a brief one. When I entered and saw him for the first time, he was wearing a gray-felt hat tilted on the back of his head and walking stiffly around the room in bright tan shoes that looked new and uncomfortable. His tight-fitting brown suit was wrinkled and baggy at the knees.

Max immediately began speaking of the forthcoming publication of *American Earth*, saying he would want to select two more of the short stories to appear in *Scribner's Magazine*, but soon he was expressing more interest in a novel than a book of short stories. That was when he asked if I had thought of writing a novel to follow *American Earth*.

As interested as he was, I still had no desire to talk about a novel yet to be written and my reply was vague and inconclusive. All I would say was that I had been thinking about a theme for a novel but that it was a work that differed so much from a short story or novelette that I was uncertain about how it should be written.

"I'll tell you this," Max said as he paced the floor. "Don't talk to anybody about a novel you are thinking of writing. That would not be good. Talking is a form of creation. Talk, and you dissipate your enthusiasm and much of the spirit will disappear from what you write later. Write the novel first and then we'll talk about it afterward."

On the way to lunch, we stopped at a small stand-up shop where Max ordered two glasses of a mixture of freshly-squeezed vegetable juices. While we stood at the counter, Max was deploring the necessity for him as an editor to live in a large city such as New York and be deprived of the natural life of man he left behind in his native Vermont.

We went next to a small restaurant in the same block where there was a counter with stools but no tables. It was soon evident that Max was a regular customer since without consulting the menu he ordered peanut butter and watercress sandwiches on whole wheat bread. Instead of coffee, he ordered orange juice.

"Young writers should never let themselves be lured to New York to live and try to write," Max remarked while we were waiting for our lunch to be served. "Young writers should live among their own people so their roots can thrive and take nourishment from their heritage. It makes me sad to see promising young writers come to New York and lose their direction. Flustered and confused, they flutter to their doom like moths to a flame. And editors and publishers with their elaborate lunches and cocktail parties are the ones who strike the match to light the candle."

Chapter Thirteen

AFTER A NIGHT-LONG BUS trip from New York, I arrived in snow-covered Mount Vernon in the frosty stillness of a sunless midwinter morning.

It was good to be home again after a lengthy absence.

During the night, there had been a snowfall of several inches that covered the crusted surface that remained from previous storms. The new snow was soft and gleamy white and made crunching sounds underfoot. Already there were a few rabbit tracks in the new snow and a solitary moose had left his hoofprints behind him.

Stationed at various intervals over the broad lawn were numerous snowmen standing like sentinels on guard between the town road and the towering gabled house. It was easy to identify the handiwork of each of my two sons since obviously Dee, the youngest, would not have been able to reach high enough to build a snowman as tall as one made by Pix, his older brother.

The lofty maple and elm trees surrounding the house were stern and severe in their leafless winter solitude and looked down upon the paint-faded dwelling with austere indifference. The same trees, lively and friendly in their breeze-blown greenery of summer, were among the countless birches and beeches that spread flaming paint-pot colors of autumn foliage in their season to the far horizons beyond the round hills of the valley.

Whatever her innermost feelings may have been as the result of my long absence, Helen was quick to greet me with eager hugs and kisses after I had stamped the snow from my shoes at the doorway. From there, and through the unheated great room with creaking floorboards under foot, we went to the kitchen which was, as usual in winter, the most comfortable room in the house and still the only one heated by a stove.

Expectant as she was—undoubtedly during the past week having waited morning after morning for me to come home—Helen immediately began serving me hot biscuits from the oven, thick maple syrup from our own tree, and mugs of heated cider. All this was placed before me on the pale-green oilcloth-covered table where I sat in my favorite captain's chair close to the broad window.

There was much to talk about as we sat facing each other at the window-side table with the deep snow of winter gleaming outside in the zero-cold of the morning. After our casual remarks about neighbors and acquaintances which as usual served as an introduction to matters more serious, I was soon to find out that food was scarce and new warm clothing was needed for rapidly growing Pix and Dee. And more, our supply of potatoes and rutabagas in the cellar, which seemed to be in abundance when harvested in the fall, was almost exhausted and would have to be used sparingly for the remainder of the winter. The apple bins in the cellar were still half full, however, and the canned rhubarb and blackberries would last through the spring.

After much urging, Helen finally admitted that the family doctor had prescribed medicine for her persistent cough but that the money to pay for it had been spent for other necessities.

There was an interval of silence in the kitchen during which Helen tried vainly to smile while tears came to her eyes.

"I know I sound like the ultimate pessimist and I wish I could stop and be quiet," she said. "But there's something else awful, too."

I asked her at once to tell me what was the trouble.

Tears began trickling down her cheeks and she waited until they were wiped away.

"It's the Longfellow Square Bookshop," Helen said then. "It's in trouble— bad trouble. Marge Morse says there are days when only two or three books are sold. And it's all my fault. I'm the one who pleaded so much to open the bookshop. And I'm afraid Marge will quit any time now and go home."

When I reached across the table and held her hand consolingly, she smiled slightly for a moment.

"That's not all," she said as more tears came to her eyes.

As related by Helen, a stink-bomb was thrown through the open door-way while several customers were browsing in the bookshop and the nause-ous odor was so strong and permeating that it would probably repel other customers for a long time.

Following the stink-bombing, which no doubt was in retaliation for our failing to contract for the window-cleaning service, Marge was further harassed to such an extent that she still might leave and go home to Massachusetts. The latter incident occurred when the young woman who previously had left a large stack of her business cards advertising a service called Companionship accused Marge of failing to distribute the cards to female customers. This resulted in a hair-pulling brawl when Marge said she herself was not interested in a lesbian affair.

I reminded Helen that the bookshop in the beginning had been stocked with review copies at no cost and that every dollar of sales was clear profit. She was well aware that it was not possible to restock the bookshop with current publications and best sellers without money of our own or estab-lished credit. However, she did smile hopefully when I told her that The Heron Press would soon publish *The Bastard* and we could order as many copies as we wished at a favorable discount.

There was little more said about the bookshop and its troubles after that, but my own thoughts were concerned with the necessity to provide food and clothing and other essentials for my family. There was no doubt in my mind that such provisions were far more important than any number of books supplied to a failing bookshop.

Aside from the hard facts of business and feeling no obligation to give aid to an ill-fated commercial enterprise, I was likewise not inclined to put aside my wholehearted determination to complete the novel I was writing and, instead, devote any amount of time and energy in trying to keep a book-shop from going out of business. In my concept for living, first things had to be first—and stay that way.

Helen and I had been sitting at the kitchen table for the past hour and sipping from our mugs of hot cider when I happened to glance aside and saw through the window, standing knee-deep in the snow, the long sad face and fuzzy antler of a full-grown bull moose in his shaggy winter coat.

"It's Winthrop," I said, moving closer to the window.

Helen nodded. "He's been here several times lately and just stands there looking into the kitchen. I think Winthrop is lonely for company."

We had given the big moose the name Winthrop the previous winter when he came to look at us through the kitchen window after the first snow of the season. This came about when we decided the moose's long, solemn face and blinking brown eyes made him look very much like an elderly widower and retired farmer named Winthrop Walton who lived in our neighborhood with his middle-aged housekeeper.

The first time we saw Winthrop-the-moose was in the previous winter when he was standing knee-deep in the snow in the hillside apple orchard behind our house and he had gnawed and eaten a damaging amount of bark from several apple trees.

To keep all the trees from being stripped of their bark, Helen and I had wrapped potato sacking around the trunks and and then shoveled the covering of snow from a terrace above the orchard. By removing the snow, a thick growth of dry summer grass was exposed. The apple orchard was saved from further damage and thereafter Winthrop was seen grazing contentedly on the uncovered wild grass.

Unlike some of the deer in the neighborhood, Winthrop had not let himself venture close enough to eat tufts of grass or clover in summer from a human hand. However, in winter he was hungry and incautious enough to snatch an apple from my hand and then after that brave foraging move he would retreat to a safe distance as quickly as possible.

As for the deer, aside from sometimes becoming tame enough to be petted by Pix and Dee in our yard, it was not unusual in our part of town to see several deer leaping over hedgerows and stone walls in the snow-covered winter. The deer always looked as if they were blithely unaware of the possibility of being sighted down a rifle barrel in the hands of a deerstalker who himself was not fearful of the likelihood of being observed by a game warden in hunting season or out of hunting season. Whether provided by buck, doe, or fawn, venison in the dead of winter was a bountiful treat that a Mount Vernon husband and father could bestow upon his family with boastful pride and utmost delight.

The longer I looked at Winthrop standing outside in the snow, and the longer he gazed at me through the window, more disturbing became my thoughts about the customary three-times-a-day fare of potatoes and rutabagas in the winter months. The only variation in the routine of dining—and probably the only possible alternative—would occur when Helen with exaggerated gestures would serve a meal in two courses. For one meal, potatoes would be the first course followed by the second course of rutabagas. The next two-course meal would be served with the procedure reversed.

From potatoes and rutabagas, my thoughts immediately turned to moose meat. Moose chops, moose steak, moose roast, moose hamburger. I had never slaughtered and quartered a creature before in my life but now I realized I would not hesitate for a moment to butcher the moose for our needed food.

Getting up from the table, I went straight to the closet where we kept a .22 caliber target rifle. After picking up the rifle and, in case they were needed, several extra cartridges, I went quickly across the room to the outside door.

Helen had left the table and she was at the door at the same time I got there. She gripped my arm with both hands.

"Don't!" she pleaded tearfully. "Don't shoot Winthrop! Oh, please don't kill him! We'll have enough to eat—someway we will! Oh, please don't do that!"

Without saying a word, I opened the door and went outside. Helen followed me part of the way down the path in the snow.

"Please promise you won't do anything while I'm gone," she begged. "I'll only be gone a minute. Please!"

Still not speaking, I nodded assent and went several steps toward the moose at the kitchen window. Winthrop turned his head slightly and gazed at me with the usual sadness of his blinking eyes.

Moments later Helen came running from the house. In her outstretched hand she held a large red apple she had brought from the cellar.

"It's for Winthrop," she said in a hurried voice. "Please give it to him— don't shoot him—let him live."

The moose had seen the big red apple and he turned and came to me with a bobbing of his massive antlered head as he walked. Becoming more cautious the closer he came, Winthrop suddenly lunged forward and took the apple into his jaws. While chewing the pulp with eager motions of his jaws he gazed at me with blinking eyes as if in gratitude for the wintertime treat. Presently, swallowing the last bite, he turned around and began walking slowly through the deep snow toward the nearby point of woods.

The least I could do was to salute Winthrop with rifle shots into the air with all the bullets I had left.

= 2 =

Winters in the state of Maine were long and confining and always tenaciously reluctant to give way to a warm and vibrant spring that would bring budding boughs to the orchards and emerging crocuses in the flower beds. When the new season did arrive with the thawing of the frozen earth, though, and with it the mud season put to an end for another year, it was the time when man and nature, their age-old conflict temporarily in abeyance, eagerly joined forces to replenish barns and cellars, to fill feed troughs and kitchen pantries with the goodness of the earth.

This, then, was the season for plowing and seeding.

Again as a friendly neighbor, Arthur Dolloff, had sent his teen-age son, Clayton, across the brook separating the two farms to plow, harrow, and furrow our large vegetable garden with his team of sturdy farm horses. Preparing the dark loamy soil for planting was almost a whole afternoon's work and when Clayton finished turning the last furrow, the tall dark-haired boy sat down with his back against the barn for a short rest before going home.

Presently, and asking a favor for the first time since coming to know him, Clayton shyly inquired if I would have any objection to his stashing a large beer-brewing pot on the sunny slope of our apple orchard. While he was explaining how he would attend to the apparatus without any disturbance to Helen and me, and coming and going in a roundabout way so he would not be observed by his father, I was wondering how I would answer to Arthur Dolloff if he should find out what his eighteen-year-old son was doing and accuse me of aiding and letting the boy make yeast-fermented alcoholic brew on my property.

There were probably very few households in the town that did not have a cider press on the premises and barrels or kegs in the cellar for storing sweet cider that could easily become alcoholic or turned into vinegar at will. And Arthur Dolloff himself had often boasted of the flavor and proof of his hard cider.

After assuring Clayton that I had no objection to his beer-making project in our orchard, I asked him why he would go to so much trouble to make beer when there was a plentiful supply of hard cider in the cellar of his own home. With a deep frown and a quick sweep of his hand, he said his father had forbidden him to take a single drink of hard cider until he was twenty-one years old. Then, with a broad smile coming to his tanned face, Clayton remarked that his father had not said a word about the drinking of beer.

First, it was the planting of corn and peas, potatoes and rutabagas, the carrots and squash, all the other vegetables for family food for another summer and following winter.

Next, with the seeding of the garden completed, including the transplanting of tender tomato plants that had been raised from seeds in the warmth of the kitchen, then it was the firewood for cooking and heating to be cut and stacked for seasoning.

And then finally, I could spend most of the time day and night finishing the novel I had begun writing in Augusta and had continued writing in New York.

By then, it was late spring, and with it the coming of the first warm days of the approaching summer. That was when I finished typing on white paper, instead of using my favorite yellow second sheets, the final revision of *Tobacco Road*. My thought was that white and not yellow paper at that time would make the typescript more impressive and professional in appearance when taken in hand by an editor and publisher.

It was to be my first full-length novel, and by then I felt I had become too apprehensive and fearful of what I had written to be able to read the manuscript objectively for correcting grammatical, typographical, and other errors. Consequently, I asked Helen to read the novel and to correct unhesitatingly whatever mistakes she could find. When she finished, and without my looking to see what changes may have been made, I sent the final typed pages of the book to Max Perkins at Scribner's. It was sent in the last outward-bound mail of the day from the Mount Vernon post office.

I had expected it would be many weeks, even months, before word from Max Perkins was received saying whether or not the book would be accepted for publication. Only ten days had passed, however, when I received a brief note from him saying *Tobacco Road* would be published in the forthcoming season and, since the manuscript needed no editing before being sent to the printer, it would not be necessary to make any changes or revisions.

It took much longer than an interval of ten days for me to return to solid ground after rising to a lofty state of euphoria. I decided it was an occasion to be celebrated and that other persons were needed to insure a satisfying time of merrymaking. Helen and I immediately invited Dorothy and Alfred Morang to be our week-end house guests.

We had become acquainted with the Morangs shortly after opening the bookshop in Portland and often thereafter had visited them at their flat and studio on the waterfront. Dorothy gave music lessons that provided some of the money for their living expenses and Alfred gave violin lessons and painted Claude Monet-inspired impressionist landscapes and figures.

As a pastime, Alfred was addicted to playing mournful tzigane music on his violin.

I never felt I was a fair judge of any artist who painted in oils with a pallet knife instead of with brushes, but I was very pleased with the pen and ink drawings Alfred did for two of my short stories that were published separately in pamphlet editions. He was in his late twenties, bearded, and had long, gleaming black hair. Besides being diminutive in size, he was extremely emaciated and had a constant hacking cough. He had the appearance of being in an advanced stage of tuberculosis.

I was probably heartless and unfair, but nevertheless I soon became unhappy as the result of Alfred's actions the first night of his and Dorothy's arrival in Mount Vernon from Portland. I had anticipated a time of gaiety and festivity but, instead, Helen and I were subjected to hours of gloomy music from early evening to three o'clock the next morning. In the beginning, Alfred insisted on playing mournful tzigane music on his violin even though several times I did not hesitate to ask him to play something cheerful and merry for our celebration instead of music that sounded like a funeral dirge.

Those requests ignored, Alfred at midnight discovered a phonograph recording that, when played on the wind-up record player, was even more sad and depressing than tzigane music. The title of the song was "Oh, How I Wish I Was In Peoria Tonight" and the wording of the song, especially the refrain, was a heart-stricken lament of a lonely prisoner far from home who was singing in the darkness of his cell. But that was not to be all. After having played the record over and over many times, at two o'clock in the morning, and for the next hour, Alfred accompanied the prisoner's song with his own sad violin music in full volume.

It was following a very late breakfast the next morning when I went aside with Alfred and told him that I thought one night of celebration had been sufficient and that he and Dorothy ought to go back to Portland and not stay for the second night of the weekend. The only indication that he may have been offended by such a forthright suggestion was when he shrugged his shoulders and walked away without a word. He and Dorothy left for Portland a few minutes later.

A month passed before Helen and I had recovered enough from the nerve-racking visit of the Morangs to consider inviting anyone else for a weekend. I was still in a state of pleasant unreality and wonderment brought about by the prospect of becoming a published novelist after so many years of endeavoring to reach the goal I had set for myself. And so it was that I was immediately agreeable when Helen said she would like to invite her friend Rijmor Neilsen to spend the weekend with us.

Rijmor, blonde and in her early twenties, had been born in Denmark and lived in Portland with her Danish parents and a younger sister. Slender of figure and friendly in manner, she was the manager of a health food and exercise establishment for women.

It was a warm week in midsummer when Rijmor came to Mount Vernon and it was ideal in time and place for the enthusiastic nudist that she was. The first morning after her arrival, Rijmor prepared herself for a day of sunbathing and blackberry picking by sitting in a rocking chair on the front porch and, with a tube of mustache wax, fashioned curls in her ample pubic hair. In no manner disconcerted when I stared at her in surprise, she remarked in a casual manner that Danes had a long tradition of fostering liberal thoughts and customs.

There were several small nudist colonies in Northern New England but, as far as I knew, nothing of the kind existed in Central Maine. However, all summer long there was modestly screened sunbathing at Elizabeth Arden's Maine Chance resort several miles away. In order to insure complete privacy, the sunbathing garden at Maine Chance was enclosed by a high boarded fence and, in addition, it was equipped with suspended canvas windbreakers to prevent anyone with binoculars from observing the sunbathers from nearby hills.

Clayton Dolloff was the first person to see the nude Rijmor from a distance. She was picking blackberries and stepping gingerly among the prickly brambles when Clayton happened to see her from the Dolloff barnyard. In a matter of minutes, he had leaped over the brook running between the two farms and was making an unanticipated visit to his beer-brewing apparatus in our orchard. For a long time, he watched Rijmor's nimble movements in the blackberry thicket. Finally, Clayton walked slowly away, passing me on the front lawn without a word spoken and went up the town road toward home.

The next person to see Rijmor from a distance was Fred Howard, the R.F.D. mail carrier, who had stopped at our mailbox to deliver several letters. Fred was usually in a hurry to complete his daily circuit, and yet this time he shut off the engine of his car and got out to stand beside the mailbox and stare intently across the lawn in the direction of the blackberry thicket.

When I left the house and reached the mailbox, Fred raised his arm and pointed at Rijmor as if asking why would a naked girl be exposing herself in full view from the town road. After explaining to Fred that she was Helen's friend from Portland, and an earnest nudist, he got into his car and drove away without a word. I realized then that undoubtedly he would be telling everybody along his route what he had seen and that rumors and gossip and common talk would spread like wildfire over the entire town.

By early afternoon, numerous curious onlookers had driven their cars slowly along the town road in front of our house while hopefully expecting to see Rijmor. It was not until early evening with the coming of darkness, though, that the telephone rang for the first time. As expected, the call to Helen was from an agitated town resident.

The woman who identified herself as being the wife of Bob Lander, a well-known house painter and town selectman, said right away that she had told her husband to see to it that an ordinance would be enacted at the next town meeting to make it punishable by fine and imprisonment for any person, male or female, to appear on the outside of a dwelling without being properly and completely clothed. In conclusion, she advised Helen and me never again to invite a nudist to visit us within the boundaries of the town of Mount Vernon.

The next morning Rijmor appeared at breakfast fully dressed and was soon to say she had decided it would be best for her to go back to Portland and not stay for the remainder of the weekend.

Chapter Fourteen

THE LESS THAN SUCCESSFUL attempt to celebrate the acceptance of my first full-length novel for publication was followed by failure of another order. This latter event occurred in the beginning of the period extending from 1929 to 1933 when four books—*The Bastard*, *Poor Fool*, *American Earth*, and *Tobacco Road*—were published in succession.

My income from writing being as scanty as it was, and nonexistent in intervals, I was unable to provide means to keep the Longfellow Square Bookshop from closing its doors. The inevitable failure of the business was hastened by the actions of the Portland Police Department and the Cumberland County Attorney. Acting on a complaint of obscenity made by a citizen, it was ordered that sales of *The Bastard* were prohibited immediately and that all copies of the book were to be shipped out of the state of Maine within forty-eight hours.

In addition to being unable to provide money to keep the bookshop in business, neither did I have the means to pay an attorney to attempt to have the charge of obscenity dismissed or defended in court. The doors of the bookshop were closed and Marge Morse, saying farewell with tears in eyes, left for home in Massachusetts.

Soon after the publication of *Tobacco Road* early in 1932, I began writing the next novel. Like the sales of *American Earth,* which was a collection of short stories, the sales of *Tobacco Road* in the beginning amounted to only a few thousand copies and I had decided to write the next novel about life in rural Maine. As fortune would have it, the book with the title of *A Lamp for Nightfall* was not published until twenty years later. This was brought about by the strategy of Maxim Lieber who used the unpublished novel on at least two occasions for what he called "fish bait."

Shortly after becoming my literary agent, Max dangled the novel as a lure to Scribner's and succeeded in voiding the Scribner option to publish my next two books. His next move was to have The Viking Press offer me a contract for my next three novels but not including *A Lamp for Nightfall.* While all this was taking place in New York, I was at home in Mount Vernon busily engaged day and night in writing a novel to have the title of *God's Little Acre.*

It was a time of much stir and bluster by Max Lieber but with little money coming to hand. The advance royalty I had received for *Tobacco Road* was barely earned, which meant there was slight prospect of my receiving additional royalties that year, and I could not keep from worrying about how I was going to be able to provide for my family. There were plenty of potatoes and rutabagas for food, but that was just about all.

It seemed to me to be trivial at the time and I soon put it out of mind after I had signed an agreement with Jack Kirkland, a playwright, for the dramatization of *Tobacco Road.* He went off to Europe for six months and I concluded that there was no prospect of his ever bringing the play to Broadway. A year later I had the surprise of my life when the curtain went up at the Masque Theater in New York on a cold December night. However, in the meanwhile, our meager diet in Mount Vernon remained unchanged day after day.

I had written *God's Little Acre* with little pause for physical relief or mental reflection. In my haste to write the novel, I had let pages fall where they would on the floor and scatter themselves under and around the typewriter table. The pages were numbered except for half a dozen and the latter had to be made to take their place in the proper order. And it was while I was in the midst of assembling the typescript and making final revision that I received the offer of a job as a motion-picture screenwriter for Metro-Goldwyn-Mayer in California.

Not only was the unexpected film offer beyond immediate belief, the breath-taking shock was followed by sensations of throbbing, uncontrollable pulsations as I tried to comprehend a weekly salary of two hundred and fifty dollars. In no way, especially in the depths of economic depression, could I reconcile the difference between such a large sum of money and my earlier newspaper salary of twenty-five dollars weekly.

Both Helen and I considered the M-G-M offer to be one that could not be ignored and had to be accepted for the sake of our family welfare. Money for food, clothing, and medical expenses was needed for her and the two children and there was no immediate prospect of appreciable income from any other source. Besides, the birth of our third child—who was to be named Janet if a girl—was expected after a few more weeks.

Wearing my threadbare gray suit of clothes, and packing an extra pair of pants and most of my shirts and neckties in a battered leather suitcase, a week later I left on the train for Los Angeles. This time, as arranged by the film studio, and instead of days and nights on a transcontinental bus, I traveled in the comfort of a Pullman sleeping car for the first time in my life.

= 2 =

After a morning arrival at the Los Angeles Union Station, I took a taxi directly to the front gate of the Metro-Goldwyn-Mayer studio in Culver City. A guard at the gate thumbed through his papers until he found my name on a list and then I was told how to find Sam Marx.

Sam Marx was a pleasant-mannered, smiling-faced young executive in the story department and he appeared to be little more than thirty years old. He was friendly and considerate and welcomed me to the mysterious world of motion pictures by casually remarking that if I wanted to know what was happening in Hollywood film-making at any time the best source of information would be in the two important trade papers, the *Hollywood Reporter* and *Daily Variety*.

I was taken to an anteroom on the second floor of the writers' building where I was introduced to Ruth Carnall, my assigned secretary, and from there we went into a much larger room furnished with deep carpeting and flowing draperies. There was a large desk and typewriter table and, most imposing of all, several upholstered lounge chairs and a long leather-covered couch. This was my office.

Sam left me there with a firm handshake and the advice to let nature be my guide in becoming acclimated and at ease in Southern California.

I had already decided not to buy or rent an automobile while working at M-G-M for only three months, which would help save money needed back home in Maine, and therefore it was logical to rent a room within walking distance of the studio. When I mentioned this to Ruth Carnall, the

Hollywood-wise young secretary, she was quick to remark that many writers bought or leased Cadillac convertibles and lived in two-room suites with wet bars and snack galleys at the Garden of Allah between Hollywood and Beverly Hills.

When I said I was not interested in an expensive scale of living, Ruth smiled and remarked that it was refreshing to meet someone in the motion-picture business who was not impressed by Hollywood-style excesses. It was my feeling then that we would have a very friendly and congenial relationship during the next three months.

For the first thirteen weeks of my life as a junior screenwriter, I spent considerable time in a third-floor, sparsely-furnished room at the Culver City Hotel. Only a few blocks from the studio, this was a plain and ungraceful small hotel with California pastel-colored walls and California Mission furniture in the lobby. The lobby furnishings included massive wooden tables and a number of uncomfortable wooden chairs and settees without upholstery or cushions.

My little room, similar to most of the others in the hotel, was furnished with a wooden bed, telephone desk and chair, two small scatter rugs, a single overhead droplight, and a creaky rocking chair. It also had a framed picture of a Rhineland castle on the wall and a tattered yellow curtain over the window.

Still being at ease and fully relaxed, as advised by Sam Marx, and after nearly two weeks had passed while waiting for a writing assignment, I became interested in the unusual activities of a group of guests occupying several rooms close to mine on the third floor of the Culver City Hotel. Every one of the group was a midget, and there were seven of them with five being males and two being females.

The midgets were strikingly uniform in physique, each standing about three and a half feet in height, and the only noticeable difference between the men and the women was the length of hair. Otherwise, all of them were muscular of body and agile in movement with similar dark-skinned gypsy coloring. And while all of them looked very much alike except for the length of hair, they also appeared to be of the same indefinite age—which may have been somewhere between twenty-five and forty-five years old.

One of the midgets, whose name sounded like "Haw-Wah", spoke a few words of English. Their own language, whatever it may have been, was incomprehensible to me.

Haw-Wah evidently understood even less of the English he heard than

134

he was able to speak even though he would always smile and nod when spoken to in English. However, the midgets were talkative among themselves in their strange-sounding language which may have been Hungarian or Slavic—or perhaps a tzigane dialect. Although I was unable to speak to the midgets, I found out at the studio that they were under contract to appear in a carnival-type motion picture featuring midgets, fat ladies, thin men, Siamese twins, and other side-show freaks and oddities which was being prepared for filming in a few weeks.

While waiting for filming to begin, the restless group of midgets seemingly devoted half of their time to taking heavy meals three times a day in the hotel dining room and much of the remainder of the time was spent rehearsing their acrobatic routines. From morning until evening, there were many hours when the small people could be seen standing and eating at their special table in a corner of the dining room.

The management of the hotel had attempted to provide makeshift highchairs for the group by placing cushion-covered boxes at the dining table. But the midgets refused to sit on such childlike seats and, instead, always stood at their meals with arms outstretched on the table top while talking excitedly and at the same time straining to feed themselves.

While it was interesting to watch the seven midgets during their mealtime activities, what was disturbing at other times was being awakened in the night by loud thumps and bumps on the walls and floors accompanied by shouts and cries similar to those uttered by performing acrobats at a circus. These rehearsals took place in the hall late at night and the sounds of the tumbling routines made sleep impossible for an hour or longer.

A few days after I had watched one of the nightly rehearsals from my doorway, Sam Marx said he had an immediate writing assignment for me and wanted me to meet him at his office at once. All the way to a meeting in another building, I was so hopeful of being assigned to work on the film with the midgets that I could think of nothing else. And by the time I had entered Sam's office, I confidently expected my hopes to be realized.

When I met Sam at his doorway, he said we would have to hurry and there was no time to talk. We walked silently across the lot to a sound stage where the filming of a motion picture had been in progress.

Work on the film had been suspended with the cast and crew remaining idle, which the producer was loudly deploring as a costly interruption. At the same time the director was insisting equally as loudly that he would not continue until better dialogue was written for the particular scene.

In a shouting match between the two, the director said he was not going to have his reputation ruined by inept dialogue and the producer stated that he was not going to permit the cost of the film to exceed the budget.

The setting of the film was the veranda of a Southern ante-bellum mansion where Miriam Hopkins, costumed in billowy white lawn and lace, moved impatiently back and forth in a swing while awaiting the arrival of a tardy suitor.

Even though I knew nothing about the story, I was told to think of something suitable for Miriam Hopkins to say that would reveal how angry and upset she was because a man would keep her waiting. I was told that the dialogue would have to be authentically Southern romantic, and with no implications of latent profanity or obscenity.

My first and only suggestion was to have her say "Aw, shoot!"

I was immediately dismissed by the director and another writer was hurriedly summoned.

When I left the sound stage and returned to the writers' building, Ruth Carnall was sympathetic to the extent of saying the incident I had experienced was not unusual at a film studio in Hollywood and that I should not feel downcast and dejected.

"The important thing is that your couch is still in your office," she said with a comforting smile. "The time to worry and fret is when two furniture movers from the property storeroom come in and carry out your couch without saying a word about what they are doing. That's the sure sign every time that a writer is out of favor and won't be around much longer."

= 3 =

About a month before the end of my thirteen-week tenure, I was called to a conference at the story department and received an assignment to prepare several film treatments and screenplays for a long-running and successful series of two-reel, weekly-released motion pictures with the general title of Crime Does Not Pay.

The story treatments were composed of episodes derived from case histories furnished by the Los Angeles Police department. Every two-reel film in the series was so designed that perpetrators of acts of theft and violence were always convicted in police court, sentenced to prison, and lived the remaining years of their lives burdened with remorse.

After several unsatisfactory attempts to prepare treatments and screenplays for the series, Ruth Carnall suggested that if I went to a screening room and looked at several previous episodes of the series I would probably find them helpful in writing my own treatments.

It was after I had spent almost two hours one morning in a screening room and was walking down the second-floor hall of the writers' building when I was stopped by a large, smiling, heavy-bodied man about thirty years old. He was dressed in a well-tailored gray suit and was wearing a pale-blue shirt and a flaming-red necktie. Almost at once he had grasped my hand with a warm clinging handshake.

"Hi," he said. "I'm Al Manuel. That's me and I'm an agent."

I nodded, wondering why he had introduced himself as being an agent, but saying nothing in return. Gazing at his sagging cheeks and drooping eyelids while he held my hand with a tight grip, it was my thought that I had been mistaken for somebody else. His smile had long since vanished and had been replaced by an expression of unrelenting sadness.

"I know who you are," he said presently. "I found out about you at the front office. You're Skinny Caldwell. Sam Marx and I called the M-G-M office in New York and they told us they found out from some publishers what your nickname is back there. You look skinny enough to need a good meal. How about a steak dinner tonight? I'll pick you up at the Culver City Hotel at seven o'clock. There ain't no need for you to get dressy—but shoes will get us in some places quicker."

I waited an hour that night in the lobby of the hotel, but Al Manuel did not appear, and it was late in the morning of the next day when I saw him again. He had apologized immediately for failing to meet me at the hotel and explained that one of his clients, who was a writer at another studio, had got into trouble in a nightclub and ended up in a police station where bail was required for his release.

Earlier that morning when I came to work and had asked Ruth if she knew anything about Al Manuel, I was quick to find out that Alvin G. Manuel was a well-known and successful Hollywood agent. His partner in an agency was Jules Goldstone, who represented among others a young actress named Elizabeth Taylor, while among Al's clients was an older writer named Theodore Dreiser. Ruth said that Al once had told her the reason he preferred to represent writers exclusively was because if they had good publishing credentials and recognizable by-lines he could sell their services to film studios sight-unseen no matter how ugly they were and they would not have to show their faces to casting directors and try to look pretty for the camera.

When Al came to see me later that morning, he was very businesslike and eager to know the amount of my weekly salary and the name of my agent. I told him I had a literary agent, Maxim Lieber, but no film agent. Then I explained that I had signed a contract at the M-G-M office in New York and, while being paid a salary of two hundred and fifty dollars weekly, ten percent of my salary was being deducted and paid to somebody else.

With an understanding and expressive motioning of his head and an outward fling of his hand, Al said he was going to arrange some changes and take charge of my interests. That was followed by his saying he did not intend for me to work another day for a salary less than five hundred dollars weekly.

"Now look here, Skinny," he told me. "We ain't going to work no more for no picture studio for the kind of money they've been getting away with. I won't permit it."

I had never known anybody before with Al's purposely illiterate way of speaking and I wondered how much it contributed to his success as a Hollywood agent.

"Now listen here while I tell you something," he continued. "I'd be so embarrassed I'd have to go off somewhere and hide my face if people in this business found out I'd let a client of mine write big words for a studio for some puny little dollars. What happened was that the story department heard about that good novel of yours and they wanted you out here on the lot. That's why they signed you in a hurry in New York without waiting for an agent to front for you. That's their business and I've got my business. Now they've got me to reckon with and I ain't no weak sister."

After that, thoroughly impressed, I was ready and anxious to sign an exclusive agency agreement with Al for motion picture representation. When this was suggested, a brief smile was barely apparent on his sagging cheeks and his drooping eyelids sank deeper on his face. With his usual melancholy expression unrelieved, Al reached forward and grasped my hand with a tight grip.

"Me and you don't need to sign nothing, Skinny," he said. "This's a handshake deal and that's the best kind of all. We can settle everything between us with a little talk. Ain't no sense in me and you doing no different."

Releasing his grip on my hand, Al then walked away without a backward glance.

"I'm going to the front office now," he said. "And I'll be seeing you later. And don't forget we've got a big steak dinner waiting for us."

After Al had left, I asked Ruth if she knew why he evidently took delight in making grammatical mistakes when he spoke.

"It's an act," she said, "and Al Manuel has made a reputation for himself with it. It's an instant attention-getter when he goes to a studio to sell a new writer or negotiate for more money for a client. If his assumed illiteracy doesn't bother you, you couldn't have a better agent in Hollywood."

Chapter Fifteen

WHEN I RETURNED HOME to Maine from California at the end of the summer of 1933, after completing what I considered to have been an obligatory financial tour of duty, I had with me more than two thousand dollars saved by perseverance and frugal living.

Perhaps with the desire to display evidence of being a good provider, as well as offering atonement for another long absence from Helen and the children, the money had been brought from California in stacks of newly printed currency and not in an indifferent bank check.

That large amount of money, together with a prize of one thousand dollars received from the *Yale Review* for a short story, "Country Full Of Swedes," was enough for a year's living. And that included the cost of trading our older Ford sedan for a more recent model and, best of all, being enabled to go to the nearest A & P grocery store once a week for food other than potatoes and rutabagas for our table.

This was the beginning of a brief period of three years from 1933 to 1936 during which several books were written and published. These were: *We Are the Living, God's Little Acre, Journeyman, Some American People*, and *Kneel to the Rising Sun*. It also was the beginning of an era of wide-spread and worrisome attempts to ban, suppress, and censor several of my books and the play version of *Tobacco Road*.

Of all the charges of obscenity and pornography in New York, Boston, Philadelphia, Cleveland, Detroit, Chicago, and elsewhere, there were only two instances when permanent legal bans were imposed. The mayor of Chicago succeeded in banning the play *Tobacco Road* in that city and the Watch and Ward Society succeeded in having the novel *God's Little Acre* banned in Boston.

It was evident that the imposition of censorship was often a capricious and whimsical act when the play *Tobacco Road* was banned in Chicago and no attempt was made to ban the production in New York. Similarly, the banning of *God's Little Acre* in Boston was not followed by the banning of the same novel in Chicago.

Upon returning home after having experienced for the first time the life of a Hollywood screenwriter, I became fully occupied for the next six months with the writing of numerous short stories. Following that, the next half-year was spent in gathering material for a volume of observations about life in the United States during the time of a stressful economic depression. The short stories were published under the title of *Kneel to the Rising Sun* and the observations were published in a book with the title of *Some American People*.

The year by that time being 1935, and I becoming increasingly unsettled by the continuing destructive designs of the censors, I was ready and willing to listen to Al Manuel when he said he had an offer from Metro-Goldwyn-Mayer that called for me to return to the Culver City studio for another three-month term. It was proposed that I would write an original film story and be paid double my earlier salary. Little persuasion by Al was needed and, traveling by airplane for the first time, I left at once for California.

I had my same office in the writers' building at M-G-M and Ruth Carnall again was stationed in the secretarial anteroom. However, Al had registered me at the Knickerbocker Hotel in Hollywood, saying the Culver City Hotel would be inconvenient as a place for one of his clients to live, and a rental car had been reserved for me for travel between Hollywood and Culver City.

As proposed by Sam Marx, and approved by Al Manuel, it was arranged that I would collaborate with Harry Behn, an accomplished screenwriter of my own age, and we were directed to conceive and write the treatment of a story and then to prepare the screenplay as a suitable vehicle for Clark Gable.

It was not only my first experience as a collaborator, I had never dictated a story, either. Harry said he could do his best work only when stretched out on a couch and dictating to his own secretary. We soon agreed that the best way for us to work together was for him to dictate while I made my notes and comments on a typewriter.

Harry and I had decided that the ideal story for a Clark Gable film would be about logging in the forests of the Northwest. The foreman of a logging camp was the hero and the daughter of a woodsman was the heroine. With enthusiasm unbounded, we made good progress with the story during the first month of collaboration. But suddenly one morning in the second month we found ourselves in a state of complete blankness.

We had reached a point in a new scene where nothing we could think of was logical and convincing as the next step. This impasse prevented us from continuing with the story for day after day while I sat at my typewriter and Harry Behn as if in a trance squirmed restlessly on the couch like a contortionist. Being tall and lithe and sinewy, he had a habit of lying on the couch and twisting his arms, legs, and torso into pretzel-shaped positions while thinking and dictating. Harry seemed to be able to do his best work while his supple body was in contortions.

It was late in the afternoon after a week of failed effort when there was a loud wail of pain from Harry on the couch.

"I'm stuck!" he yelled a moment later. "I can't do it! Get me out of here!"

"Don't worry, Harry," I told him sympathetically. "We'll get this story going again soon. What we ought to do now is quit for the day and start again fresh in the morning."

"I don't mean that!" he said in an anguished voice. "It's not the story—it's me! Help! I can't get untangled—I've got cramps in both legs!"

Going to the couch, I saw that Harry had crossed his legs behind his knees in such a manner that one of his arms was gripped so tightly in a leg-lock that his hand had become pale and bloodless for lack of circulation. I tried to pull one of his feet free but stopped when he yelled in great pain.

At that moment, Harry's secretary came running from the anteroom where she and Ruth had been talking while waiting to be called for dictation. She was a small, dark-haired girl and frail in appearance. As soon as she saw what had happened, she knelt down on the floor beside the couch.

"You've put a Boston crab hold on yourself, Mr. Behn." she said reprovingly. "How did you manage to do that?"

"I don't know," Harry replied weakly. "But hurry and do something—quick!"

The young secretary pressed against one of Harry's knees while deftly twisting a foot. After another maneuver, both of Harry's feet shot forward with a crackling sound in his knee joints and his arm fell limply from his shoulder. His left hand was deathly white and perspiration covered his face.

When I asked the secretary how she knew what to do in order to release Harry from the wrestlers' holds, she said she had been going to professional wrestling matches on Wednesday nights where she observed how holds and locks were broken. And evidently it was not the first time Harry had tied himself into knots when deep in thought and struggling with a film story.

After that incident, and when little more was accomplished while Harry and I tried to develop the difficult scene to our satisfaction, the story editors took a long time to decide if our screenplay about a handsome logger who spent more time in saloons along Skid Row than he did among the firs and pines would be suitable for Clark Gable. In the end, it was decided by the story department to suspend work on our film story while it was being thoroughly evaluated.

Harry Behn went on a vacation in Arizona where he said he hoped to discover at leisure the correct solution for the failed scene in our Northwest logging story.

For my part, I was anxious to get back to Maine and begin planning a long summer trip through the Deep South. I had earned and set aside a sufficient amount of money to finance a comprehensive tour of the economically and socially troubled states in the South resulting from the Great Depression. The purpose of the investigation was to provide photographic and factual material needed to refute the continuing charges by unenlightened critics, censors, and editorial writers that my depictions of social and economic conditions in *Tobacco Road*, play and novel, were exaggerated, defamatory, and pernicious.

= 2 =

The spring of 1936 was late arriving in Central Maine. The fields and pastures remained soggy for a long time after winter's belated thaw and the brooks were still full to the brim with the runoff of icy water from the melting snow.

Arthur Dolloff, who usually was unperturbed by the vagrant courses of the climate, came sloshing down the town road one morning in his knee-high rubber boots to complain at length about being unable to plow in his own garden at the proper time of year and saying he would be surprised if he could plow my garden until after the Fourth of July.

"Don't foresee the likelihood of having sweet peas on the vine for the Fourth of July this year," Arthur proclaimed. "Can't always count on having garden vittles to eat at will when nature chooses to have a contrary mind of its own."

Unmindful of the weather, Pix and Dabney had already planted a few rows in their own garden on the sunny slope of the orchard. They had used seeds gathered and saved from the previous summer and green shoots appeared for them long before Arthur and I could begin our plantings.

By that time, I had become determined to vindicate my writings about the South and I had formed a clear idea about the kind of book I wanted to prepare. For one thing, it was to be factual study of people in the cotton states living in economic stress and it was my intention to show that my fiction was as realistic as life itself in the contemporary South. And, to be completely authentic, as I was well aware, the book would have to be thoroughly documented with photographs taken on the scene by a perceptive photographer.

The title of the book had already been selected. It was to be called *You Have Seen Their Faces*.

I asked Maxim Lieber to prepare a list of accomplished photographers who would be desirable collaborators. First of all, a meeting was arranged with Margaret Bourke-White, a spirited young woman with an engaging personality who had published a highly-regarded volume of industrial photographs. In addition, she was well-known for her photographs of Russian industrial and agricultural operations.

Margaret Bourke-White immediately expressed enthusiasm when the purpose of the book was explained and stated without hesitation that she should be the one to take the pictures for the project. At that point, I was not sure that I wanted to collaborate with her since I was not fully convinced that the work I had in mind would be suitable for a female photographer to perform. However, she insisted slightly tearfully on our having an immediate agreement and nothing I said after that daunted her spirits. So as it was, there and then it was decided we would meet in Augusta, Georgia, in the first week of July and travel westward through the Southern states by automobile for six or eight weeks.

Following the meeting with my collaborator, I became concerned about the need to keep complete notes and make typings of other material for use later when the text of the book was being written. And I realized, too, that secretarial help would be needed to keep accurate accounts of such travel expenses as meals, lodgings, gasoline, and miscellaneous supplies.

The person I thought of at once who would be ideally suitable for the secretarial work was Ruth Carnall. And as I had hoped, when I phoned Ruth to ask if she would be interested in arranging to take a leave of absence from her M-G-M position and join the tour, she shouted with joy and said nothing other than the death of her cherished tawny cat would keep her from meeting Margaret and me in Augusta.

As I had anticipated, the steamy canopy of July heat had settled over the valley of the Savannah River like a suffocating blanket and the only stirring of the humid air was to be found under the ceiling fans in the public rooms of the Richmond Hotel.

The summer heat was familiar to me and, except for occasional cooling showers, it would prevail in state after state for the next two months. And although I had purposely sought to travel in the South during the heat of summer, which I considered to be the best time of year to observe people in their true workaday way of life, I did begin to wonder what effect it was going to have on Margaret and Ruth.

Ruth arrived at the Richmond Hotel in Augusta after having traveled from Los Angeles at times by train and airplane. Margaret, loaded down with several suitcases and bundles of photographic equipment, arrived in the afternoon of the same day on a train from New York.

I had arrived in Augusta the night before from Maine in my Ford sedan and had limited my impedimenta to a single suitcase and portable typewriter. It was soon evident that the automobile was going to be packed and stacked to the limit with little space left on the back seat for one of the two women. No matter what happened, I had decided I was not going to consent to ride for six or eight weeks in the heat of summer while sitting cramped three abreast on the narrow front seat.

During the first evening we were together, the three of us had a pleasant dinner in the hotel dining room. That was when I had the first opportunity to describe to Margaret and Ruth what we would probably observe during our tour.

I began by saying that in general what we would observe would be people living in various conditions of economic and physical distress. As an extreme example, I cited the plight of chain gang convicts in their black-and-white striped clothing who were physically handicapped by being hobbled at work in steel balls-and-chains. As shocking as such a sight might be, I suggested that what would probably be more common would be our coming into close contact with human beings whose faces and bodies revealed the continuing ravages of hunger, disease, and utter deprivation. I explained that I had such people in mind when I was visualizing a book illustrated with photographs and having the title of *You Have Seen Their Faces*.

After assembling in the hotel lobby the next morning, Margaret took me aside and said in an agitated voice that she had been unable to sleep most of the night for fear she would have to ride on the back seat of the car. Pleading, and almost in tears, she begged me to assure her that she could sit on the front seat. Unprepared to act upon such an unexpected request for favoritism, I could only suggest that she and Ruth should decide which one would sit on which seat.

While the automobile was being loaded with our belongings, and Ruth evidently having perceived that Margaret would claim the privilege of riding on the front seat, it was announced by Ruth that she was going to ride in the rear all the time.

Ruth's unexpected announcement did not end with that statement, however. She elaborated by saying in a jesting yet somewhat caustic manner that her position was that of a hired girl and that untemperamental hired girls knew their place in life and expected to sit at second-table. Ruth's comments ended when she said, looking directly at Margaret, that she had often wondered if it would give her a delightful feeling of superiority to be temperamental.

There was a series of briefly sharp glances between the two young women after that and we next took our places in the car to start on our travels. I was beginning to realize that I might have prevented the occurrence of unpleasantness by offering to sit on the rear seat myself and let someone else drive the car.

= 3 =

Our travel through the central region of Georgia and Alabama during the first week of our trip was pleasingly productive and without obvious conflict between Margaret and Ruth. In each state, we were in the geographical region of the fall line between the hilly piedmont and the coastal flatlands. And it was here, among the gullies and sand hills and eroded red-clay hillsides that the most devasting effects of the great American economic depression were seen in the tragic lives of defeated people in the confines of their shacks and shanties.

The constantly recurring sight of so much dire poverty and untreated illness afflicting children and adults of all ages may have served to reduce to a minimum, at least temporarily, any feeling of animosity existing between the aggressive photographer and the unassuming secretary.

Regardless of what the cause may have been, the result was that Ruth often put her notebook aside and offered to change a flashbulb or move a reflector when Margaret was setting and lighting a scene for a portrait or interior photograph. Moreover, neither did she become impatient or annoyed when Margaret, devoted as she was to time-consuming and meticulous preparations, would spend two or three hours and take dozens of photographs before being satisfied with what she had put on film.

It was not clear to me what may have brought about a sudden change of attitude on the part of both Margaret and Ruth toward each other. It was the kind of situation that I had imagined might happen sooner or later and I had always wondered if there would be anything I could do to prevent a verbal, or perhaps even a physical, clash between two girls.

The inevitable abrupt turn from congeniality to hostility took place in late afternoon at the end of our fourth week of travel soon after we had stopped for the night in a hotel in Jackson, Mississippi. Immediately and loudly objecting to her room in the hotel, which was one of three similar rooms Ruth had arranged for us to occupy as she usually did, Margaret loudly insisted on having a more comfortable room on a higher floor and with a pleasant view from the window.

I came to the doorway of my room when I heard the argument between the two become excessively loud and boisterous. What I saw was that they were facing each other across the hall from their opposite doorways. Later that evening, I wrote in my notebook much of the conversation heard in the hallway.

Margaret: You did this on purpose.

Ruth: Did what on purpose?

Margaret: Put me in this awful room with a view of absolutely nothing. I won't stand for it. It's too awful for words. I simply won't stay in it. I won't—I won't—anything!

Ruth: All the rooms in this hotel are alike. You probably want a hotel room that costs more.

Margaret: I don't care what anything costs!

Ruth: But why do you want something different than what you've got?

Margaret: Because I'm me. That's why. I'm me!

Ruth: I'll never doubt that as long as I live.

Margaret: What do you mean by that?

Ruth: Whatever you want to make of it. Only a blatant egotist would make your kind of demands.

Margaret: That's insulting. Are you going to do something about changing my room?

Ruth: No!

Margaret slammed her door with a crashing sound that echoed up and down the hall. Later, she had dinner brought to her room. When I tried to call her several times during the evening, she would not answer the phone and she was not seen again until the next morning.

I was beginning to wonder during breakfast with Ruth what could be done to dispel the cloud of ill-feeling between Margaret and Ruth so that work on the book could continue without disruption for the next three or four weeks. It was then when unexpectedly Margaret came into the dining room. She was smiling and pleasant when she sat down at our table without the slightest indication of any lingering resentment after the angry scene in the hall the previous evening. She even leaned over the table and patted Ruth's hand in a friendly gesture. Ruth slowly withdrew her hand from the table.

In view of Margaret's display of excessive friendliness and seeing Ruth's reaction to the patting of her hand, I decided at that moment to change our working plans. For the good of all, it seemed to me that instead of staying several days longer in Mississippi it would be wise to drive all the way to Little Rock, Arkansas, for a well-earned rest of several days after having been together continuously for almost a month.

It was my feeling that not only would there be relief from the effects of so much enforced close association, also there would enough time for hairdressers and movies and other amenities to please Margaret and Ruth. As for myself, after finding a barbershop and a convenient pool room, I wanted to have time to review the month's accumulation of notes and to make plans for the remainder of the tour through the rice and cotton plantations of Arkansas and from there through the entire length of Tennessee.

The day-long trip from Jackson to Little Rock was pleasant and uneventful. After having lunch and crossing the Mississippi at Greenville, off and on for several hours the two young women would suddenly begin singing a song they discovered was familiar to both of them.

When we arrived at the Albert Pike Hotel in Little Rock, and saying she wanted to be sure of having a comfortable room with a pleasing view,

Margaret went with Ruth to arrange for our accommodations. We had an early dinner that evening at a candle-lighted table in the hotel dining room.

Afterward, good-nights having been said by all, I was walking across the lobby on the way to my room when Margaret grasped my arm and hastily asked me to stop later at her room for a few minutes to talk about a particular type of photograph for our book. Ruth was too far away to hear what was being said, but the expression on her face was revealing enough to indicate that she was not without understanding.

There was only silence when afterward I knocked several times on Margaret's door. It was not locked, though, and when I stepped inside the only illumination in the room was the glow of city lights coming through the open windows. Although there still was no sound to be heard in the room, I soon saw Margaret in bed with the covering tossed aside in the balmy air of the summer evening. With gradually increasing vision in the dim light, I was soon aware that she was partially clothed in a very thin garment. It was dusty rose in color and had an opening from neck to waist that had not been closed with dangling ribbons and bows. Also, one of her shoulders was bare and likewise a portion of her bosom.

"I waited too long," I said, going to the foot of the bed. "I'm sorry to be so late."

"Oh, that's all right," she said with an unexpected softness of voice. "It's still early in the evening."

I went closer as she began smoothing the bed covering over and over again as if engrossed in thought. I was near enough to her then to be able to smell the odor of a sensuous perfume and was becoming increasingly impassioned. Ever since starting on our tour, I had been constantly impressed by Margaret's enticingly lissome figure and her provocative femininity. However, I was not prepared to find myself in a hotel room with her by invitation.

"And now that you're here," Margaret said, "you can sit down so we can talk for a little while."

Even though there was only the dim glow of city lights in the room, I could see more distinctly than ever the bold bareness of her arms and shoulders, the roundness of breasts under the lacy gown. Still far apart, I had the feeling of being drawn closer and closer to her with the desire to put my arms around her. As if to provide ample space for me, she made a subtle movement toward the far side of the bed. I immediately lay down beside her.

"This is what I've wanted to do for a long time," I told her. "And now that I'm here—"

"But you must stay like you are—this time," she said with a direct firmness. "You could take off your shoes and coat to be more comfortable in this warm night. But nothing more—"

"Can't I even take off my necktie?"

She laughed. "Well, yes, if you wish."

It was midnight when, putting on my shoes and then carrying my coat and necktie, I went down the hall to my room. Restless and wide awake for several hours, I finally fell asleep at dawn.

It was not until midmorning that I woke up and went down to the hotel lobby on my way to breakfast. First with a casual glance and then with a closer look, I saw an envelope in my box at the mail desk. I knew at once what to expect. It could be nothing else. It was a note from Ruth.

Fearing the worst, I went to a corner of the lobby and sat down before ripping open the envelope and hastily reading Ruth's brief note.

From the first few words, I knew she had left Little Rock to return home to California. And I was certain long before reaching the end of the farewell letter that it had been written with tears in her eyes. And, sure enough, at the bottom of the page there was the still damp and unmistakable impress of a teardrop.

Chapter Sixteen

I CAME HOME TO NORTHERN New England in the latter days of September at the time of year when in the daylight hours the pale-blue sky always seemed to be the farthest away and the twinkling stars closest to the earth at night.

This was the season when the first bold colors of autumn foliage began sparkling in the sunlight. Almost overnight there would be flaming colors of russet and red and gold in the tall stands of gray and white birches in the lowlands and along the shores of the placid blue lakes. Beyond the birches, and waiting patiently in their summer greenery on the ridges and higher ground, were the groves of hard maple that soon would spill their brilliant paint-pot colors over the countryside as the leaves of the soft birches began fading into obscurity.

For the first time, my homecoming gave me the unmistakable feeling of being a stranger in the presence of my wife and children—and in my own house, too. It was a disturbing sensation. I felt as if I had been forewarned of an impending calamity over which I had no control. And for a moment I even tried to think of an excuse to turn around and leave without a word of explanation.

Helen as usual was tenderly loving and joyously excited from the moment

I had arrived. And, even more so than ever before, she was curious about the events in my life while I was away from home during the summer. In the course of all that, Pix and Dee were pulling my hands and arms in their eagerness to have me hear about all their feats and exploits during the summer as swimmers and divers and rafters at our lake below the woodlot and orchard. Little Janet, withdrawing shyly herself like a stranger in my presence, observed my homecoming with a wistful expression on her face.

On her part, Helen was not at all satisfied with my cursory remarks and sometimes evasive answers to her penetrating questions concerning my life and adventures in the company of two comely young women. In particular, she wanted me to describe in detail the type of clothing they wore and to tell her what they did when competing for my attention. And over and over again she wanted to know which one of the two did I consider to be the most attractive.

When the questioning became too pressing, I tried to direct talk to the purpose of the trip through the South.

"You must remember, Helen," I said, "we were working all the time on the book and—"

"Book my foot!" Helen retorted in a sarcastic tone of voice. "Two unmarried girls and you on the loose—day and night—and all that time together. Oh, my!"

"But I wasn't unmarried—I am married," I protested.

"Oh, sure!" she said with brief laughter and the flinging of her arms around me. "It's good of you to remind me of that. I wouldn't want to forget it."

The two boys had an entirely different kind of curiosity about my travels. First it was Pix, then Dee, and neither of them saying a word, came close to me and sniffed my clothing like inquisitive puppies as if trying to detect some strange odor that mystified them. Their obvious puzzlement made me wonder what scent could be of so much interest to them.

At first, I thought that since I had been exposed for such a long time to gasoline fumes and engine exhaust it was probable that my clothing would be saturated with that particular odor. Next, I decided that I might be exuding the pungent smell of onions and garlic resulting from a recent restaurant meal. Not one of the explanations satisfied Helen and later, after the boys had left the room, she said in a positive tone of voice that a musk-like female scent was emanating from my clothing.

"Do tell me, Skinny-boy," she said with a fluttering of her eyelids, "what was the name of the perfume you were exposed to? I'd like to try it myself."

I passed off Helen's questioning as quickly as I could. But the fact that a scent was noticeable reminded me of the times when I was very young that my father would return home from a trip on a train with his clothing, and even his hair and wool hat, saturated with the exciting odor of coal smoke.

While I would be begging my father for the colorful timetable of the coal-burning Southern Railway or Atlantic Coast Line, on one of which he usually traveled, my mother would be greeting him in pretended surprise. Her remarks, as I clearly recall, would begin with her saying: "Hello, stranger!" or sometimes, "Well, well! Are you somebody I've seen before?"

Now that I was at home again with Helen and the children, and even after several days of companionship and close association, I still had the uneasy feeling—and sometimes the guilty feeling—of being a stranger among strangers. Since I was far from being completely readjusted, finally I had to be reminded of the fact that it was cider-making time.

The McIntosh apples in the orchard were tree-ripe and rosy-red while in the cellar the storage bins were empty as were all the cider jugs and wooden kegs. The boys and I went to work early one morning in the first week of October gathering apples from the trees and hauling them in the wheel-barrow to the cellar door on the south side of the house.

The big wooden cider press was only a few steps inside the cellar door-way. We took care to wash the apples thoroughly in a large laundry tub until they were free of all dust and insects before carrying them inside and dump-ing them a bushel at a time into the hopper on top of the press.

As each pressing was finished, the squeezed pulp was carried outside and spread on the sunny terrace. In the evenings in the twilight after sunset, we would watch from the windows of the great room as rabbits, squirrels, woodchucks, deer, and sometimes even Winthrop-the-moose would come to eat until every fragment of apple pulp put there during the day had disappeared.

In the forenoon of our fourth and final day of cider-making, Arthur Dolloff came down the town road from his house to have a look at our operation. Arthur sat on a stool in the cellar doorway for a long time smoking his pipe and observing the flow of apple juice into measuring buckets while the big iron wheel above the press was turned tighter and tighter. Presently, as if unable to remain silent another minute, he got up and walked to the press.

"Can't say you're making a botch of your task, young man," Arthur said in his customary way of offering a compliment. "Your apple juice is running thin and clear. Haven't observed any seeds and fluff getting past the strainer. Fact is, you can count on having a good year's supply of sweet cider for the womenfolk and young ones."

"Well, thanks, Arthur," I said in appreciation of his approval of my cider-making.

"That may be all fine and dandy for those folks, but when are you going to start squeezing the makings for your man-drinking hard cider? You don't have many apples left for a run of cider for that purpose."

"I've taken care of that," I told him. "I'm going to put aside a few jugs of this run of cider for the other kind. I had that in mind all along. Doesn't all cider start out the same, anyway? There's no difference between sweet cider and the hard kind in the beginning, is there?"

"Wouldn't consider it worth boasting about if my man-drinking cider wasn't made the proper way."

"What is the proper way, Arthur?" I asked, wondering what he could mean by that.

"Every batch of apple cider intended for turning properly and tasty hard for man-drinking has to have a working worm. You take one chosen apple for every pressing that has a working worm inside. And just one of those healthy worms is enough to get the job done properly every time. Never known it to fail. But if you don't find the proper worm right away, just look under your trees for a windfall that's been on the ground long enough to have the necessary makings inside. That'll start your cider on the way to perfection. Otherwise, your whole cellar full of cider will be only fit for the womenfolk and young ones."

"Does everybody else make hard cider the way you do?" I asked Arthur.

"Anybody who properly appreciates a tasty toddy would. Can't say all the folk in the town would, though. Bound to be some blockheads with other notions. If you want to take my advice, you'll get busy and find a wormy apple or a suitable windfall. And if you make a proper run of it, I'll walk over some winter day for a testing of it with you."

= 2 =

After working day and night to complete the text for *You Have Seen Their Faces*, I left Mount Vernon on the day of the first snowfall of winter to meet Margaret Bourke-White in New York where we were to make the final selection of the photographs for our book. Following that, it was to be my task to write the captions for the illustrations.

When I arrived in New York, instead of renting a top-of-the-stairs hall bedroom in a cold-water tenement or brownstone, this time I moved into a small apartment in a modern building near the East River.

As a member of the staff of *Life*, Margaret was frequently out of town on photographic assignments but our book was finally finished, with little time to spare, for publication in early 1937. Other than the time spent writing several short stories, I was insufficiently occupied. And with so little to do I let myself be persuaded to sign a contract with Frances Gossel, the congenial manager of a lecture agency, to make a series of appearances on a public speaking tour.

Speaking from a public-lecture platform was the last thing in the world I would have consented to do if I had had my wits about me. But a victim of my own folly I was and, as the time for my first appearance drew near, I lay awake night after night in dread of the impending ordeal while trying to think of some manner of escape. In desperation, I thought of saying I would have to withdraw due to illness in my family, or because of illness of my own, but that seemed like issuing an invitation to fate to respond with a fatal calamity.

Fortunately, only a few days before I was scheduled to give the first lecture on my tour, the engagement was canceled by mutual agreement. That advent of good luck gave me the opportunity, and the courage as well, to plead with Frances Gossel to release me from all the remaining engagements she had arranged.

My first lecture had been scheduled to take place at Hamilton College, Clinton, New York. As it happened, Carl Sandburg also was beginning a lecture tour that season and I was asked by the college at the last moment if I would consent to the cancellation of my appearance in favor of the poet.

I was so relieved and elated to have been freed from my obligation that I had no thought of inquiring why I had been asked to yield to the college's request. However, a few days later I read in Leonard Lyons' syndicated newspaper column that the reason for my nonappearance at Hamilton College was because all I could offer an audience was mere talk whereas Carl Sandburg played his guitar while reading poetry.

Later in the year, after having prepared a collection of short stories to appear with the title of *Southways*, and still restless and seeking more activity, I committed myself to the obligation to write a brief story a week for a year to be published in a new weekly magazine. The magazine was an ambitious project with the title of *Midweek Pictorial* and the editor and owner was Monte Bourjaily. Monte, who had been the general manager of a successful newspaper syndicate, was a pleasant, obliging, fleshy man a few years older than I and was affectionately known on Madison Avenue as "The Affable Arab."

Soon after I had written half a dozen brief stories for Monte's magazine, I realized that being faced with a journalistic deadline once a week for a year was far more than I wanted to endure. After begging for my freedom as I had done with Frances Gossel previously, and with Monte Bourjaily's reluctant well wishes, I soon was to go in search of a less demanding activity to enjoy in my free time.

First of all, though, I moved across town from the East River to a larger apartment at the Mayflower, a residental hotel on Central Park West. With that accomplished, I had the good fortune to obtain the services of a thoroughly capable secretary to take charge of my jumbled and neglected financial matters.

Margaret Salter, a conscientious young married woman who commuted to New York from her home in New Rochelle, brought immediate order to my checkbook and established a plan for payment of past due and current income taxes. To my surprise, book royalties were amounting to several thousand dollars monthly while my one-half share of play royalties from the Broadway and touring company productions of *Tobacco Road* amounted to several thousand dollars weekly.

Perhaps it was a logical coincidence or perhaps a diabolical trick of fate to separate me from my money, but regardless of the cause I found that my next activity was that of being a backer of a play on Broadway with thousands of dollars involved. The play was not *Tobacco Road*. It was a dramatization of the novel *Journeyman*.

Journeyman, the play, opened at the Fulton Theater in New York on a wintry evening in January 1938. The reviews of the play the next morning were so unfavorable that it did not appear to be rational to open the doors for a second performance. The playwrights themselves walked out on their own dramatization and never returned.

The producer, Sam Byrd, was a determined man, however, and he would not permit himself to be discouraged by adverse criticism. Sam said many plays in the history of the theater had survived and prospered after receiving unfavorable notices and that he intended to raise enough money to pay salaries and theater rent so the play could be kept running for a full week or longer. I was persuaded to write a check forthwith for five thousand dollars. As I was to find out shortly afterward, that amount was only the first installment.

After several installments, when I protested against putting more of my money into the money-losing play, Sam said I should be able to find somebody else who would be willing to invest five thousand dollars for a share of future profits.

"Sam," I said, "I don't know where to find anyone who would put good money into a play that's already a cold turkey."

"It'll be easy," he assured me. "You can find backers on Broadway for a hundred thousand-dollar production of a dog scratching fleas—and it wouldn't have to be a shaggy dog, either. Just find the right people and talk fast. That's all there is to financing on Broadway."

"You've been on Broadway longer than I have," I told him. "You'd know where to find the right people to talk to."

"I've got to stay close to the theater and keep my eye on the box office. All successful producers do that."

When the play closed at the end of three weeks, and after I had written a series of five thousand-dollar checks it was necessary to write a final check for even a larger amount to pay outstanding bills. As I watched the scenery being hauled away, I vowed to decline the privilege of backing a Broadway play the next time I was invited to be an investor.

= 3 =

Having been confined within the boundaries of the skyscrapers and restricted to walking the pavements of New York for almost a year, in addition to feeling bruised and battered as a money-losing backer of a failed Broadway play, I was restless with the urge to travel again in the outside world.

I was thirty-four years old then and had never been outside the United States, with the exception of a brief trip into Canada, and it was easy to convince myself that the time had come for me to go abroad. With that prospect foremost in mind, I put aside all thought of staying in New York for the next six or eight months to write the next novel.

When I suggested to Margaret Bourke-White that we should consider collaborating on a second book of photographs-and-text and go abroad for subject and material, she was immediately interested. She was quick to say that she was so pleased with our first collaboration that she was hoping we could do another book together.

For several days we talked about various possibilities and made a close study of maps of Europe until finally deciding that Czechoslovakia was the place to go. Our decision was based on the fact that Adolf Hitler had indicated very clearly that he intended to invade and subdue Czechoslovakia as his first move for world domination. Our objective was to observe the people there and describe their way of life in word and pictures in a time of peaceful existence before Hitler's invasion. We decided well in advance that the title of the book would be *North of the Danube*.

After crossing the Atlantic on the *S.S. Normandie* late in May, and crossing France and Germany on trains, Margaret and I arrived in Prague early in June. It was cold and damp in that region of Middle Europe and the upland countryside was green with pines and white with the unmelted drifts of winter snow.

At the beginning of our travels in the western provinces of Bohemia and Moravia, we had little difficulty in making ourselves understood by using a few words of German and English when speaking to taxi drivers, policemen, and restaurant waiters in that part of the Slavic-speaking nation. However, later going eastward into Slovakia and Carpathian Ruthenia, where Polish and Hungarian languages were more familiar to the natives, we frequently had difficulties and misunderstandings.

Many were the occasions when obtaining a simple restaurant meal was a time-consuming and frustrating ordeal. Fortunately, both Margaret and I had a fondness for schnitzel, which was one of the favorite foods of Middle Europe, and this was usually the only item on a menu that could be readily obtained without argument and delay in hotel cafes, railway-station restaurants, and rural eating houses. With the help of waiters who appreciated schnitzel as much as we did, for several weeks we were content to eat schnitzel for lunch and dinner. The time came, though, when for breakfast I wanted eggs—fried, scrambled, poached, or boiled—and not another schnitzel.

In desperation one morning in the eastern province of Carpathian Ruthenia at a restaurant between Ozhgorod and the border of the Russian Ukraine, I quit trying to make it known to a waiter with words that I wanted eggs— no schnitzel, just plenty of eggs. Instead of uselessly trying to make use of words, I began clucking like a hen and flapping my arms as if they were chicken wings. At the end of that exhibition, I picked up a small round roll and held it in my hand triumphantly to indicate the production of an egg.

Evidently both mystified and amused by my behavior, and alternatingly nodding and shaking his head, the young waiter with a full-grown black moustache and wearing a starched bibbed apron disappeared through the kitchen doorway.

There was a long wait at our table and then, smiling and moving briskly, the waiter returned with a tray on which there were two large bowls filled to the brim with red caviar and a heaping plate of buttered toast. Placing the bowls of caviar in front of us on the table, the attentive young waiter bowed and then stood aside with a smiling expression on his face.

"Nein schnitzel," the waiter said proudly, pointing at our bowls of bright-red caviar. "You like?"

"If you have that much understanding of German and English," I said, "why did you bring us fish eggs instead of chicken eggs?"

As if he had actually comprehended the exact meaning of what I had said, the waiter with both arms outstretched and a pleased smile began making the vigorous motions of a swimmer.

Then with a sudden change of expression on his face, the waiter shook his head with forceful motions and began flapping his arms like the wings of a chicken. Next, with a backward tilting of his head, he startled everybody in the restaurant with the raucous sound of *Cockle-doodle-doo! Cockle-doodle-doo!*

"I suppose I should be doubled up with laughter," Margaret said without a smile, "but you and the waiter have been so silly that I'd better be serious and keep my sanity. Let's hurry and finish our breakfast and go before you and the waiter do any more of your imitations of fishes and fowls."

Where we went that morning, having been almost two months in Czechoslovakia, was to Paris to stay for several days before returning home on the *S.S. Aquitania*. It was my first visit to Paris, though not for Margaret, and I was content to spend most of the time at the Cafe de la Paix dining on bountiful servings of ham and eggs while Margaret was selecting perfumes and attending style showings at various dress designers.

The last night of our stay in Paris was devoted for the most part to dining and dancing in a Montmartre nightclub. And it was there where early in the evening, much to my surprise and to Margaret's amusement, that I was mistaken for a professional gigolo.

My first thought at the beginning of the incident was to wonder how there could be such a mistake of identity. There were several authentic gigolos in attendance, readily noticeable in their black bow ties and black suits and black patent-leather shoes while I was wearing an ordinary gray suit and brightly striped necktie and tan shoes. It was soon evident that I had been approached by a confused young woman who was under the influence of an excess quantity of cognac or champagne.

Margaret and I, as were other couples, had been dancing between dinner and the first show of the evening. At her urging, I had been persuaded to demonstrate one of the dance steps I had learned at Arthur Murray's before leaving New York. That was when I was tapped on the arm by a bold young woman with frizzly brown hair and an unconfined tremulous bosom. Speaking with an unmistakable British accent, she said she admired my style of dancing and was claiming me for the next dance.

"I'm here for the fun of it, lov," she said crisply as she opened her purse. "And I always pay for my fun in advance."

At that moment, Margaret began nudging me with her elbow.

"Go on and dance with her," Margaret whispered to me. "Go ahead. I want to see what happens."

"Don't you turn me down, lov," the determined woman told me. "It's not my style to like being turned down."

The tall man with whom she had been dancing, and who evidently was her husband, was trying to pull her away from the dance floor. She stamped her foot angrily.

"Dance with her just once—that's all," Margaret pleaded. "She'll be satisfied then and leave us alone."

The music stopped and the dancing couples began returning to their tables. It was not long until the show began and we never saw the two tourists from England again.

Chapter Seventeen

IN LATE SEPTEMBER OF 1938, a few weeks after Margaret and I had returned to New York from Czechoslovakia, I was served with notice of a divorce suit filed in Maine by Helen. My first reaction was the poignant realization that I would probably be separated from my three children. My next thought was to ask Helen one more time to come to live with me in New York or Connecticut. When I did ask her to do so, again she promptly refused.

The uncontested divorce was granted in due course and Helen received permanent custody of our three children. The terms of the divorce settlement as negotiated by my attorney, Julius Weiss, provided for monthly child support and my relinquishment of any interest in the Mount Vernon property.

With little time lost, I gave up my Mayflower apartment in New York and rented a furnished cottage on Pratt's Island near Noroton, Connecticut, on Long Island Sound. For the next two months I worked steadily to complete the text of *North of the Danube* for publication the following year.

Then late one night while Margaret and I were selecting photographs for the book, a violent storm swept across the Sound and waves carried away the cottage's front and only stairs. The complete staircase was hurled across the inlet to the rocky shore and smashed into splinters. The next morning we had found that we had been left stranded high and dry nine feet above ground and had to wait until neighbors discovered our predicament and brought a ladder to rescue us.

Being aware that winter would soon be closing in on the wind-swept island, and realizing that another violent storm could demolish the high-stilted cottage, I bought a new, white, two-story, Cape Cod house on a wooded hilltop several miles away in Darien.

Taking possession of the Darien property was a happy occasion and that was probably the reason for my naming it Horseplay Hill. It was there at Horseplay Hill that Margaret and I finished our second collaboration before the end of the year.

Within a week after we had bought furnishings and had moved into the new house, Margaret surprised me by having the walls of my work room recovered with wallpaper designed with the neatly-written alphabet in Spencerian script. Repeated endlessly in letters three-fourths of an inch in size, the alphabet from a to z was in alternating lines of black, orange, and blue.

When I asked Margaret how she had managed to find such an appropriate wallpaper for a writer, she readily admitted that she had designed it herself and had prevailed upon a friendly advertising agency to have the hand-written alphabet reproduced and printed in three colors on rolls of ordinary white wallpaper. In awe and still amazed by the sight of the ingenuous display of the alphabet on the walls, I sat down on the couch and gazed around the room. In a moment, Margaret sat down beside me.

"Are you going to like it—it won't become too monotonous?" she said with a concerned tilting of her head. "I wanted so much to give you a present you would really like."

"I'll like it forever," I said at once. "And almost as much as I like you."

"Are you sure—about me?"

"I'm sure—about you."

"But how can you be so certain?"

"It's a gift, I suppose," I told her. "Anyway, I'll start right now to prove it and make a believer of you."

I put my arms around her and pressed my cheek against her cheek. Her face was warm and flushed and for a while there was a slight trembling of her body. Presently she curled up closer to me and at the same time kicked off her slippers and drew her legs under her on the couch.

"I feel like a kitten—I'm so happy I want to purr," she said, snuggling closer in my arms.

"I won't believe it until I hear you purr," I said, shaking her gently. "Let's hear you purr like a kitten."

With a quick movement, she pressed her face against my ear and made a purring sound like a kitten could have done.

"Now you've done it!" I told her. "You've made a believer of me. You are a real live kitten. And from now on you won't be Margaret—my name for you will be Kit. How does that sound to you?"

"Oh, I like that!" she exclaimed. "I do, I do! That's the name I want you to have for me. And just like your literary and publishing friends, now I can call you by the name I like best—Skinny. Kit and Skinny. That's us!"

"Then we should get married," I proposed immediately.

"No," she was quick to say. "Not now. Not this year."

"Next year is only a few weeks away. What about that, Kit?"

"That's something that can wait until next year—or later, Skinny."

What would not wait were the plans we wanted to make for collaborating on a third book of text and photographs. This had already been decided upon as being our next project and would be devoted to a study of life in selected regions of the United States. More than anything else, we hoped to write about and photograph the ordinary activities of Americans. For our purpose, we felt that the commonplace was more worthy of depiction than the sensational or the exotic. The title chosen for the study was to be *Say! Is This the U.S.A.?*

It was necessary for Kit for the third time to arrange for leave of absence from her position as staff photographer for *Life* magazine. This was not always easily accomplished since the magazine's publication schedule was planned for months in advance. However, Henry Luce, the editor-in-chief, had been impressed by our previous collaborations and had indicated that we could again count on his cooperation.

For my part, though, I was in the process of changing publishers again and, although Maxim Lieber assured me that we could easily obtain a release from my contract with The Viking Press, I did not want to leave home for lengthy travel until the matter had been settled to my satisfaction. The cause of the uncertainty was due to the fact that Harold Guinzburg, the Viking president, had said he was willing to continue publishing my novels and short stories but would not agree to publish under my editorship a series of twenty-five volumes with the general title of *American Folkways*.

I had become completely absorbed in my interest in editing a series of books describing regional life in the United States and was determined to get the books written and published. By chance, I happened to accept an invitation to one of New York's literary cocktail parties on an opportune occasion. And it was there that I met Charley Duell, who with Cap Pearce and Sam Sloan, had established the new publishing house of Duell, Sloan, and Pearce, Inc. The three partners promptly offered me a contract to publish the twenty-five-volume series of *American Folkways* under my editorship in addition to publishing any books of fiction and nonfiction I would write.

During the interval between Christmas and New Year's Day, when it appeared that we would soon be able to make final plans for travel across the United States to gather material for our new book, Kit came home late one afternoon from New York with a gaily-wrapped package and handed it to me as a present. This was her second gift to me since we came to Horseplay Hill to live and, having given her nothing more fanciful than perfume, I was embarrassed and disconcerted. Being as negligent as I was to reciprocate properly, I could not keep from wondering if Kit's gift-giving proclivity was going to continue indefinitely.

What Kit had brought me that holiday season was a pair of suspenders fashioned by Elizabeth Hawes, the clothing designer, who had used strips of a colorful red, white, and blue banner that was claimed to be the original creation of Betsy Ross. There were both stars and bars woven into the material and it looked to me as if a genuine United States flag had been desecrated to make the Uncle Sam suspenders. I regarded the gift in silence for a while.

"Now please don't worry, Skinny," Kit said presently in a tone of concern. "It's all right. At first, I thought an original Betsy Ross flag had been used, too. But Elizabeth Hawes showed me authentic documents proving that the red, white, and blue silk cloth with the thirteen stars and thirteen stripes had been designed by Betsy Ross as a banner and not a flag. As soon as I heard about the Uncle Sam suspenders I wanted you to have a pair of the only ones in existence. And now you do. Well, maybe not the only pair— but one of the very, very few."

= 2 =

Mindful of the ending of the old year and the beginning of the new year 1939, and having restrained myself until the middle of January, I knew I could not wait much longer to ask Kit for the second time to marry me. It was then a cold and windy winter day on Horseplay Hill, with alternating gusts of snow and sleet pelting the windowpanes, and we had been sitting in the warmth of blazing logs in the fireplace while reading the Sunday newspapers for the past hour or longer.

Presently, after Kit had glanced across the room at me several times with an obviously inviting gesture, I tossed my paper aside and went to sit beside her on the sofa. As she often did when she was at leisure, she made herself comfortable by kicking off her slippers and drawing her legs under her.

"I'm glad you finished reading your paper at last," she said, smiling shyly. The expression on her face was a familiar one by then and I always knew that something pleasant would soon follow. "And now that you've finished your reading, there's something I want to tell you."

"What is it, Kit?" I asked at once.

"I've been given a week's assignment by the magazine to do some work in Hollywood. Actors and actresses at home and studio scenes and so on. Movie picture stuff. That will be in a few weeks. Early February. And I thought you'd like to know this far in advance—just in case—"

"In case of what?"

"Well, there was a certain question I didn't want to answer the first time. And so I thought if you wanted to ask me once more—"

"Will you marry me, Kit?"

"Yes, Skinny."

"When?"

"As soon as we get to Reno."

"Reno? Why Reno?"

"Because it's on the way to California. And by going a few days early—"

"But Reno—why—?"

"Because there are many places near Reno that would be just perfect for us. I want to be married this time in a ghost town or abandoned mining camp or something of the kind. The first time was a horrible experience. It was so stuffy and formal and boring. I don't want to go through anything like that again. Please understand."

"Is that the only condition you intend to impose?"

"Well, I wouldn't want to give up my professional name. My name means so much to me in my career and—"

"Now hear this, madam," I said emphatically. "As far as I'm concerned you can be Margaret Bourke-White from here to the world's end as long as you are Kit to me."

It was on our airplane trip from New York to Reno, and shortly before

167

we were to land in Reno, that Kit prevailed upon the captain to divert the flight and make several low-level passes over a group of abandoned mining camps and ghost towns between Carson City and Reno.

While the airplane's wings dipped time after time over the rugged dry mountains a short distance east of the Sierra Nevada range, Kit selected for the wedding ceremony an abandoned small town that had a steepled church standing among a clutter of decrepit shacks and gaping mine shafts. The name of the town, the captain informed us, was Silver City.

It was midmorning when we landed in Reno and got into a taxicab for the trip out of town. The black-bearded driver and owner of the cab, who said his name was Herman and who had the rough-hewn appearance of a hard-rock miner and prospector, immediately became enthusiastic when told of the purpose of our trip to Silver City. Herman advised us to take a minister with us, since there would be no justice of the peace or anyone else there to perform a legal ceremony, and he heartily recommended Brother David to be that person.

On the way to the Washoe County courthouse to obtain a marriage license, Herman told us that Brother David early in life had been an aspiring motion picture actor in Hollywood and had abandoned that precarious profession for a more rewarding career on a live stage. And, according to the taxi driver, Brother David had become owner of a profitable Reno wedding chapel and, while wearing the vestment of a priest, never attempted to refute the rumor that he was an excommunicated minister.

By the time Kit and I had obtained our marriage license, Herman returned to the courthouse with Brother David and a small bouquet of daisies. Making several bows, Herman handed the daisies to Kit and introduced us to the supposedly defrocked priest who greeted us with a congenial smile and long and warm handshakes.

"I am extremely pleased to meet such a beautiful bride and handsome bridegroom," Brother David said, bowing first to Kit and then to me. "I'm proud to have the privilege of inducting you two into the holy state of matrimony. Herman told me that we will be going to Silver City for the ceremony. So, let us be off. Some things in life deserve to be speeded up—and foremost of all is love."

After going several miles, we came to a suburban cluster of buildings where a blinking electric sign indicated the location of a bar. Brother David tapped Herman on the shoulder with one hand while pointing at the bar with his other hand.

"It's coming up high noon any minute now," said the affable Brother David. "And in this part of our great land high noon calls for civilized refreshments. We owe it to ourselves and to our descendants to cherish and sustain a time-honored tradition."

The smoke-filled barroom, noisy with jukebox music, was occupied by half-a-dozen casually-dressed patrons who had not waited until the stroke of twelve noon to begin their routine of drinking for the day.

Behind the bar and facing the slouching drinkers, the elderly, shirt-sleeved, potbellied bartender sat on a high stool staring glumly at the row of ranch hands and truckers with the stub of a dead cigar clenched between his teeth.

Some of the men at the bar glanced at Kit and me with mild interest when I asked for two glasses of white wine. A moment later, when Brother David ordered a double slug of rye whisky and a beer chaser, the same men nodded approvingly and went back to their own drinking. The taxi driver, waving aside an offered glass, was content to hold his bottle of beer in his hand.

Half an hour later, we arrived at the dusty hillside ruins of what in the past had been rich and riotous Silver City. In an abandoned mining town as ghostly by day as a remote graveyard in moonlight, and situated somewhere between Carson City and Virginia City, we were in the midst of sagging mounds of tailings where numerous rusting winches were scattered over the bleak landscape. As she looked at the wind-swept hillocks and tumble-down shacks, the smile on Kit's face indicated how happy she was with the place she had selected to be married.

The door of the only church structure remaining in the town had been nailed shut in order to protect the interior from additional vandalism but Brother David found that it was not too difficult to force it from its hinges after he had traveled all that distance from Reno.

"Ordinarily, I would not approve of using force to enter a sacred building," Brother David said, brushing dust from his black coat and adjusting his clerical collar, "but I am here on an ecclesiastical mission and nothing shall prevent me from performing my duty."

After entering the church and taking our places at the dusty altar, where Herman handed Kit the bunch of wilting flowers and stood before us as the only witness, Brother David married Kit and me in a hurriedly intoned ceremony accompanied by the loud squawking of disturbed pigeons fluttering overhead between the altar and the vaulted ceiling.

= 3 =

I went home to Darien in early spring 1939 with the determination to complete the novel I had begun writing the previous year, *Trouble in July,* and to deliver the manuscript before the end of the year to Duell, Sloan, and Pearce for publication in 1940.

Kit's photographic assignment in Hollywood had been extended an additional week and then, unexpectedly, she had been asked by editors at *Life* to stop for several days in Kansas City to photograph a livestock show.

We had planned to spend our honeymoon at Horseplay Hill and the enforced interruption, although lamented by Kit at length in nightly telephone calls, did not serve to mollify my resentment toward magazine editors who would heartlessly prevent a loving couple from continuing the customary consummation of marriage.

As if motivated by a heartfelt desire to make amends for his magazine's inept action in delaying Kit's homecoming after her marriage, on a midmorning following her return home, there was delivered in a furniture van a huge, totally-enveloped, red-ribbon-tied object from Henry Luce as editor-in-chief of *Life.* Too large to be taken through the doorway of the house, it was placed on the lawn beside the swimming pool where, unwrapped, it was revealed to be probably one of the largest and most luxurious king-size outdoor bundlebeds ever constructed. It would easily have accommodated two couples without discomfort. Attached to the bundlebed was a scrawled note that said: "To Margaret and Erskine for a happy marriage from Henry Luce."

After finishing the novel, I left Darien later in the year on a cross-country automobile trip in search of a number of able regional writers to contribute volumes to *American Folkways.* As it happened, Kit left home at the same time on a long assignment in Europe. I was lonely and the separation was like being divorced against my wishes. It was a bitter foretaste of a greater loneliness to follow.

During my first few weeks of travel, I visited Otto Ernest Rayburn in Arkansas who agreed to write *Ozark Country,* Stanley Vestal at the University of Oklahoma who would write *Short Grass Country,* Haniel Long in Santa Fe who would use the title of *Pinon Country* for his contribution to the series, and in California it was Edwin Corle who wrote *Desert Country.*

Edwin Corle was the only one of the four authors I had not corresponded with previously. Ed was somewhat belligerent when I finished explaining why I had come to see him.

"I'd certainly like to write the book about the Southwest deserts," he said, "but nobody's going to slash up my work with an editorial pencil. If there's any editing to be done, I'll do it myself."

"I'm not doing the kind of editing you are thinking about, Ed," I assured him. "Every *American Folkways* author should plan his own book. All I do is offer suggestions if asked."

"Well, that's different," he said agreeably. "I've wanted to write this kind of book for years and years—and now I'll do it even if you and I get into a quarrel over every chapter I write."

It was late in November then and after leaving California I stopped in Arizona in December to visit Harry Behn at his home in Tucson. It was the first time I had seen Harry since telling him good-by at the M-G-M studio in Culver City. He had bought a home and was teaching courses in radio writing at the University of Arizona.

During the time I was in Tucson, Harry tried diligently though unsuccessfully to persuade me to buy a home on the desert and live there part of each year. It was my first trip to the Southern Arizona desert and I was not impressed by the famed grandeur of its barren expanse and towering dry mountains. After part of a lifetime in the South and East, I could not understand why anyone would willingly leave a favored region of leafy trees and green grass for sun-baked sand and the prickly cactus of a desert.

Before leaving Tucson, however, I became aware of a haunting premonition that I was going to miss watching the shadows as they began falling into the crevices and canyons of the purple mountains in the late afternoon. After all, it was inescapably fascinating to be there to watch the constantly changing hues of the purple haze from the sun-bright days to the clear star-lit nights.

After a week or longer in Arizona, I started driving to Florida. My destination was Miami Beach where I planned to stay for two weeks over the Christmas and New Year's holidays before going back to Connecticut in January to be with Kit when she returned from Europe.

The highway distance from Tucson to El Paso, Texas, was slightly more than three hundred miles. Several hours before reaching El Paso, I began to feel dizzy and weak and several times I stopped the car beside the highway until I felt capable of driving again. Seizures of intense feverishness and dizzyness came over me at twenty-minute intervals. I hoped I was not going to die but I had never before felt so sorely stricken and utterly helpless to be able to keep myself alive.

I had intended to go to a hotel in El Paso, but when I got out of my car at the Plaza in the center of the city at midnight and tried to stand up I could not do so. My knees buckled under me and I fell to the pavement. Recovering enough to crawl back into the car, and after sitting there for a while and wondering what would be infallible signs of impending death, I called to a nearby taxi driver and asked him where I could find the nearest hospital.

"Three blocks down that street on the right hand side," he directed me, pointing across the Plaza. "You can't miss it. Look for the big holy cross in front. That'll be it, bud."

"What's the name of the hospital?" I asked him.

"Hotel Dieu."

"What?"

"That's it. Hotel Dieu."

"But I don't want a hotel—I need a hospital," I told him, pleading desperately.

"That's what I'm telling you, bud. Don't you know what you hear when you hear it? I told you that's a hospital—Hotel Dieu. Religious people run it but they'll take in anybody—even the devil himself if he's got the money to pay his way. Now why don't you get going if that's what you want?"

I gazed blankly at the exasperated taxi driver, wondering why any man would torture another human being as he was doing. He had left his cab and was standing a few feet away and staring at me intently.

"Is there another hospital in town?" I begged.

"Sure. Go about three miles down that other street over there and you'll come to the City-County Hospital." Speaking with a Texas drawl, he directed me with a waving of his hand in the way I should go. "Maybe you'll like that other hospital name better, huh? And if you want to know the truth, I'm not so much for liking foreign names, either."

After thanking the friendly cab driver, I drove from the Plaza in the direction of the City-County Hospital. The distance seemed to be much longer than two or three miles and it was far after midnight when I arrived and parked my car near the emergency entrance.

Slowly making my way across the parking lot, and with the little energy I had left, I staggered into the emergency room. There were two nurses on duty and a drowsing young intern was slumped head downward on a desk. The intern was shaken awake by one of the nurses and all three of them watched me suspiciously as I walked unsteadily across the brightly lighted room.

First of all, the sleepy-eyed intern smelled my breath. After that, he took my temperature. With that examination completed, I was given two pills and a glass of water to drink. And I had a vague remembrance of giving up my pocketbook and being led down what seemed to be an endless hallway.

A nurse and one of the staff physicians woke me up at dawn to inform me that I had chicken pox and would be quarantined for about a week as a Christmas present from the City-County Hospital. By the end of the first day, I felt so good to be alive that I could even smile when I saw that the doctor or perhaps a nurse had hung an Infants Ward sign on my door.

I reached Florida shortly after New Year's Day and took a room at the Wofford Hotel on Miami Beach. I had been there for several days when an attractive, raven-haired, young woman came to the hotel and asked for an interview for a student publication at the University of Miami. Her name was Mildred Zinn.

Having talked so enthusiastically and intelligently during the hour-long interview, I told Mildred as she was leaving that there was a job for her as secretary and editorial assistant any time she wanted to come to work for me. She said she expected to graduate from the University of Miami at mid-term in February and after that would be looking for a position.

Mildred came to Darien at the end of February. She was pleasant company in my loneliness.

Chapter Eighteen

WHEN I WAS SOON TO COME upon the age of forty, a figure chosen arbitrarily to be half of the expected years of my life, I found myself being acutely aware of the quickened chirping of birds and the accelerated ticking of clocks and the speedy conclusion of thoughts and judgments unlike the deliberate pondering in the past. Time was trying to catch up with me.

There was so much to do and so much desire for accomplishment that there was a constant urgency to eliminate this or to select that other thing in order for the best among the good to be chosen. To travel to this destination or to that destination? To write a lengthy short story or a short novel? To do something now or defer to a later time? To read the first novel of the young writer or the classic tale of the master?

Already decided upon was the completion of the manuscript for *Say! Is This the U.S.A.?* and that the book to follow would be a volume containing seventy-five short stories selected from the more than a hundred previously published in magazines. The latter project was to have the title of *Jackpot* and it soon came to be a far more arduous task than merely choosing a title. When the time came to type the material for the printer, it was discovered that there were no copies of many of the magazines in my files and it became Mildred Zinn's task to see to it that many stories were reproduced from magazine copies in the New York Public Library.

The next project that could not be delayed or eliminated was the selection of the quartet of volumes in the *American Folkways* series to follow the original four. Fortunately, the writers in the newest group were eager to contribute to the series and they submitted their manuscripts promptly. These books were: *Blue Ridge Country*, by Jean Thomas; *High Border Country*, by Eric Thane; *Palmetto Country*, by Stetson Kennedy; and *Mormon Country*, by Wallace Stegner. Among the others who helped to fill the yearly quota each time were Gertrude Atherton, Harnett Kane, Carey McWilliams, and Meridel LeSueur.

I was not always successful, however, in my attempts to persuade some of the carefully selected writers to contribute to *American Folkways*. One of the persons who flatly rejected my proposals was Clare Boothe Luce who would not consent to write a volume describing suburban life and tribal manners in the mansions in the Lower Hudson River Valley and including Westchester County, New York, and Fairfield County, Connecticut.

After I had followed Clare from New York to a duck-shooting blind in the South Carolina marshes near Charleston, where her companions at the flyway were a hunting guide and a state game warden, it was there that she had effectively put an end to my pursuit.

"No, thanks," was Clare's tart reply to my persistent entreaties. "You ought to know I'm not one to tell tales on my own kind. The person you are looking for is someone who has lost his badge of honor. That person is not me and I don't intend to lose mine."

"But may I keep on and ask you a second time?"

"Please don't bother," she replied firmly.

After politely shaking hands with everybody in the duck blind that morning, and not waiting for the fly-over, I walked back in a subdued mood to my waiting car for the return to Charleston and from there to New York.

I had been at home in Darien for only a few days when Kit returned home from Europe after a long absence. And again I was presented with one of Kit's always surprising gifts. This time she had brought me a portable, Swiss-made, Hermes typewriter in a light-weight carrying case. Before that, I had neither seen nor held in my hand a writing machine that was so small and compact and seemingly weightless in comparison with the domestic portable typewriters I had been accustomed to using.

The small typewriter, which possibly could have been carried in a large overcoat pocket, proved to be sturdy and practical and not a mere toy when I typed with it for the first time. I was eager to take a trip as soon as possible so I could test its usefulness while traveling.

I did not have to wait long—in fact, only two weeks—until I could take my Hermes on its first trip after being brought to America. That occurred when Kit's next photographic assignment was to be a tour of several weeks in Mexico and she had suggested that I might like to go with her. I was immediately interested in the prospect of being with her and traveling with her for the first time when we were not collaborating on one of our text-and-picture books.

We left in the early summer of 1940 for Mexico and for the next several weeks we traveled on busses and trains and rented automobiles to various photographic locations in the states of San Luis Potosi, Coahuila, Chihuahua, Durango, and Zacatecas. During that time, I was able to complete six or more short stories—all of them typed of course to good advantage on the Hermes—and afterward placed for publication by Maxim Lieber in *Harper's Magazine* and *Town and Country* and *Esquire*.

Back home at Horseplay Hill, with *Say! Is This the U.S.A.?* delivered to Duell, Sloan, and Pearce for publication in 1941, Kit said one evening after dinner that she was so pleased with the books we had done together that she wanted to collaborate on a fourth volume of text-and-photographs. My thoughts had been solely about writing a series of connected short stories about boyhood and family life in Georgia that had come to mind and I was not sure I wanted to put fiction aside even temporarily and devote the time to working on another book of non-fiction.

When I did not respond immediately to Kit's comment, I could see that she was twisting her fingers nervously and glancing at me hopefully in the silence.

"But how could you work on another book so soon—and work for the magazine, too?" I asked presently.

"Oh, I can do both," she said at once, her expression bright with delight. "I've already talked about it with the editors. All of them are very enthusiastic."

"That's very kind of them," I said, "but you can see that I'm not jumping with joy."

"That's because you don't know what I have in mind—where I'd like for us to go."

"Where for us to go?"

"The U.S.S.R."

"Russia?"

"Yes, Russia."

177

"Why?"

"Because it's the thing for us to do, that's why," she said at once. "It'll be an exciting experience for you and me—for both of us. We'll be together all the time—just like it was when we went to Mexico together. And you'll like the Russians. They can be so friendly when they want to be. Almost without exception, everybody was so helpful and kind when I went there the first time. And something's going to happen there soon. That'll be exciting—"

"War is going to happen there, Kit. That's what will happen. You know that. The Germans—Adolf Hitler—"

"Of course!" she exclaimed excitedly. "That's it exactly. Now, don't you want to go, Skinny? Please say you do!"

= 2 =

It was mid-March when Kit and I left New York on a United Airlines plane for Los Angeles to board the *S.S. Lurline* for Honolulu. From Hawaii, we had booked passage on a flying boat, the *China Clipper*, to Hong Kong.

Many weeks prior to leaving the United States we had made formal applications for visas to travel to the Union of Soviet Socialist Republics. Several weeks had passed before word of any kind was received regarding our applications. Then, finally, a notice was received instructing us to go to Washington and apply in person a second time for visas.

Constantin Oumansky, the Soviet ambassador at the time, showed no enthusiasm whatsoever for our plans to go to Russia to gather material for a book. He tried to discourage us by saying the western borders of the country were already closed to travel, that the U.S.S.R. soon might be on a wartime alert, and that as foreigners we might become prisoners of war for the duration. The effect of all his dire warnings brought renewed effort to Kit's endeavor to obtain the visas. I could see indications that at any moment her pleas might become tearful. And I had never known a time when her tears had failed to be productive.

It was at that moment, possibly as an acknowledgment to the inevitable, when the ambassador wearily lifted both arms in a gesture of surrender. He said that if we could succeed in making our way from Hong Kong to Chungking, Chiang Kai-Shek's provisional capital during the Japanese-Chinese War, that he would arrange for our visas to be issued to us there at the Soviet Embassy.

Elated by the ambassador's assurance that we would be permitted to enter the Soviet Union, we went home to plan and prepare for our trip to Moscow.

Many travel agents were eager to sell us tickets as far as Hong Kong but none would offer help through China. The route we had to plan for ourselves through a nation divided and partly occupied by the Japanese Army appeared to be a logical one in the beginning. In the end, it was a journey that succeeded with help of luck and perseverance aided by enforced human endurance.

The trip on the amphibious *China Clipper*, normally quicker in more favorable seasons of the year, was for us a journey of eleven days due to frequent delays caused by typhoons or the threat of squalls or typhoons in the vicinity of Guam and the Phillipines. The crew of three and the nine passengers spent nights at Pan American Airways hostels on atolls inasmuch as flights were made only during daylight hours.

After waiting a long time in Hong Kong, where Chinese tailors and shoe-makers overnight duplicated shirts and shoes for me and numerous garments for Kit, we were at last taken aboard a small aircraft for a midnight flight to Chungking. Several hours later, after evading planes of the Japanese Occupation Force in the moonless night, we arrived stiff-legged and sleepless at the Chungking landing field. The visas to enter the U.S.S.R., as promised, were waiting for us at the Soviet Embassy.

However, the office of the Chinese-operated Eurasia Aviation Corporation claimed that it had no record of having booked and confirmed passage for us from Chungking to Hami, Province of Sinkiang, where we expected to connect with a flight on the Soviet airline to Moscow.

Bowing and apologizing time after time, the manager of the E.A.C. office assured us that our names would be placed high on the waiting list for seats on the weekly plane scheduled to leave for Hami six days later. After that, saying he wanted us to have a pleasant place to stay while waiting in Chung-king the airline office manager took us to a tea house at the bottom of one of the city's many hills were we had a large ground-floor suite with a wide veranda and adjoining private garden.

Only a few minutes after being taken to the tea house, we were adopted at first-sight by an English-speaking, twenty-two-year-old Chinese cook-boy with an ingratiating smile who said he was a refugee from Japanese-occupied Shanghi where he had been a chef's apprentice. As for the cook-boy's name, he said he wished to be called Sonny since it sounded almost the same in both Chinese and English.

After unpacking our baggage and arranging our clothing in an orderly manner on hangers and in drawers, Sonny produced his highly-treasured, batik-bound book of recipes. The indexed volume contained numerous listings of recipes for hamburger and veal, soups and vegetables, savories and sweets, while most of all were recipes for no less than two hundred flavors of souffles.

"You must hurry and choose one of my souffles at once to celebrate your arrival in Chungking," Sonny implored with an eager smile. "That's to be for now. After that, there will be a different souffle for your every meal. And in between, maybe at nap time and at midnight, I will prepare some other souffle for your pleasure."

"I think a chocolate souffle would be very suitable now," Kit told him.

"You bet!" he said in enthusiastic agreement. "You choose well, missy. And Sonny will prepare well."

Sonny took it upon himself to be not only our personal cook-boy, he also became our interpreter, translator, butler, valet, guide, bodyguard, messenger, and counselor.

"You people must go with me every day at noon to sit for exactly thirty minutes in a safe cave while the Japanese drop the bombs," Sonny told us sternly. "I insist for our lives. We do not wish the Japanese to kill us with their bombs. We must stay alive for our own sakes."

Since Sonny was much interested in the large amount of photographic equipment Kit had brought on the trip, I told him that she was a photographer for an American magazine.

"Then you must go and take the pictures of the great Chiang Kai-Shek," he said to her. "I will arrange right away for you to do that. It's very important to have the Americans see the great Chiang Kai-Shek in the magazine."

"Do you really think it can be arranged before we leave on the airplane for Hami?" Kit asked.

"Of course," he told her. "Because it's important."

Two days later the three of us were admitted to the compound where Generalissimo Chiang Kai-Shek's living quarters were guarded by a large detail of heavily-armed soldiers. We were then taken into a plainly furnished reception hall where Kit at once became busily engaged in her usual prolonged method of photographing a subject from every possible angle.

While Kit was frequently changing lenses and lighting levels during the next hour, and not hesitating to urge the stern-faced Chiang Kai-Shek to smile for the camera, Sonny and I at the other end of the reception hall were served tea and cookies by the unsmiling Madame Chiang Kai-Shek.

= 3 =

The ancient, noisy, German-made, single-engine aircraft we boarded in Chungking on a sunny spring morning with the expectation of arriving in Hami the same day landed instead several hours later at Lanchow, Province of Kansu. It was there that the pilot told the passengers with a cheerful smile that we would be grounded for a little while because of a slight mechanical breakdown.

During the time he was speaking to us, the smartly costumed pilot was fingering one after another the dozen or more zippered pockets and other openings that adorned his Hong Kong-tailored jacket. While the jacket of many zippers was actually not a part of the uniform, it was proudly displayed as being appropriate for a licensed airplane captain.

The mishap that had grounded us in Lanchow resulted in a delay of almost a week while we waited in the beginning for several days while mechanics tinkered without success in making repairs to the collapsed landing gear. After that, more time passed while we waited for the promised replacement aircraft to take us the remainder of the way to Hami.

The enforced waiting time was spent photographing local citizens and scenes, typing notes and memorandums on the portable Hermes, playing Chinese checkers with a board and the marbles that were to be taken around the world with us, and making twice-daily trips to the E.A.C. office to ask with constantly diminishing hope when another aircraft would arrive. It came to be a time when patience was on the verge of giving way to rage and wrath.

Finally aboard the replacement plane to fly the final segment of our trip over China, we were somewhere over the Gobi Desert in the vicinity of Mongolia when suddenly we plunged into a dense sandstorm that pelted the plane's windows with a sound like pebbles being hurled at a tin-sided shack.

It was only a moment until there was a loud cry from the pilot when the windshield of the airplane was suddenly sandblasted with such force that he had to turn the aircraft abruptly around to avoid further loss of vision through the pitted windshield. Diving earthward then, we could see the gleaming windswept surface of the Gobi hurling itself at us until it seemed certain we would be crushed against the shiny monolithic surface of the earth like the splattering of a ripe tomato under foot.

Appearing to be close to destruction, but probably still safely above the earth, we went away from the awesome sight of the Gobi Desert until we landed at a military airfield about five or six minutes later. The door of

the plane was promptly sealed by armed soldiers and we were still wondering two and a half hours later if Constantin Oumansky had Mongolia—or
wherever we were—in mind when he said we might find ourselves being
held prisoners of war.

When the door of the airplane finally was opened, the crew and all
passengers were ordered to climb aboard an open-bed military truck. After
traveling several miles in the darkening twilight, we were delivered to a
sprawling barracks surrounded by guard towers and barbed-wire fences.

Marched single-file like so many army recruits—or prisoners of war—
we were taken to an area in one of the single-story buildings where in the
center of which were hundreds of cots. There we were ordered to remain
and not attempt to go anywhere else during the remainder of the night.

Each person was assigned to a cot, men and women alike, and given the
choice of sitting on the cot or standing beside it until we would be taken
back to our airplane the next morning to resume daylight travel. Beside each
cot was a large pitcher of water, a wash basin, a square of cloth, and a private slop jar.

Shortly before the lights were dimmed for the night, a detail of soldiers
brought each of us a mess kit containing an ample dinner that had the appearance and taste of chow mein. It was one of the best meals we had been served
during our entire time in China.

The delay caused by the violent sandstorm over the Gobi resulted in our
arriving at the Hami airport a day too late to make connection with the Soviet
plane to Moscow and we were told we would have to wait six days for the
next weekly flight. The gracious airport manager expressed much sympathy for our plight and called upon the only available English-speaking person in Hami to help him make our enforced stay as pleasant as possible.

"It is too cruel for Americans visiting us to be delayed for such a long
time," the manager instructed the interpreter to tell us. "Americans need
to be in a hurry at all times because they are Americans. I am sorry this
delay had to happen anywhere in China."

The manager said he wanted to be as helpful to us as possible and would
provide us with a donkey cart to take us to the nearby Hami market. Later,
when we returned to the hostel, we brought back jars of tasty black caviar
which had cost the equivalent of a dollar a pound and vine-ripened Per-
sian melons that had cost five cents each.

The day before we were scheduled to leave for the Soviet Union, Alice-
Leone Moats caught up with us on an undelayed flight from Chungking.

We had last seen her at the Soviet Embassy in Chungking where she was waiting for verification and issuance of her visa to the U.S.S.R. as a magazine correspondent.

When Alice-Leone was offered bread and a spoon with which to eat from a jar of chilled black caviar, she nodded approvingly after a tentative sampling.

"I can tell you this," she said. "A horde of self-esteemed gourmets in New York society will gag and retch if they ever find out that ordinary people are privileged to eat dollar-a-pound caviar as good as this is. They would probably say that was committing an unpardonable sacrilege. What I'll say is that I'll have another helping of this delight—or two or three more."

Chapter Nineteen

THE OUTBREAK OF THE German-Russian War, soon after our arrival in the Soviet Union, brought to an abrupt end the elaborate plans Kit and I had made for travel in the many regions of the U.S.S.R. to seek material for a book of text and photographs similar to the study we had made in Czechoslovakia.

Instead, as events would have it, Kit took the assignment of being full-time photographer for *Life* and I went to work filing daily radiogram dispatches to North American Newspaper Alliance, a syndicate, and broadcasting news reports via short wave radio to the United States twice daily for the Columbia Broadcasting System.

In the beginning, all our activities in Moscow were routine and uneventful. With the first of what came to be nightly German air raids, though, our way of life became unpredictable and unsettled and otherwise subject to the hazards of modern warfare.

On the night of the first German air raid, which was two weeks after invasion by land began on June 22, 1941, and when the wailing sirens were sounded for the first time, we were promptly ordered by rifle-carrying wardens to go down to the subway under the street between the National Hotel and the Kremlin. And there we sat with scores of other persons in the silent underground station from midnight until three o'clock in the morning. During all that time, Kit was frequently complaining about being required to stay in the subway and be unable to take pictures of the bombing of the Kremlin while knowing, she said, that the scene was brilliantly lighted by flares floating downward from German aircraft.

"Nobody and nobody will ever make me come down here like this again to an air-raid shelter," Kit said with firm determination. "It's absurd to make me do something like this and keep me from photographing history-making German air raids on the Kremlin. I'll never let them do this to me again."

"The air-raid wardens have a lot of authority," I reminded her. "And they carry rifles, too. That says something about them."

"The only thing it says to me is that we let them herd us down here in this subway with those other people like so many sheep," she said angrily. "I'm ashamed of myself for letting them do it. Well, I'm not going to stand for it another single time. I just won't! That's what!"

"Do you have any ideas about how we can evade the wardens the next time?"

"I don't know about that now but I do know I'm not going to let anybody keep me from photographing the Kremlin when it might be set on fire or bombed to smithereens by the Germans. If that happened, and I was prevented from photographing the historic event, I'd be so embarrassed and chagrined I'd simply die. Can you imagine my being in Moscow and failing to get a thing like that on film? How awful that would be! I'd never be able to live it down!"

The next night, and nightly thereafter, the raids began with the dropping of flares and the *Boom! Boom! Boom!* of anti-aircraft guns mounted on the rooftops of the tall buildings surrounding the fortress-like Kremlin. Viewed from the National Hotel on the west side of Red Square, the Kremlin on the opposite side was far more awesome and formidable in appearance at night in the dazzling light of German flares than it could ever be as a daytime scene of serenity for a picture postcard sought by tourists.

Our rooms at the National Hotel were on the second floor in a corner suite with a wide balcony and we had an unrestricted view of the Kremlin and the parade grounds of Red Square.

The richly furnished suite—parlor, dining-lounge, bedroom, and bath—was affordable because of the large amount of rubles I had earned in royalties from the translations of *Tobacco Road* and *American Earth*. The most imposing room of all was the large oval parlor embellished by an ornate crystal chandelier, a grand piano, an enormous white bearskin rug, and over-stuffed red leather chairs and sofas. Hovering overhead on the pale blue ceiling were chubby pink-and-white cupids armed with bows and heart-shaped arrows.

In keeping with our sumptuous living quarters, as well as being aware of the impossibility of being able to convert blocked Soviet currency into American dollars to take home, we soon became accustomed to having meals served in our suite without regard to cost. Typically, our fare would include dark caviar and chilled vodka followed by chicken *a la Kiev* and champagne. Between-meal snacks would usually be open-face red caviar sandwiches and hunter's vodka or Georgian champagne.

As expected the second of many nightly air raids to follow had begun with the horrifying wails of the city's sirens within a few minutes of midnight. Almost immediately, the telephone rang in our suite. Knowing it would be a summons to go at once to the shelter of the subway, the call was unanswered. Then, minutes later there was a loud knocking on our door and we were certain it was one of the air-raid wardens,

With all haste, Kit and I crawled as planned under the enormous wooden bed and remained there out of sight for the next half-hour while maids and wardens relentlessly searched for us in closets and behind sofas and everywhere else in the suite except under the bed. And during all that time I could hear our names being called in aggravated tones from as far distant as some of the many second-floor hallways.

After waiting as much as an hour and then deciding the search for us had ended, all lights were turned off, the bedroom door was barricaded with a large chair, and then Kit mounted her camera on a tripod at a window facing the flare-lighted Kremlin. During the remainder of the air-raid, there she waited fully contented while nervously alert for what might happen at any moment.

The next day many hours were spent at a government bureau in a bleak gray building while I was applying for an unrestricted twenty-four-hour pass as an accredited correspondent. Such a pass would permit me to be on the streets and in hotels and other public places at all hours day and night and not be compelled to go to air-raid shelters at any time.

The bureau with the authority to grant such a pass finally issued it to me after I had waited from early morning until late afternoon. That did not occur until the commissar was convinced at last that a permit without limitations was needed by me in order to be able to travel the mile and a half in both directions without hindrance between the National Hotel and the state broad-casting studio for my nightly three o'clock news transmission to CBS Radio in New York.

The pass I obtained was similar to an automobile driver's permit with detailed physical description and a photograph. In the haste to issue the per-mit shortly before the bureau's closing hour, my picture was taken in a shadowy light with the result that I had the appearance of looking more like a sinister spy than a reputable reporter. Consequently, there were occasions when I was suspected of being the former and not readily accepted as being the latter.

Because of time-consuming wartime censorship regulations, I found it was necessary, as did American correspondents Henry Shapiro, United Press, and Henry Cassidy, Associated Press, to have reliable transporta-tion. This meant buying a secondhand automobile and hiring a driver.

In my case, in addition to transmitting a censored daily news dispatch to NANA, I needed approval of the censor's office for my afternoon and early morning broadcasts for CBS. The chauffeur's name was Boris and he proudly carried a pistol under his jacket at all times. I soon found out that Boris was actually a corporal in the Red Army and had been assigned to act as my political advisor and bodyguard. Together with a succession of government-approved, English-speaking translators whose task it was to read to me the official news in *Pravda* and other newspapers, I was well protected against any unauthorized source of information.

After having been issued a twenty-four-hour pass, the wardens at the National Hotel no longer knocked on our door to compel Kit and me to go to the subway shelter during the nightly air raids. This suited Kit to the point of rapture. She said she would no longer have to leave her watch at the window to crawl under the bed during a furious German bombing of the Kremlin. And, moreover, she said that without the annoyance of the wardens she could continue trying to think of and devise possible ways to achieve her ambition to obtain permission to do a complete photographic take-out of Josef Stalin in the Kremlin.

I did not want to call upon Boris to work all day and to stay up for several hours in the middle of the night to take me to the three o'clock broadcast at the studio. Instead, I walked the entire distance from the hotel and back again during the raids.

Until I became accustomed to the frightening sound of demolition bombs exploding in all parts of the blacked-out city, I had not experienced such fear since the time I was very young and was taken on a snipe hunt one night by a group of older boys who ran away and left me alone in the darkness of a forest far from home.

I had been walking along the dark streets in the middle of the night going to and returning from the broadcasting studio so many times that I had come to be recognized and passed by the regular air-raid block wardens without incident until early one morning I was challenged by a new block warden.

Firmly insistent and obviously suspicious, the tall stern-mannered warden took me to a lighted room in the basement of the blacked-out apartment building where I was ordered to remain until my pass could be verified. After a lengthy telephone conversation in Russian, the mistrustful warden with some reluctance returned my pass with a few words of English. That was when I found out that he was a teacher of English in a Moscow lower school.

"You work for the Hearst newspapers in America, don't you?" he said in an accusing tone of voice.

"No, I do not," I told him. "I'm a correspondent for a newspaper syndicate and a radio broadcasting company. Neither of them has any connection with the Hearst operations."

"But you admire Hearst, don't you?"

"No more so than I admire some of the other newspaper publishers. What do you know about the Hearst newspapers?"

"The Hearst newspapers are always full of lies about the Soviet Union. They are our enemies. They are always trying to get us into war. And now the Germans are doing exactly what Hearst tells them to do."

"Are you sure about that?" I asked.

"Of course I'm sure—everybody in our country knows that," he said sharply, opening the door and directing me toward the stairway to the street. "Even the school children know that to be the truth. They read about it in our newspapers. Now go on about your business. I'll find out more about you tomorrow. That'll settle the truth about whether you work for the Hearst newspapers or not."

= 2 =

Under a grayish overcast sky on a chilly afternoon early in October 1941, Kit and I boarded a hard-class coach on a passenger train going from Moscow to the northern port of Arkhangelsk on the Barents Sea.

In addition to several suitcases and Kit's cameras and my Hermes typewriter, we carried with us a quantity of bread, sausage, red wine, and bottled water for sustenance during the journey of two days and two nights on unpadded wooden benches provided for wartime hard-class sitting and sleeping.

Our fellow passengers for the most part were bearded herdsmen and mustached artisans, sailors and soldiers in uniform, babuska-draped girls and women of all ages, and crying children. Strolling in the aisle with authoritative strides was an ever-present militiaman with rifle slung over his shoulder.

A month before our leaving Moscow it had been arranged with the help of Sir Stafford Cripps, the British ambassador to the Soviet Union, for us to have passage on a British ship in a convoy sailing from Arkhangelsk through the Barents Sea, the White Sea, and the Norwegian Sea across the North Sea to the Firth of Clyde in Scotland.

Before permission for the passage was granted, we had been solemnly warned that it was a dangerous trip inasmuch as several ships in previous convoys on the same route had been sunk by German U-boats. Nevertheless, it was an appealing adventure and we chose to take the risk rather than return to America by retracing our travels through China.

As much as a month before leaving Moscow, Kit and I had decided that after more than three months in the Soviet Union, regardless of how productive and exciting our lives had been, we should not let more than six months, including travel time, elapse from the date we left New York until our return. I was anxious by then to go home where I could resume writing the fiction that mattered so much to me and Kit was satisfied with her accomplishments in Moscow—including a long photographic session with Josef Stalin in the Kremlin—and she wanted to seek new challenges elsewhere.

When the time to leave Moscow to board the ship in the convoy was only a few days away, I could feel the pangs of withdrawal and realized how reluctant I was to sell my Soviet-made sedan and have to say good-by to Boris, my constantly good-natured, pistol-toting driver and political advisor.

Likewise, it had been no less anguishing to give up the luxurious corner suite at the National Hotel where I had become accustomed to gazing fondly at the winged cupids on the ceiling while reclining on the sofa and passing the time with chilled black caviar and Georgian champagne. Hopeful that it would make the leave-taking less sorrowful, even though it had been early morning, I asked Boris to wait while I sent for a liter of champagne so I could offer a toast to our lasting friendship.

It was snowing lightly in the cold, gray afternoon when we arrived in Arkhangelsk and went directly to the dock to board the cargo ship that was to join the convoy the next morning. There were accommodations for twelve passengers and, since we were the only ones to be on board, we were given the choice of several cabins on the stern deck. After an early meal with some of the officers, we hurried to the comfort of bunks with mattresses after two fitful nights on the wooden benches of the hard-class train.

We were soon to find out that the only heat on board was in the engine room, since the ship had been built for service in the tropics, and for the duration of the voyage we lived in our clothing, usually including overcoats, around the clock.

During the brief hours of daylight, we could watch some of the activity on the forward deck of the Soviet freighter that followed closely in our wake. The ship's crew had two cows in a pen on deck, which were milked at various times, while nearby was a wire-screened hen house where eggs were gathered almost as soon as they were laid.

The convoy of fourteen ships was about midway of the voyage when we were surprised to see that a black-hulled freighter flying the British flag had taken the place of the Soviet ship in our wake. When asked what had happened to the freighter flying the Soviet flag, the captain of our ship was silent for several moments with a tightening of his lips before answering.

"The poor chaps took a torpedo from a German submarine during the night," he said finally. "We had to move one of our own freighters up to take the place of the Russians."

"Do the crews of all the Soviet cargo ships in a convoy always sail with cows and chickens on deck?" he was asked.

"Wouldn't be a bit surprised," he said. "Very practical people. No nonsense. The British could learn a lesson or two from them. We ought to be able to do better than sail the seas with our ubiquitous evaporated milk and powdered eggs."

The convoy reached Scotland with no more losses at sea and Kit and I took a train from Glasgow to London. The people of bomb-devastated London were enduring a greater degree of hardship than I had observed in Moscow and yet the spirited British people were more interested in reading about what was happening in the Soviet Union than in talking about their own plight.

During two weeks in London, I wrote a series of articles for publication in the *Daily Mail*, collaborated with Kit to produce a text-and-photographic book with the title of *Russia at War* for publication the following year by Hutchinson and Company, and with the help of notes and extracts from my diary I wrote a book of observations under the title of *Moscow Under Fire* for publication by Hutchinson.

At the end of our fortnight in London, and more anxious than ever to return home to Darien, it was necessary to spend almost a full week waiting for passage on a British courier plane from England to Portugal.

There was no other way with relative safety to travel from London to New York because of the German submarine blockade in the Atlantic Ocean and while the danger of being shot down in the air by German warplanes was ever present. Our waiting place for passage to Lisbon was an ancient, damp, uncomfortable, almost-deserted resort hotel in Bath where we were instructed to remain in readiness for a moonless, clouded night that would make travel to Portugal as safe as it would ever be as long as the Germans were at war in Europe.

At last, after sleeping in our clothes for warmth and nursing frostbitten ears and fingers on the convoy freighter without heat, we arrived in Lisbon from blacked-out England and saw the glowing lights of a city at night for the first time in several months. Equally startling it was to feel the clinging warmth of the balmy air and to see the late-blooming flowers of summer in the window-boxes and dooryards of Lisbon's ever-present red tile-roofed cottages.

We had come to Lisbon to wait for passage to New York on a Pan American World Airways amphibious plane by way of the Azores and Bermuda. And wait we did.

Planned flights were postponed or canceled and then once again scheduled for departure. Until that time the German air patrols still had not shot down a Pan Am flying boat over the Atlantic. However, there were numerous German agents and spies in Lisbon to report the movements of ships and airplanes and for that reason the island-hopping amphibious flights across the Atlantic were on a wait-and-see basis.

During the long waiting period for departure, the young Clipper captain and his navigator invited Kit and me to go swimming with them in the Tagus River. The river was the only available place for swimming, since neutral Portugal's beach at Estoril was off-limits to foreigners for the duration of the war in Europe. And after experiencing the subzero cold of the arctic regions, as well as being without heat in the dampness of England, the water of the Tagus felt pleasantly warm in the chilly mornings.

Each time we went swimming in the river I wondered if the captain's purpose was to keep us from becoming bored because of the long delay or if it were to condition us for survival at sea in the event we were shot down by a German patrol plane. Whatever the reason, there was no longer any need to speculate about it when we finally landed safely in New York, rumpled and weary, at the conclusion of our journey of six months around the world.

Extremely glad to be at home on Horseplay Hill where I could devote myself to writing for the next six months or year, I was not prepared for the disappointment of hearing Kit say only a week after our return that she had decided to take an assignment to go back to England and from there to North Africa for wartime photography.

My immediate reaction was to ask her why she wanted to leave home so soon after an absence of half a year.

"Because war is going on and I've got to be there," she said. "Photography is my life, my career, my everything."

"But what about us—our life together?" I asked.

"That can wait."

"Your everything—that's more important?"

"Yes. That's the way it is. It has to be. I'm sorry."

"Kit," I pleaded, "think about us. Please don't go away so soon. Maybe you'll change your mind—"

"No, Skinny. Not maybe. I've got to go."

Several days passed before anything more was said about Kit's planned departure for Europe. By then I was so unhappy about our impending separation that I had to try once more to persuade her to stay at home or at least to postpone the trip to a later time. That was the evening she returned to Darien on a commuter train from New York with another present for me.

This time the present she brought me was a long-haired, black-and-white, loudly-purring, female kitten which was immediately named Fluffy.

"Kit, I'm as pleased as can be to have a gift that will remind me of you every time it purrs," I told her, "but it still won't be the same without you in person no matter how loudly Fluffy can purr. You and I have had a lot of happiness together and we can have a lot more. And you must know how lonely I'll be here without you. But if we can't stay together—then what's going to happen to us?"

"I'd hate myself for leaving and knowing you are so anguished and unhappy," she said with an expression of concern coming to her face. "I'd feel guilty—like being a despicable traitor. But something can be done—"

"What can be done?" I asked hopefully.

"I want you to go to see Harry Stack Sullivan. I'll make the appointment for you. It's important. Very important."

"Who's Sullivan? And an appointment for what?"

"Dr. Sullivan is a highly-regarded psychoanalyst. He's one of the very best in the profession. He treated me with such good results long before you and I were married that I was completely liberated. It was a wonderful experience. It probably saved my sanity."

"But why me?"

"Because if you undergo analysis you'll be freed of all hostility and any feeling of loneliness. You'll be a contented person with yourself. But you must cooperate with Dr. Sullivan and not be skeptical. And when I come back you'll be well-adjusted. Your different self will be the most wonderful present you could ever give me. Please, Skinny! Please go to Dr.Sullivan! Please say you will!"

"I suppose so," I agreed after a while. "If it means so much to you, I'll give it a try. And it may result in being a worthwhile experience for me. I've often wondered how I would react to being psychoanalyzed. Yes, Kit, I'll do it. For you I will."

Chapter Twenty

NO LESS PERSUASIVE THAN Hutchinson and Company had been earlier when I was prevailed upon to write two books and collaborate on a third volume for publication in England, Duell, Sloan, and Pearce in New York began urging me the day after I returned from Europe to begin working immediately on two books for publication about my wartime experiences in the Soviet Union.

The first of the two books scheduled for American publication in 1942 was based on features written for North American Newspaper Alliance and Columbia Broadcasting System. The title was *All Out on the Road to Smolensk* and the contents were selected and prepared with the help of Mildred Zinn. When I told her how much I was in need of her expert help, Mildred had come back to Darien to resume working for me as secretary and editorial assistant.

The second book was to be a novel of guerrilla warfare in the Soviet Union and the purpose for writing it was to depict, in fictional form, the patriotic activities of civilians in wartime.

It seemed to me that partisan warfare, as it was called in the Soviet Union, was to become an important factor in international conflicts in the future. The title of the novel was *All Night Long*. First it was serialized in *Redbook*. Later, film rights were bought by Metro-Goldwyn-Mayer.

My visits to the office of Harry Stack Sullivan, planned so as not to take any more time away from my writings than necessary, may have served no need other than to fulfill my promise to Kit and I soon began to resent taking any time at all from my writings. And as for Harry Stack Sullivan's attitude, it had been evident from the beginning that he was suspicious of my motive in coming to him to be analyzed.

"Now, Mr. Caldwell," the stern, full-faced psychiatrist said, tilting his head backward and gazing intently at the ceiling, "let us clarify matters once and for all. Is it your intention to make use of our analytical sessions for the purpose of acquiring for commercial purposes the material for a sensational novel or other writings?"

"I hadn't thought of anything like that," I told him.

With a quick movement of his body, he leaned forward and looked at me with an unblinking gaze.

"Would you be willing to make such a statement on your word of honor—or a similar statement under oath?"

"Yes."

"Then what was your reason for coming to me for analysis?"

"To find out what it would do for me."

"That's all?"

"That's all."

"Then what do you think is your difficulty?"

"My inability to persuade my wife to spend more time with me and to get her to consent to have a second home somewhere in the West." .

"That's very interesting," Dr. Sullivan said with a slight movement of his head. "Let's pursue that idea for a moment. Where would you like to go—and have your wife spend more time with you?"

"There are several likely places—Colorado Springs, Santa Fe, Tucson—"

"Were your discussions with her conducted in a pleasant, fully relaxed manner?"

"Not always."

"Then your discussions with her sometimes led to arguments, disagreements, ill-feelings, moments of violence?"

"Yes."

"What form of violence?"

"Face slapping."

"Who slapped first?"

"I did."

"Then after you and your wife traded slaps on the face, which one of you made the first conciliatory gesture?"

"I don't remember."

"Well, then," Dr. Sullivan said, "that would be a good starting point for our next meeting—if—if there is another meeting."

After a month in Europe, Kit had come home and within a week had left again for the northern regions of Canada on another assignment. That was followed immediately by a trip even more lengthy that took her to several state capitals from Nebraska to Florida.

I had become morosely lonely by the time the manuscript of *All Night Long* was finished and delivered to Duell, Sloan, and Pearce. I had no desire to begin writing another book immediately and, to escape from the loneliness of Horseplay Hill and an empty house, I telephoned Harry Behn in Tucson and told him I was ready to buy a house on the desert.

Harry was elated to hear that I was at last going to have a home in Tucson and he said the only decision I would have to make would be to decide whether to buy an existing house or contract with a builder and wait for one to be constructed. I chose to wait for a new one to be built at a cost of twenty-five to thirty thousand dollars. What I then planned to do was to go to Tucson and be on the scene so I could make any desirable changes in the plans while the house was under construction.

A few days before I planned to leave for Arizona, Al Manuel telephoned me from his office in Beverly Hills. In his usual bluff, relaxed manner when there was a lucrative motion picture deal at hand, Al said he had received an important screenwriting offer for me from Warner Brothers and that he wanted me to leave for Los Angeles on a plane or train without delay.

I knew something about the Warner Brothers offer because the New York office had told me a few days earlier about a film to be made at the request of the Department of State that would be based on *Mission to Moscow*, a book by Joseph E. Davies. It was my impression that the reason I was wanted to work on the film was because of my knowledge gained in the Soviet Union as a correspondent there for several months. Still not eager to commit myself, I had asked that the offer be referred to my agent in California.

"I don't think I want the job, Al," I told him on the phone. "I'm tired. I've just finished the fourth book to be published here and in England. That's enough writing for a while. Besides, I've already planned to go to Southern Arizona from here. That's what I'd rather do. Other things can wait."

"Stay away from that hot desert, Skinny," Al said discouragingly. "It's too hot down there in summertime. Forget it. That sand will blister your toes through your shoes."

"I know about the summer heat, Al, but I'd still rather do what I've planned. I want to stay away from any kind of writing for a while. I want to wait till I feel better. I told you—I'm tired."

"Skinny, your trouble is that you're hungry and don't know what ails you. You ain't eating right. You've been hopping around all over the world writing books and things and not getting enough down-home grease in your stomach. Now you listen to me. I've got Theodore Dreiser and Richard Aldington out here now and they both say they ain't had it so good before in their lives. They mean good eating. When you get here, you'll start eating plenty of blue-ribbon steaks and greasy fried potatoes. Don't that sound good, Skinny? Don't it make you hungry right away? Sure it does! That hot sand down there in Arizona will cool off some by October or November and you can walk around barefooted if you want to and not get no blisters on your feet. I'll see you out here right away, Skinny. Good-by."

= 2 =

I went to work at the Warner Brothers studio in Burbank a few days after arriving in Hollywood with Mildred Zinn.

First I wrote a detailed outline for the film version of *Mission to Moscow* in collaboration with Robert Buckner, an earnest young producer, and next I wrote a complete screen treatment of the story. With all that work completed, I felt I had done my share on the film and was willing to let the screenwriters who followed me put the screenplay into final form for the director and his camera crew.

It was at this point that I found myself unwittingly involved in a heated political controversy. Considering myself to be an innocent bystander in the conflict between two opposing factions, who were card-carrying members of the Communist Party of the United States and dissident Communist fellow travelers, I disclaimed any political motives involving the Soviet Union and *Mission to Moscow.*

In outspoken moments, I had let it be known that, based on what I had heard unofficially in Moscow, I did not consider Joseph Stalin to be an admirable, benevolent, humane leader of his people. It was plainly evident that the film was being made to serve as a propaganda vehicle to gain the approval of the American people to accept in wartime the close alliance of American democracy and Soviet Communism. I was aware that propaganda was an essential factor in modern warfare and decided it was my duty as an American to strive to help win the war and bring about the defeat of Adolf Hitler.

Having voted for President Roosevelt because of his concern for the welfare of people in the United States during the Great Depression, perhaps I had been influenced by his patriotic appeal for cooperation with the Soviet Union in a war to defeat Hitler. However, I was eager to remove myself from any involvement in the bitter controversy between the two Communist factions in Hollywood film studios. I sometimes voted for reputedly honest and qualified candidates in town and state elections as well as for my choice for President of the United States every four years. Otherwise, my political activity was of little note and effect.

Supremacy attained by one of the two Communist factions, the two screenwriters who followed me—and with the aid of the Screenwriters Guild—succeeded in having my name removed from the screen credits of *Mission to Moscow*. When this news was brought to me, the first thought to come to mind was that I might have put my time to better use by writing another episode of *Crime Does Not Pay* at MGM.

However, the result of the contention among the political activists was of little interest to me by that time inasmuch as I had completed my thirteen weeks of service for Warner Brothers and was free to leave for Arizona and my new home.

Saying without hesitation that she had no desire to leave Hollywood for voluntary exile on the desert, Mildred Zinn indicated that she was grateful for my not trying to persuade her to change her mind and go with me to Tucson. Being the considerate person that she was, Mildred spent much time helping me find a capable, suitable person to work as my secretary and assistant and who would like to live in Southern Arizona. That person was Polly Stallsmith.

Living in Pasadena with her parents and being a recent college graduate, the personable, vivacious, dark-haired Polly Stallsmith was exceedingly anxious to leave home as soon as possible and go to Tucson with me. Polly had confided in Mildred, saying that the reason for her enthusiasm about the opportunity to go to Arizona was because a recent romance with a youthful Air Force pilot in training had ended abruptly, and evidently

Polly had suffered much emotional distress. The version of the incident that I heard from Mildred was that Polly, being in love and having consented to marry the young officer, was told only the day before they were to be married that he had changed his mind and was going to remain single.

When Polly Stallsmith and I left California in my sedan for Arizona with our solidly-packed belongings, my sympathy for her distress was expressed for the most part by telling her of my own failing romance with Kit and saying something about the unhappiness and loneliness that had settled upon me. During the long trip that day, my laments were frequently interrupted when Polly would burst into a spell of unconsolable weeping as her own sorrow could not be suppressed. It would have been difficult to gauge which one of us was the most miserable at day's end.

A short time before arriving in Tucson in the golden glow of a desert sunset, Polly had fallen asleep after the long day of tearful anguish. When we reached the Santa Rita Hotel, I was sorry she had to be awakened. However, she was calm when she opened her eyes and I was glad to see a slight smile come to her face. I was sure at that moment that our commiseration for each other's unhappiness would result in mutual respect and lasting friendship.

That evening, being anxious to see the new home I had bought sight-unseen, and too impatient to wait until the next morning, I called Harry Behn on the phone and arranged to meet him half-an-hour later at a Rillito River bridge near the new residential development in the Catalina Foothills.

Harry had seen the new house while it was under construction, though never at night, and he was no more able than I to find the location in the darkness. There were no street lights and no street signs had been erected. After searching for a long time with only a flashlight to help us, we decided at midnight to come back the next day to look for my house.

Early the next morning Harry and I went to the office of the builder who had constructed all the dwellings in the new development and asked for directions for finding my new home.

"Very simple," the friendly builder said, drawing a series of zigzagging lines with directional arrows on a map of the Catalina Foothills. "Very easy to find your place. Can't miss it. All you have to do is follow the directions on this map and look for Job No. 78."

We soon found the rambling, flat-roofed, desert-modern, white stucco house that was surrounded by a high, white-painted, concrete-block wall and situated in the midst of three acres of spreading palo verde trees and twenty-foot sahuaros.

Attached to a stake at the driveway entrance, there was the boldly lettered identifying sign: Job No. 78.

"Now that we've found your house," Harry said, "what are you going to name it? How about Casa Blanca? Rancho Grande?"

"It's already named, Harry," I said, pointing at the sign at the driveway entrance. "Why change it?"

"Job No. 78?"

"That's it. Job No. 78. That can't be improved upon."

= 3 =

I had come to Tucson to be free of any involvement with motion pictures, at least for a while, and to be able to devote my time to the writing of fiction that was pressing itself upon me. First of all, I intended to write the concluding chapters of *Georgia Boy* to follow the earlier portions written in Darien, Chungking, Moscow, and elsewhere. That book was to be followed by a novel depicting the disintegration of an American family in wartime and the title of which was to be *Tragic Ground*.

Little could be done with my writing, though, until my new home was carpeted and furnished. A local decorator assured me that this could be accomplished in no more than ten days and he went to work immediately with much purpose and enthusiasm. This was a period that gave me the opportunity to write more letters and send more telegrams to Kit pleading with her to consider spending part of the year with me in Tucson.

The results of my daily appeals this time were no different than my unsuccessful efforts had been during the three months when I was writing and telegraphing from Hollywood several times a week.

No, my letters were not returned unopened; and, yes, my telegrams were unfailingly delivered.

As hopeful as I was from day to day, I gradually came to realize that Kit was unyielding in her decision not to live with me in California or Arizona. This was difficult for me to accept and I was determined not to give up all hope for a reunion.

However, in time it became plainly evident that we would be able to live together again only on Kit's own terms and that even then there would be no assurance that we could live in harmony for the remainder of our lives. And so, in effect, I had to accept the fact that our marriage could no longer exist and that my presence in Kit's life had come to be unwelcome. I still had great respect and fondness for her but such personal feelings could be remembered only as part of my sorrow.

As surely as it was destined to be, about three weeks after coming to Tucson I reluctantly engaged a local attorney to guide me through the disagreeable intricacies of an immediate Mexican divorce that would be valid throughout the United States. The legal procedures required only weekend travel by airplane on three occasions from Tucson to the State of Morelos in Mexico.

The most costly feature of the divorce in terms of money was the loss of my house, fully paid for, on Horseplay Hill in Darien. Kit was firm and unyielding in her determination to have sole ownership and occupancy of Horseplay Hill and refused to compromise by letting it be sold and dividing the proceeds between us in any proportion.

The only concession that Kit would make, after retaining the real estate, the household furnishings, some personal belongings, books, and, of course, the alphabet wallpaper in what had been my workroom, was to offer to ship to me in Tucson via air express the then fully-grown, long-haired, black-and-white former kitten named Fluffy. Her resonant purring still as endearing as it had been in the beginning, Fluffy divided her time between people in the house during the day and with the gophers and rabbits on the desert at night.

As soon as the interior decorator had completed his furnishing of the new house, and when I was beginning to engage in the unpleasant routine of obtaining the Mexican divorce, Harry Behn said he was perturbed about my marital troubles and the depressive effect it was having on my life.

Shortly before I began legal proceedings, Harry arranged for me to meet, in a seemingly accidental manner, one of the students in his radio writing class at the University of Arizona. The personable young woman, June Johnson, had recently come into her twenties and was to graduate in the coming year. June was dark-haired, tall, slender, with a ready smile, and preferred being casual in manner and dress.

A few days after meeting June Johnson, I invited her to join me for horseback riding along the Rillito River and on the bridle paths in the Catalina Foothills. We spent a pleasant afternoon together. In the early darkness of the autumn night, as the lights of the city began twinkling on the desert below the mountainside, I asked June to stay for dinner with Polly and me. It was pleasant being in her company and the casual conversations kept my thoughts from dwelling solely on my misfortune. I was glad when June accepted the dinner invitation with an eager smile.

In the days that followed, and with my urging, June came to the Foothills with increasing frequency for our horseback rides and dinners together. In fact, only a few weeks had passed until we were meeting daily and our time together was extending from an afternoon of several hours to far into the night. After that, it became not unusual for June to spend the night in the lounge adjoining Polly's bedroom. That was when, to make it easier for her to travel between my house and the university, I provided her with the use of my smaller sedan.

Perez, my mulatto-skinned Mexican houseman of many talents, probably had suppressed the comments he wanted to make about my close association with June until he could no longer withhold them. Perez was a free-spirited, handsome, well-developed man, still not yet forty years old, who had taken thorough training in California in the duties of chef, butler, valet, chauffeur, and housekeeper. Every day at work Perez wore a freshly laundered and starched white jacket, gray slacks, and a boldly purple bow-tie. Also, he spoke English with the same ease and enjoyment he had with his native Spanish.

"Now, Mr. Erskine," Perez said one morning with much concern evident in his manner, "there's something I ought to say to you. It's about your personal life. I know you're getting a divorce in Mexico. I know you are greatly depressed about your shattered romance. And I know the meaning of certain signs when I see them—"

"Then what do you want to tell me, Perez?" I asked him. "What signs do you see?"

"Let me tell you this first, Mr. Erskine. What I've learned about the behavior of people is important, I think. I don't believe I'm wrong most of the time when I come to conclusions—"

"What is it you're going to tell me?" I spoke up.

"I'll say it this way, Mr. Erskine. A woman who has been disappointed in love—or separated from her lover by death—she is likely to hold fast to her grief and sorrow and let nothing keep her from enjoying the pleasure of mourning as long as possible. The women will do that and I can see it happening to Miss Polly. She's told me about her lost romance and it was a mournful thing for her to talk about. And she's never going to be happy again until she's able to wring the last sob from her heart. I admire a woman being in love but when it hurts like it does—"

"Maybe so, Perez," I said with some impatience, "but what's that got to do with me?"

"Mr. Erskine, you're not behaving like Miss Polly does. That's what I'm trying to tell you. You're behaving like a man always will. You're trying to keep your unhappiness about your divorce and the loss of your romance out of thought by romping like a carefree playboy with Miss June. Some men would soak themselves in gin to forget their heartache when a woman leaves them, but what you're doing is—"

"What's wrong with what I'm doing?" I protested.

"Mr. Erskine," Perez said slowly and carefully, "Miss June has her eyes on you. You act like you don't know that, but I do. She's out to get you as sure as shooting comes out of a pistol."

Perez's long suppressed concern about my personal welfare had not been revealed until sometime after the middle of December 1942. Shortly after that, with Christmas at hand, June and I were married and took the train that same night to New York on our honeymoon.

Chapter Twenty One

FROM NEW YEAR'S DAY 1943 to the end of that decade seven years later, I was continually finding myself coming to terms with so many irresistible causes and appealing choices that it was not easy for me to be able to allot six months or more to my cherished preference for writing a novel or series of short stories in undisturbed isolation.

Even though I knew I would continue living the life I had made for myself, often there were yearnings for a quiet retreat as comforting and productive as it had been my good fortune to enjoy in Mount Vernon for many years.

However, I considered myself being still young at forty with the second half of my envisioned span of years in the world to be lived with no less enthusiasm in the future than in the past.

The first of the many choices and decisions to be made in the coming seven years confronted me in late morning of New Year's Day. This was when Al Manuel, no respecter of holidays and periods of leisure, or of honeymoons either, telephoned me at the St. Regis Hotel in New York from his office in Beverly Hills.

Sleepy and wavering I was, and it seemed to me that it had been only a few brief hours since June and I had been happily tooting New Year's Eve horns and tossing streamers at the Stork Club. The time then being eleven o'clock in New York, it was eight in the morning in California.

"Wake up, Skinny!" The sounds of the first words spoken by Al were so loud and penetrating that for a few moments all I could hear was a buzzing in my ears. "Wake up! Wake up! It's late where you are. You ought to be up and wide awake by now. I've been up a couple of hours and it's still early morning here."

"What's this all about, Al?" I asked drowsily.

"Now hear this," he answered in a booming voice. "We've got a good deal cooking. It's at Twentieth Century-Fox this time. I've been talking to Boris Morros and Sam Spiegle and they want you to write a screen treatment for a film they're going to produce. It's a story based on the Grand Street Boys—you've heard of them. It's a thirteen-week job and they'll reach down deep in the pocket for our kind of money. That fast-passing short time will let you get back quick to your other trade, whatever you want to call it, and we'll have some worthwhile money to play around with. How could there be a better deal?"

"When would I start?"

"You've already started," Al said at once. "The contract time started ticking when I called you on the phone. Now get yourself out here right away. I'll reserve you an apartment at the Beverly Wilshire Hotel. You and June can keep your honeymoon going for the next three months. What more would you want out of life?"

I phoned Maxim Lieber to let him know I was going to leave New York sooner than I had planned. I had given Max two copies of the typescript of *Georgia Boy* when I arrived from Arizona, one copy to be submitted to Duell, Sloan, and Pearce for publication, and the other copy for whatever use he thought would be of some value.

While talking to Max on the phone, I found out that he had given the second copy to Jed Harris to read and Jed had said he wanted to talk to me about the possibility of his directing and producing a dramatization of the story on Broadway before the end of the year 1943. The dramatization of *Tobacco Road* had had a successful run on Broadway for seven and a half years and Jed had said he believed a play made from another book of mine would have a good chance to achieve a profitable run.

I did not have to wait long before hearing from Jed Harris. He phoned me early the next morning to say he needed more time for a careful second reading of the story while assuring me that he expected to be no less enthusiastic then about it as a stage play than he had been after reading it for the first time. Jed said he had already been thinking about the casting and wondered if there would be any way to persuade Eleanor Roosevelt to play the part of the mother in the story. In the end, it was decided that we would meet in Beverly Hills in a few weeks to talk at length about the possibilities for a Broadway production.

When I saw Jed Harris at the Twentieth Century-Fox studio several weeks later it was February and he was in a hurry to prepare a Broadway production for an early fall opening. He said it would be helpful and save a lot of time if I would speak to Marc Connelly and persuade him to dramatize *Georgia Boy*. When I hesitated, saying I thought Jed as director and producer should be the one to talk to Marc, he said he was afraid that he and Marc would get into an argument about how the play should be staged and thereby endanger a friendship of long standing.

I saw Marc Connelly several times on the Fox lot, and on each occasion, no matter what excuse I offered for Jed, Marc appeared to be displeased because Jed had sent me to talk about the play instead of speaking of it himself. Finally, I told Jed that I thought we would have to look elsewhere for somebody to dramatize *Georgia Boy*.

Jed then decided that Nunnally Johnson would be the dramatist for the story. I was very pleased to hear that, because I had a great liking for the screenplay Nunnally wrote for the film of *Tobacco Road*, although I was very unhappy about the inept ending that a producer at Fox had arbitrarily substituted for the realistic conclusion of the novel and the play. I spent several afternoons in Nunnally's office at the studio waiting for an opportunity to talk to him about the play Jed said he intended to produce on Broadway.

Each time Jed arrived for a meeting with Nunnally, Damon Runyon was with him and no one wished to do anything other than listen to Damon Runyon get started telling one of his long-winded tales about Broadway eccentrics. At the end of the week, the play had not been mentioned a single time and that was when Jed said he had to return to New York immediately.

Before leaving, however, Jed assured me that Nunnally Johnson was going to write the dramatization and finish it in time for fall production.

"Has Nunnally ever said outright that he wants to do the play?" I asked Jed.

"Well, no, not exactly," Jed said, "but Nunnally intends to do it. I'm sure of that. He'd be deeply hurt if we let anyone else do it now. He's set his heart on getting a play on Broadway. And he's a very sensitive person about such things. But Nunnally's peculiar, too, in his own way. I can understand that and make allowances for it. If he didn't want to do a certain thing, he'd talk your ears off about it. He hasn't said a word to me about this play and that's how I know he's very anxious to do it."

After Jed had gone back to New York, I asked Nunnally if he expected to hear from Jed about writing a play for Broadway.

"No," he said. "Jed Harris is a very peculiar person. He won't come out in the open and discuss a project he's anxious to get me to do. Anyway, from what I hear on the grapevine, Jed is looking for a play that has a part for Eleanor Roosevelt. And that's absurd. Mrs. Franklin D. Roosevelt is not going to appear on a Broadway stage for Jed Harris or any other producer."

"Then did Jed say anything to you about dramatizing *Georgia Boy* for him to direct and produce?" I asked.

"Not a single Jed Harris word. That's the first I've heard of it. If he had mentioned it, I'd have been sure he wouldn't want me to have anything to do with it."

"Then how can you and Jed get together?" I asked.

"We can't—not until he stops being peculiar."

Three months later the option Jed Harris held on the dramatic rights to *Georgia Boy* expired. The option was not renewed.

= 2 =

The first thing I wanted to do when June and I returned to Tucson in the spring was to buy a larger house. This was accomplished with little delay by trading the smaller house as part-payment for a newly constructed larger house that was more than double in size and price. Our new home with four bedrooms in the Catalina Foothills was situated at an elevation much higher than the earlier location and it had been built with two wings that provided, on the west side, ample service quarters while the east side had a small suite consisting of library, office, and bar-lounge.

The editorship of *American Folkways* was a fascinating task, though time-consuming, and I had come home to Tucson to find it was necessary to work overtime in order to fulfill the plan of publishing four titles yearly. Consequently, there was little I could do about my own writing of fiction until additional able authors were found to contribute to the series. This could be accomplished to my satisfaction and that of the publisher only by frequent travel and continuous correspondence. Fortunately, I had little difficulty in persuading Donald Day, Homer Croy, Hodding Carter, and

Carey McWilliams, among others, to write about the varied regions of the United States in which they lived.

My own region, more or less having been decreed by Harry Behn, was now Southern Arizona, Tucson in particular, and I was called upon as a responsible citizen to help establish a new radio broadcasting station. The new radio operation had been planned by Harry Behn to be both a commercial enterprise and, emphatically so, a project programmed primarily for civic betterment.

Regardless of the noble purpose, the cost of hearings by the Federal Communications Commission, which were necessary in order to obtain an operating license for KCNA, together with the outlay for expensive equipment, amounted to a surprisingly large sum of money. As a consequence, Harry, with mention of his salary as a professor at the university, asked to be relieved of any further financial obligation. His action was soon followed by the request of other original investors to withdraw for similar reasons. Eventually, I became a reluctant owner and unqualified operator in an industry in which my previous experience had been limited to that of a speaker at a microphone in Moscow.

Like many other writers during World War II, I was called upon to write a series of radio announcements for the War Finance Division of the Treasury Department. I had no idea how many war bonds were sold as a result of my one- and two-minute patriotic appeals to citizens on the home front. However, it was good training for what was to follow.

What did follow was the request by the Treasury Department for me to join a bond-rally tour with other writers to appear at auditoriums, theaters, colleges, and civic centers to promote the sale of United States war bonds. The members of the tour other than myself were Vicki Baum, S. J. Perelman, Irving Stone, and Kathleen Windsor.

Our group traveled up and down the state of California, always by automobile or bus, for several weeks of one-night stands. The results of our personal appearances were said to have been satisfactory to the Treasury Department although there were reports of remarks by observers at the rallies to the effect that we looked like a group of ordinary people and not like glamorous actors and actresses.

Even though during this period I did take frequent brief trips to other parts of the United States, in particular to consult with writers for *American Folkways*, I wanted to stay at home as much as possible to work on my own writings. There was one trip I did take more by impulse than by acting with some deliberation. This occurred when, scarcely without forethought, I decided that I wanted to own a second home in Santa Fe. And so I went there and bought a whitewashed adobe cottage that appealed to me at first-sight because it had a red tile roof and hollyhocks were blooming in the dooryard.

Completely satisfied, I returned home from Santa Fe and resumed work on the first of a new group of novels I planned to write. The first of these was *A House in the Uplands* and it was to be followed over the years by *The Sure Hand of God*, *This Very Earth*, and *Place Called Estherville*. The only welcomed interruption for a long time took place when June and I made a hurried trip to the hospital where she gave birth to my third son who was immediately named Jay.

I had joined the long-established Old Pueblo Club in Tucson, the membership of which for the most part was composed of the socially elite among the descendants of the first families and a few of the better-mannered among the wealthy newcomers.

My reason for applying for membership in the club was because it did have a good library and a quiet reading room, a pleasant paneled bar and lounge, and undoubtedly the best dining room and men's grill in the city. I had been accepted for membership, along with a very few writers and university professors, for the probable reason that one of my profession might enhance the image of the club in some way.

The Old Pueblo Club maintained its austere atmosphere of respectability to such a degree that uninhibited pool shooters found themselves to be far less welcome than were quiet-mannered billiard players. There were many interesting younger people in Tucson who were employed by the newspapers, the radio stations, and others were on the university faculty. Most of them had a liking for pocket pool more than for billiards and the only gathering places for them were noisy bars and grimy saloons. With that in mind, Vic Thornton, the city editor of the *Arizona Daily Star*, and I decided to establish the Tucson Press Club with pool and poker players in mind and with membership offered to newspaper reporters, radio newsmen, and resident or transient literati.

The Tucson Press Club thrived from the beginning and it was soon serving jumbo hamburger lunches and taking reservations for Wednesday night nickel-ante poker games. The latter became so popular and widely famed that it attracted the attention of Tucson's chief of police. Previously, the editor and owner of the *Arizona Daily Star*, William R. Matthews, had

Virginia Caldwell and son Drew Fletcher (rear), Erskine and son Jay Caldwell (1958).

Actor Buddy Hackett clowns with Virginia and Erskine (1957).

Salut, Calder

Left: Caldwell portrait by Alexander Cald
Paris (1976). Below: Virginia and Erskine
a Paris park (1979).

Caldwell speaking in Sofia, Bulgaria (1984).

irst editions and translations of Caldwell's books (1976).

Erskine Caldwell at work, Dunedin, Florida (1971).

written a series of editorials calling for the prosecution of the chief of police on the charge of allegedly committing numerous acts of malfeasance. The charges were so serious that the chief of police had fear of being convicted and sent to prison.

In retaliation, the chief of police led a squad of four policemen on a raid of the Press Club one Wednesday night and threatened to jail Vic Thornton, me, and other poker players. The charge against us was for operating a gambling establishment as employees of William R. Matthews and refusing to disclose his whereabouts. While the charge was being read to us, the squad of policemen was confiscating the playing cards, poker chips, and money from the table as evidence and placing it all in canvas bags. Still not satisfied, the angry chief ordered his men to rip the green felt covering from the table and confiscate it for evidence.

The gambling charge was never brought to court. When I applied at police headquarters for the return of my money, which amounted to at least five dollars including the nickels and dimes in the pot that I would have won with my full house of sevens over jacks, I was told that there was no record of such property being held by the police department.

$$= 3 =$$

I became aware for the first time in my life of the strange reality of an institution that had come to be known as a writers' conference. This particular intellectual rally took place late in June 1948 at the University of Kansas, in Lawrence, a short distance from Kansas City, Missouri. I had been invited to the conference to participate in round-table discussions on the subject of contemporary American literature.

As I was to discover before the end of the conference, I was far afield among tried and true intellectuals who with few exceptions were young new-wave poets and instructors in college creative-writing courses. As a former newspaper hack, an indifferent student, and a struggling fiction writer, I had felt uncomfortable from the beginning in the presence of people whose topics of conversation were derived almost exclusively from the lofty heights of the academic world.

Undoubtedly, my reception by the intellectuals at the writers' conference would have been much different if it had not been for an incident that took place in Kansas City and was reported in newspapers a few days before I arrived in Lawrence.

When told of my plans for being in Kansas City on my way to Lawrence, I was asked by Roscoe Fawcett and Edward Lewis, both being field representatives for my paperback book publisher, New American Library, to come to Kansas City a day earlier than I had planned and take part in a plan to promote the sale of my reprinted books.

When I arrived in Kansas City, I found that Eddie Lewis had arranged for me to sign copies of my books in one of the large Katz Drug chain stores near the Muelebach Hotel. The location of the store was at a busy downtown corner and Eddie had plastered the streetside display windows with colorful streamers and show cards. Passers-by were urged to "Step inside and for only twenty-five cents (25¢) buy a sensational new novel autographed personally by the author while you wait."

The well-planned sales campaign was so successful that the stock of books on hand was exhausted in early afternoon. Customers continued to be attracted by the signs on the windows but, since temporarily no books were available, for a while all I could do was sit on a stool at the soda fountain and drink cokes while waiting for more copies to be delivered from the warehouse. While waiting, Eddie would rush to the telephone every few minutes to complain to somebody about the slow delivery of the needed books.

Eddie Lewis and I were still sitting at the soda fountain when several newspaper reporters and photographers came into the drugstore. At the sight of the news people, Eddie became instantly alert. He jumped to his feet and began waving his hands above his head. Then, calling out in a loud voice, he invited all the waiting bookbuyers to come to the soda fountain and be his guest for cokes, milk shakes, ice-cream sodas, or whatever. The noisy din and waves of hilarity in the drugstore did not cease until the new supply of paperback books arrived from the warehouse.

One of the results of the festive occasion at the Katz Drug soda fountain was the appearance in newspapers the next day of sprightly news items and photographs of the gathering of young people waiting to buy books.

One of the reporters described the scene in the drugstore as being a welcome new departure from the traditional autographing ceremony in the formal atmosphere of a bookshop whereat an elderly author sips tea and reads passages from a slender volume of poetry.

Another reporter wrote a column extolling the soda-fountain scene as being the ideal modern replacement for bookshop receptions for one-book authors where watered-down punch was served to palpitating housewives.

Soon after arriving at the University of Kansas campus to take part in the writers' conference, I became aware of unmistakable aloofness and coolness on the part of some of the academics when I was in their presence. This mild rejection became so obvious that I finally asked Walter Van Tilburg Clark, one of the other authors at the conference, if I may have done something or said something to affront anyone.

"Well, yes, it's a possibility," Walter said. "I have overheard some talk about that."

"Then what was my misstep?" I asked.

"The Kansas City newspapers are widely read here and—"

"The news items and photographs—the drugstore—"

Walter nodded. "One comment by a professor was critical of your bringing disrepute, as he expressed it, to the profession of authorship by engaging in an undignified publicity stunt. Another person said it was humiliating to all participants at this conference for one of them to autograph books in a drugstore—and the books being twenty-five cent paperbacks to make the affair even more disgraceful and shameful."

Chapter Twenty-Two

MY FIRST TRIP TO EUROPE following the end of World War II was in the late spring and early summer of 1947. The purpose of the European travels at that time was to visit and become acquainted with publishers, editors, and translators of my books in Finland and Czechoslovakia and various other countries. At the conclusion of the trip of several weeks there was no doubt in my mind that the most memorable incident had occurred in Italy.

This particular European journey was not June's introduction to life abroad inasmuch as in the previous year we had traveled to Cuba and had spent several weeks on both coasts of South America. It was June's nature not to be inclined to have the carefree attitude of an enthusiastic traveler and, on frequent occasions, she made little effort to adjust to local customs.

Patently homesick and unhappy, and seemingly indifferent to the surroundings and expressing no interest in the people we met, June had found no enchantment at Copacabana Beach in Rio de Janeiro or enjoyment at the race track in Buenos Aires. In Italy, her consuming interest when not expressing a morose desire to go home was to engage in prolonged cryptic conversations with English-speaking hotel bellboys and porters.

Several of my books had been translated and published in Italy and my authorized publisher was the impassioned Count Valentino Bompiani whose publishing house was in Milan. Valentino happened to be in Rome the day of our arrival from Prague and he immediately sent word to me at the Excelsior Hotel that he had obtained a court order assessing damages against the unauthorized publisher of a pirated edition of *Tobacco Road*. He also sent an eager-minded young newspaper reporter, who was accompanied by a bustling young photographer, to meet me in the hotel's bar-lounge for an interview.

It was soon evident that the enterprising reporter was much more interested in the clothing I was wearing than in any books I had written or in any impressions I may have received as a first-time visitor to Rome.

The fabric of my dark gray suit was a tightly-woven, smooth-finished worsted and, since it had been skillfully steam-pressed before I left the United States, the creases in the coat and trousers continued to hold their press to a remarkable degree after weeks of travel.

Ignoring the crease in my trousers, the reporter began questioning me about the crease in the sleeves of my coat. For one thing, he wanted to know if many well-dressed men in the United States considered it to be fashionable to have their coat sleeves creased instead of being ironed lightly in order to preserve a natural roundness as exemplified in Italian fine tailoring. While the questioning continued, the photographer was busily engaged in taking numerous pictures of me from various angles.

The next day, displayed in a full-page feature in one of Rome's leading newspapers, the interview appeared with several enlarged photographs of me with highlighted creases in the sleeves of my coat. It was evident that in order to emphasize the existence of the creases, some of the photographs had been cropped to portray me only from the neck to the knees.

Later in the day, I was informed by one of the waiters in the hotel restaurant who had read the interview that it was stated that while I had the reputation of being a well-known American writer it was not likely that my clothing would establish a new style for well-dressed Italians.

Early in the day following the publication of the interview and photographs, I was visited by two emissaries from a motion picture studio who informed me that they had come to prepare me for a meeting with Anna Magnani.

When I asked why there should be such a meeting, I then was told that Anna Magnani had read the interview in the newspaper and had decided that she wanted me to provide an Americanized version of the screenplay of a new film in which she was to be the star. It was said that she and her advisors wanted to take all necessary steps to prevent her film from being prohibited by censors. The title of the motion picture was *Volcano*.

As it was explained to me, the reason Anna Magnani had an urgent desire to film *Volcano* and have it distributed world-wide was because Roberto Rossellini, who had made a star of her in his production of *Open City*, had rejected her for his new film, *Stromboli*, and in her place was starring Ingrid Bergman. And true to her nature, Magnani was intent upon retaliating at all costs.

The two films were similar in theme and content, each having a Mount Vesuvius-type volcanic eruption as the background, and the intense, unrestrained love scenes provided ample opportunity for both actresses to display their talents.

The two emissaries impressed upon me the fact that the filming of *Volcano* would begin within a very short time and that my Americanized version was essential for the success of the motion picture in the United States. It was explained that certain love scenes would have to be filmed in two versions in order to be sure that one with sufficient restraint would be accepted by American censors. In addition, since the dialogue would be in Italian, sub-titles in English would be necessary.

Promptly at the appointed moment, Anna Magnani arrived at the Excelsior Hotel with a flurry of movement in the company of three smilingly affable young associates. Immediately after introductions, she nudged one of the well-dressed young men with a sudden thrust of an elbow and whispered to him with a fluttering of her eyelids. He nodded constantly while she was whispering.

"We sincerely beg your pardon," the young man said as he looked directly at me. "Anna Magnani asks a personal question. She would like to know if the suit you are wearing is the same one mentioned by the newspaper reporter."

The actress and her group of young men waited for my reply with eager smiles.

Smiling in return, I shook my head and told them that I was traveling with two suits of clothes and that the one I was wearing was made of softer material than the other and did not hold a crease very well.

The moment that information was made known to Magnani, she frowned with a disappointed shrugging of her shoulders. Then again with a flutter of her eyelids she whispered with intense seriousness.

"Now as for an arrangement," said the young man who was acting as her spokesman. "Anna Magnani wants you to know you will receive all possible assistance in preparing your English version of her film. There will be an English translation of the screenplay, freedom to work wherever you wish, and there will be full cooperation in all respects."

When I did not agree immediately to contribute an Americanized version of the scenes that would keep the film from being banned by censors, the actress with annoyed waving of her hands and arms whispered loudly to the interpreter.

"Anna Magnani wants me to assure you that you will be made an instant millionaire," he hastened to tell me with a beaming smile. "Anna Magnani says that if you've ever had the ambition to be a millionaire, now your wish will come true. She intends to treat you with all the respect, too, that you will be entitled to for your valuable services."

In the excitement of the moment, I neglected to reckon the difference in value between Italian lira and American dollars. And it was with great anticipation that June and I left Rome a few days later to complete our Italian tour in Naples, Capri, Genoa, and San Remo.

Day after day I mailed pages of my Americanized treatment for *Volcano* to the film studio in Rome fully confident that I would return to the United States a millionaire. In the end, however, Al Manuel could only stare at me in silent wonder with an occasional sympathetic moving of his head from side to side when I asked him how much payment had been received from the producers of Anna Magnani's *Volcano*.

= 2 =

Beginning with my first visit to France after World War II, and during subsequent visits, too, I always spent much time in the company of Marcel Duhamel. Our first meeting had taken place in the office of Gaston Gallimard, my French publisher, and thereafter as friend and translator Marcel introduced me to numerous disparate attractions ranging from the sight and sound of the original French discotheque to the cool recesses of the Paris sewers as a refuge at night from the sweltering summer heat.

Always brimming with energy and untiring in activity, Marcel's life was devoted to translating American novels and plays, skiing in the French and Italian alps, and swimming and beachcombing on the Riviera. And through it all he had an enduring friendship with Pablo Picasso.

It was during an early visit to the Riviera at the invitation of Marcel and his wife Germaine that I became aware of the widespread admiration and esteem for Pablo Picasso on the part of the French people. In a restaurant near Marcel's villa in the hills above Antibes, there was a large, plainly framed, pencil drawing by Picasso that had been carefully mounted on an ordinary sheet of cardboard. There was no signature or identification of the artist to be seen.

On close inspection, it could be observed that the drawing had been made on a restaurant placemat and, according to the legend, Picasso himself after doodling on the blank paper had torn it into shreds and minute scraps and thrown them on the floor under the table where he had been dining. As soon as the artist had left the restaurant, it was said, the owner had retrieved every scrap of paper and with meticulous effort had restored the drawing in the manner of a jigsaw puzzle.

As could be expected, considering Picasso's fame as an artist, it was not long after the hanging of the restoration in the restaurant that numerous imitations were being made along the Riviera by scrawling figures and shapes on restaurant placemats, tearing the paper mats into shreds, and restoring the drawings by gluing them on cardboard.

When sold in Nice, Antibes, and Cannes to gullible art-seeking tourists, the fraudulent Picasso drawings brought large sums of money to the street-corner hawkers whose ordinary stock-in-trade was pornographic postcards. One of the most successful peddlers, a well-dressed family man benign in appearance, boasted that his fake Picasso drawings had enabled him to become a respectable businessman and that he no longer had to resort to selling obscene postcards to tourists for a living.

"I'll tell you this about Pablo," Marcel said as we sat on the terrace of his villa facing the Mediterranean, "he was born a Spaniard but he's the best-loved and most respected Frenchman living today. His art touches everybody. I can't explain why. But it does."

I asked Marcel if acclaim by critics had been responsible for Picasso's popularity or if concerted schemes by art dealers and galleries had resulted in fame and world-wide attention for Pablo Picasso.

"Superficially, yes," he said, "but basically, no. That's my opinion about both suppositions. In my judgment, he is accepted and loved because his works have the magic touch that reaches the hearts of people. It's the simplicity and human appeal of his art. No amount of critical acclaim combined with commercial promotion could come within hailing distance of Pablo Picasso's inborn genius."

Before leaving the Riviera and returning to Paris that summer, Marcel and Germaine took June and me to the Antibes beach one warm August evening. In one of the small, open-front cabanas along the seawall, a slightly-built, tanned-skinned man of middle age in brief swimming trunks was lolling in a canvas beach chair among several younger members of his family. He beckoned to us with a friendly waving of his hand.

"It's Pablo," Marcel said as we went toward the cabana. "He wants to speak to us."

There was a brief introduction in a mixture of French and English languages and that was followed by a spirited conversation between Marcel and Pablo that lasted for several minutes. As we were shaking hands and preparing to leave, I ventured to ask a well-intentioned question. When it was interpreted by Marcel, Pablo frowned slightly with a staring of his dark eyes.

"No," he replied harshly. "I do not approve of scoundrels imitating my work and selling it for the genuine. Now tell me the truth. Did you buy one of those abominable deceptions?"

"I did not," I was quick to assure him. "You can be sure I'd never do that."

"You are a good American," he said with a smile. "I admire good Americans."

= 3 =

When I returned home in 1949 after my second postwar European trip, I discovered to my surprise that I was no longer being represented by a New York literary agent. Overnight and without notice, Maxim Lieber had closed his office and gone to Mexico.

Weeks later, writing from a Mexico City address, Max informed me that he was conducting business as usual and that my interests would not be jeopardized to any degree by reason of his absence from New York. His letter contained no explanation for his abrupt closing of his office and his announcement from Mexico City.

After having experienced many years of not always favorable treatment by publishers, I was not inclined to be represented thereafter by an absentee literary agent and I immediately called upon Julius Weiss for legal advice.

The particular year in which the disappearance of Max Lieber occurred was during an era of intense investigation by the United States government of suspected subversive activities. Not only professed Communist party members, but also fellow travelers, labor union rank and file, radical intellectuals, and just plain liberals were suspected of planning the overthrow of democratic government and the establishment of a dictatorship of the proletariat.

The campaign to eliminate any Communist influence in American government was originated during the 1932 presidential election year by Elizabeth Dilling who subsequently published a who's who and handbook of radicalism under the title of _The Red Network_.

Thousands of Americans, ranging from Jane Addams, the founder of Hull House, to Rabbi Stephen Wise were cited for unpatriotic activities by Elizabeth Dilling. The charges against me were for having publically approved of some of the stated policies of presidential candidate William Foster, although I voted for Franklin Roosevelt, and also for having published a short story in _New Masses_.

Inasmuch as Max Lieber had often freely expressed more than casual interest in and, in fact, had stated that he had a favorable attitude toward the political activities of certain individuals under investigation for alleged subversive acts, it was my assumption that he had decided it was expedient not to be questioned in the matter of the government's investigation of Alger Hiss and Whittaker Chambers. Moreover, the trial and execution of Julius and Ethel Rosenberg at a later date on the charge of espionage indicated to me that Max had found it more comfortable to be in Mexico than in the United States during that period.

Whatever the reason for Maxim Lieber's absence from New York, his attorney readily agreed to accept a settlement proposed by Julius Weiss. This left me free to seek another literary agent to represent me. The selection of a new agent was not made without considerable deliberation and patient inquiry.

Among a score of available authors' representatives was one young man who insisted that my name would have to be changed to one that had more literary significence. Another agent wanted to be paid a fixed monthly sum to represent me rather than the customary percentage of royalties. And a third prospective agent tried to persuade me to devote myself exclusively to the writing of mystery novels.

All this search for a capable and worthy agent required a number of trips between Tucson and New York and each time I left home I felt increasingly deprived of June's assistance and companionship. However, try as I did, no amount of pleading would persuade her to go with me during that period.

In that time of arduous search for a reliable and congenial literary agent, I was able to complete the writing of a novel, *Episode in Palmetto*, for publication by Duell, Sloan, and Pearce. With that accomplished, I began writing a nonfiction book with the title of *Call It Experience*.

And as it was to come to be, these two books, together with the final volumes of *American Folkways*, were the last of mine to be published under the DS&P imprint.

As if planned by some occult power to take place simultaneously, Duell, Sloan, and Pearce was bought by and merged with Little, Brown and Company while at the same time James Oliver Brown and I were happily reaching agreement to become associated as author and literary agent. The difference between the two events was that the former took place in one evening of negotiations after business hours and the latter was accomplished only after weeks of careful consideration.

The swift, overnight merger of the smaller New York publisher with the larger Boston publisher, which brought about the disappearance of DS&P within days, resulted in a successful move by Little, Brown and Company to acquire for its list a number of conservative authors whose reputations would help to counteract any speculation that it's editorial staff may have been subjected to influence by political agitators.

This was a bold move by Little, Brown, and a successful one, during a period of grave concern on the part of all publishers while the Rosenbergs were awaiting execution for espionage and when Senator Joseph McCarthy had acquired unlimited power to charge and condemn any person or establishment suspected of having Communist leanings. Although I did not see myself as being a ranking conservative, and was prominently listed in Elizabeth Dilling's *The Red Network*, I was never called upon to account for my political preferences by Little, Brown.

What I was called upon to do was to meet on several occasions with Arthur Thornhill, Sr., the spirited president of Little, Brown and always with James Oliver Brown being the third person present. These gatherings usually took place at lunch at expensive East Side restaurants in New York and always the time spent at table was never less than three hours.

Arthur was an affable, stout-chested, ruddy-cheeked Bostonian who took delight in lavishing gratuities and good cheer upon any restaurant employee, hat check and busboy included, who came within his sight. He and Jim Brown had had friendly business relations for many years and were never at a loss to trade good-natured banter. And if the considerate attention paid to me was consistent with the treatment received by other Little, Brown authors we undoubtedly were among the best wined and dined in the profession.

One of the comments Jim Brown had made about Arthur long before my first meeting with him at lunch was that he would probably impress me as being more like the lordly owner of a Kentucky bourbon whisky distillery than as the presumably dignified president of a conservative Boston publishing house.

And so it was when within moments after I had been introduced to Arthur Thornhill that he first of all gave me a hearty slap on the shoulder and then handed me a double dry Manhattan cocktail. Soon he was raising his own glass to me in a cordial salute.

"Greetings and welcome to Little, Brown and Company on the road, Skinny," Arthur said with deep chuckles. "We'll have to make-do the best we can in this city until we meet again in Boston the next time. When Jim told me about you, I said I was glad you've got an old-fashioned nickname I can remember. Have you written any good books lately?"

Not waiting for any response from me, Arthur continued speaking without pause.

"Now listen to me, Skinny. When your next book is ready, send it to Jim and he'll give it to me personally. We've had a lot of turnovers in the editorial department and until we can get straightened out nobody knows who'll be there tomorrow. Some of the people we've had think they did a day's work when they took a one-book author to lunch at Locke Ober's. You write your books and be your own editor for a while. All you need now is Jim Brown and me."

Chapter Twenty-Three

SOON TO ATTAIN THE AGE of nine, and freed from schooling for the summer months, my son Jay was eager to go into the world and explore the animal kingdom wherever zoos existed.

Jay's mother was begged and even offered bribes by both of us to take the month-long zoo-hopping trip from coast to coast in a new Lincoln sedan. But June was too deeply absorbed in the pleasurable throes of psychoanalysis to permit her obsession to be shared with something she considered to be of no importance to her.

Tolerant I was to the end, being mindful of the obsession that was compelling her to be confined in Tucson as the patient of a psychiatrist, nevertheless I urged June to make a careful study of *The Locomotive God* by William Ellery Leonard before becoming entirely devoted to analysis.

The book by Leonard was an autobiographical revelation of the mental torture of a highly intelligent university professor who had been held captive by the fear of travel away from the immediate boundaries of his life. *The Locomotive God* was a chilling study of an obsession long remembered from my days as a book reviewer. However, my suggestion did not appeal to June and she was likewise opposed to any effort to encourage her to liberate herself from her anxieties.

As for myself, I was unwilling to give up and abandon my innate need to observe and ponder and participate in life beyond the horizon. Consequently, I was pleased to hear Jay's eager pleas for me to conduct him into the world outside the confining rims of the Catalina, the Rincon, and the Santa Rita mountains of Southern Arizona.

Our tour of American zoos began in Los Angeles on a balmy day in early summer after our arrival there with a new portable typewriter and two reams of yellow paper for me and a bundle of maps and a wildlife encyclopedia for the boy.

After a drive of two days along the foggy California coast, we groped our way through fog even more dense at the San Francisco zoo.

Portland was sunny and mild. In Seattle, though, it rained steadily for two days and so finally we outfitted ourselves with proper rain gear and went sloshing among the cages and quarters of the local denizens. By that time, the bears began having a familiar appearance and they returned our gaze as if we had seen each other previously in Los Angeles or San Francisco. The seals and zebras were definitely look-alikes from the beginning of our zoo trip.

On our way eastward from Seattle, we changed our course and program several times. For instance, in Utah we spent a twelve-hour day riding as fare-paying passengers in the caboose of a scheduled Union Pacific freight train operating between Ogden and Park City and back to Ogden. Again, after the Milwaukee zoo, instead of traveling to Detroit by way of the Chicago zoo, we took the automobile ferry across wave-tossed Lake Michigan.

By that time, Jay had recorded in a notebook a comprehensive listing of names for locally inspired variations of hamburgers that had been observed on roadside billboards or on menus of eating establishments. Among the names catalogued were Bestburgers, Goodyburgers, Papaburgers, Whataburgers, Yourkindaburgers, and on and on.

Our zoo trip ended in Boston. By that time, it had been decided that it would be an undesirable climax to a memorable trip if we stopped at The Bronx zoo in New York, or at any other zoo, on our way home to Arizona.

Jim Brown joined us in Boston where we had a hurriedly-arranged meeting with Arthur Thornhill in his office overlooking The Common from the corner of Beacon and Joy Streets. Author's first comment was a lament about our meeting place.

"What in the world are we doing here?" Arthur said. "This is not the St. Regis or the men's grill at the Waldorf in New York. If I took you people to lunch here, I'd be humiliated. At the Ritz Carlton or Locke Ober's, I'm permitted by the Little, Brown board of directors to have only a two-hour lunch. It's a terrible state of affairs."

Anxious to leave after a hasty lunch, and with Jim Brown riding with us, we drove directly to New York. I took a room at the Essex House and for the next few days Jay and I spent most of the time going to theaters, sight-seeing on tour busses, and wandering in Central Park. Our trip home from New York was swift and uneventful.

I had been able to write several short stories during the month of travel. These stories, together with several that had already appeared in magazines, were soon ready for book publication by Little, Brown. It was decided by Jim Brown and me that the title of the collection should be that of one of the stories in the volume. The name of the book was *The Courting of Susie Brown.*

First of all, however, I put aside everything else until I could finish revising the early novel that had been a contributing cause of my moves from Charles Scribner's Sons to The Viking Press to Duell, Sloan, and Pearce. The fourth publisher involved, Little, Brown and Company, was to bring out the novel with the original title of *A Lamp for Nightfall.* The manuscript went directly to Arthur Thornhill as suggested by Jim Brown.

It had been my hope that after a month's absence I would return home to find that life in Tucson would provide a gratifying existence. I soon realized this was not to be. I had long before accepted the fact that my life was subject to frequent change—a condition similar to that of a company man being periodically transferred from one branch office to another in a corporate empire.

Consequently, it did seem to be an inevitable move when I sold our house in Catalina Foothills and bought an even larger house in downtown Tucson that was in a preferred residential area near the University of Arizona. The immediate advantage provided by the move was that I was within easy walking distance of university football and basketball games. Also, it was convenient for June and her many social activities.

The attempt to find contentment by moving from one house to another house was not a successful one, however. Other than providing access with less travel to athletic events, the downtown location soon became disappointing to a person in my increasingly unhappy state of mind. There were undoubtedly many reasons for this.

For one thing, it disturbed me when I came to realize that Tucson was too small for any further investigative prowling. Then, too, I had become acquainted with too many people. My telephone, even with frequent change of unlisted numbers, rang to distraction. And then, perhaps most perturbing of all, there were June's ever-increasing demands, probably to test my tolerance by willfully burdening me with debt, made evident by scheduling more and more hours for psychoanalytical sessions with the encouragement if not the connivance of her psychiatrist.

My capacity for tolerance was not enhanced by the subtle and usually vulgar jokes about analysts and their adulterous female patients that were overheard from time to time at the Tucson Press Club.

$$= 2 =$$

In a desperate effort to offer a carefully planned surprise that would overcome June's unwillingness to leave Tucson in the manner of William Ellery Leonard and travel with me, I bought tickets in advance for a compartment on a train to New York, purchased tickets in advance to a popular musical on Broadway, and reserved a suite at the Waldorf Astoria Hotel.

This surprise package was presented to June at a bedside ceremony on the morning of the day of departure. From that moment through the final minute as the train was leaving that evening she remained firmly adamant in her refusal to cancel appointments with her analyst and go with me.

When I returned to Tucson ten days later, I sold the house recently bought near the university and rented a smaller one in the eastern suburb of the city. The move was of little concern to Jay since he was more interested in the friendships he had made at the private school he attended than he was in neighborhood playmates.

June, however, expressed great unhappiness by saying she was fearful that her social standing as a member of the Junior League would be jeopardized when it became known that she no longer lived in an area of distinction and had gone to live in a small house beyond the city limits.

Blaming my dissatisfaction with the results of my writing in the midst of the turmoil that had been created as well as on my own restlessness, I was in an ill-tempered mood the day I was confronted by June with the demand that I pay her psychiatrist immediately his bill for three months of treatments.

By that time, due to the increased number of appointments, the charges amounted to a considerable amount of money. It was June's complaint that by failing to make orderly payments I was creating a strained relationship that would damage the progress of her analysis.

I fully expected eventually to pay in full what was owed but for the present I did not have several thousand dollars in hand for nonessentials. Many thousands of dollars had been invested in the construction and operation of radio station KCNA in Tucson. More thousands had been invested in partnership with John Mills, of Dallas, and John Mullins, of Denver, to construct and operate KPHO-TV in Phoenix. And there was a considerable amount of money invested in a chain of five weekly newspapers in South Carolina. As I had previously advised June, there was no extra money available for the additionally scheduled hours of analysis and that the time being spent on the psychiatrist's couch should be reduced.

But that was not the way it was to be.

June insisted, even demanded that I sell the house I had bought in Santa Fe for a second home and use the proceeds to pay off the debt for her analysis. It was her insistence that it was the Santa Fe property that was to be sold and not the valuable acreage in the foothills near Tucson. As it was to be revealed later, she had other plans for the acreage.

It was a journey of sadness for me when I went to Santa Fe to arrange with a real-estate broker to effect a forced sale of my house in the Placita Rafaela compound. Alfred and Dorothy Morang, who had moved from Maine to New Mexico several years earlier, were living in the house as caretakers for me and it was a painful ordeal to have to tell them that the house would be sold and that the new owner would probably require rent that was higher than they could afford.

Eventually as expected, Alfred and Dorothy were forced to move out of the house. And that was the sorrowful beginning of a series of unfortunate events.

It had been emotionally devastating to Alfred Morang to be compelled to leave his home and studio so unexpectedly and it was not surprising that the trauma of what amounted to an eviction was to some extent responsible for the hasty divorce of Alfred and Dorothy.

That divorce, however, was not to be the final event in the life of Alfred Morang. While still distressed and unsettled, he married a new acquaintance with two teen-age daughters. This unfortunate marriage lasted for two tempestuous years before ending in another divorce.

Then came the final episode. Living alone in an abandoned shack, in an enforced reclusion that for him had become a way of life, Alfred went to bed one night with a comforting bottle of wine and a lighted cigarette. He died in the fire of his bedding during the night and his death went unnoticed until his body was found several days later by boys playing in the rubble.

Following cremation, Alfred's ashes remained unclaimed for several years while being kept in an urn in the storeroom of a mortuary. After that length of time, several friends claimed the ashes and sprinkled them along the footpaths of Canyon Road and the Acequia Madre where Alfred had often been seen walking in his rapid but staggering strides during the latter years of his life in Santa Fe.

With money obtained to pay every dollar owed for June's psychiatric treatments, I promptly made a declaration of my own. I announced that I had decided to leave Tucson and move to Phoenix. Following that statement, I suggested that by going with me June could probably find it beneficial to consult a different analyst in Phoenix who might really help her.

That suggestion was not acceptable.

Moreover, June declared that she had no intention of ever leaving Tucson and her favorite analyst. Each of our decisions steadfast and irrevocable, the impasse indicating the inevitability of divorce, all that remained to be done after that was to reach an agreement about the division of community property.

I had no feeling of remorse or regret when I spoke with my friend Harry Behn or my attorney William Kimball about the impending divorce and my moving to Phoenix. Both of them were sympathetic and understanding when I explained that privacy for writing had vanished and that it had become difficult to support unrealistic demands for psychiatric treatments.

Neither Harry nor Bill, as indicated by their silence, found it necessary to inquire further about the cause of the forthcoming divorce.

The financial settlement finally agreed upon by June and me consisted of the conveyance of the valuable undeveloped foothill acreage to her in lieu of the nonexistence of a home to pass along to her and ample alimony payments directly from me. Also, she was provided with the income from a fund for yearly support for life. And, of course, adequate child support. This was the third time I had been called upon to divide assets.

First I shared with Helen, next with Margaret, and then with June. I was left wondering what would be left to divide if it should happen a fourth time.

= 3 =

It was early in the 1950s when I bought a medium-sized, gabled-roofed, recently-built house on a large tree-shaded lot situated on Central Avenue in a northern residential section of Phoenix. In addition to a swimming pool and extensive plantings of oleanders and roses, there was a modern three-room guest house on the property that provided an ideally secluded place for writing and was a quiet retreat at other times.

I was so pleased with my new living and working establishment in the quiet residential neighborhood that during the first few weeks in residence I rarely left my compound and then only for meals at a nearby restaurant or to meet friends at a downtown bar or club.

It was during those early days in Phoenix when I became a life member of the Phoenix Press Club. My reason for joining the club was to continue fellowship with writers that had its beginning in Tucson. What this led to in Phoenix was what was lightly called the performance of a civic duty.

In this case, my involvement occurred in the era when many cities were establishing annual celebrations featuring parades and football games between two leading college teams. The Phoenix entry was the Salad Bowl, a suitable designation since lettuce and tomatoes were produced in large quantities in the area. And as a member of the Phoenix Press Club, I had been appointed to be one of the five judges to select the beauty queen for the parade and the opening event at the football game.

I voted with the majority for the young woman to receive the honor of being judged the fairest of them all. However, I disapproved loudly and persistently when it came to having the winner called Miss Salad Bowl.

Insisting that such a name for a comely young woman was demeaning, I contended that her name should be Miss Tomato. My attitude undoubtedly becoming obnoxious, I was cautioned by one of the judges to stop using intemperate language while trying to convince the panel that an ordinary head of lettuce used as an ingredient for a salad lacked the esthetic appeal of a luscious red-ripe tomato. The winner was not named Miss Tomato and I was never again asked to be a judge for the annual selection of Miss Salad Bowl.

My first task at my new workplace was to find a reliable secretary to bring order to my jumbled accounts and neglected correspondence. This was accomplished when I obtained the services of Betty Pustarfi. Betty was a student at Arizona State University, specializing in English, and since all of her classes were in the morning she was able to come to North Central Avenue five afternoons a week or six times when there was extra work to be done.

Recommended by an employment agency, Mrs. Edith Heald came to work for me as a part-time housekeeper. She was an energetic widow sixty years of age, lean and sinewy to the extent of being almost emaciated in appearance, with the weathered face of a Kansas farm wife, and she was endowed with a freely given smile.

Sometimes as often as twice a week Mrs. Heald insisted upon baking for me a large pan of a dozen soda biscuits. The browned-to-perfection biscuits were so irresistible that I could not keep from eating a whole panful with orange marmalade or apple butter at one sitting while they were still warm from the oven.

Then there was John-Henry Rushmore. John-Henry was a gray-bearded refugee from the Arkansas Ozarks who had come to Arizona with the hope that the drier climate would bring relief to his wife's painful arthritic condition. According to John-Henry, his wife complained as much as she ever did back home in Arkansas. However, he was hopeful of being able to make a better life as a part-time gardener and handyman in our neighborhood than he had been able to do as a farmer on the stony ground where he had been born nearly sixty years earlier.

Other than not having the stamina to perform day-long outdoor labor for a man of his age and not being able to tolerate the desert heat as easily as native-born Arizonians and Mexicans, John-Henry knew no more than I did about attending to oleanders and roses and other plantings on the one and a half acres of property. He was a likeable person, though, always willing to be instructed, and I found it easier to praise him for his efforts than to scold him for his ineptitude.

In the middle of an afternoon while flooding one of the levels of the lawn with water from the nearby irrigation canal, John-Henry beckoned to me while I was on the way from the garage to my workroom in the guest house.

Prior to that, John-Henry had been trimming an oleander bush and he still held one of the several severed stems in his hand as if he did not know what to do with it. While I was walking toward him, he whisked the stem back and forth several times as though it had been a hickory switch to drive a cow to the barnyard for milking.

"I just want you to know one thing, mister," John-Henry said in his drawling manner of speaking. "I sure do miss my coon hunts out here in this strange territory. I've been around here now for nearly three years and I ain't seen a single solitary common old coon in all that time. It just don't seem like natural living not having a couple of coon hounds around the house and striking out with them through the brush on a moon-lit night to tree a couple of them rascals. You know that kind of feeling, don't you, mister?"

I nodded. "It's been a long time since I lived in a coon-hunting part of the country, but I think I know what you mean," I told him.

"Sure you do, mister. Once you done it, you'll always miss it. And the best way is starting out real early when you're no more than a scant young-ster. But if you're too little and short-legged to keep up with the hounds, then the next best way to get started is to be sent on a snipe hunt. That'll start the manhood juices boiling up inside you."

Turning away and muttering to himself, John-Henry went back to attend to the flow of water over the lawn. The next time I saw him several days later was when he was clipping withered hips from the rosebushes.

"Mister, I've been thinking some more about them coon hounds I left back there where I came from," John-Henry told me, "and it got me to feeling mighty downright homesick. For a while I thought I'd just belly-up and die if I couldn't get back there to see them pretty groves of oak trees shaking the dew off of their sleepy-eyed leaves in the sunrise and watch them devil-ish red squirrels scampering over them rocky ledges after a mouthful of grasshoppers which they'd spit out as soon as they got the first bitter taste of them."

John-Henry stopped, swallowing hard, and looked at me with an imploring gaze.

"Mister," he said in an earnest manner after a short pause, "if you'd write a little story about what you remember about coon hunting back there where you come from—mister, if you'd do that, I'll promise you one thing."

"What would you promise?" I asked.

"I'll promise you I'll read every word you write—well, not exactly me, because I never learned most words at sight. But my wife knows nearly all the words. She'll read the little story to me. That's the promise I'll make. And I'm a truthful man. I'll swear before the Good Lord Almighty on the biggest Bible I can find to prove how truthful I'll be about reading what you write about the coons."

I could not promise John-Henry that I would write a story about coon hunting but I did thank him for the suggestion. I was working days and parts of nights on a novel that interested me very much and I did not intend to let anything divert my attention to anything else until the final page was written.

Chapter Twenty-Four

DURING ONE OF OUR MEETINGS in New York, Jim Brown and I had decided that it would be to our advantage for us to go to London, Milan, and Paris for the purpose of becoming better acquainted with the literary agents who were representing me in those publishing centers. We had agreed that an agent should be retained or replaced as the result of our findings.

Earlier, while being represented by Maxim Lieber for American rights, I had been willing to let Laurence Pollinger in London be in complete charge of not only British rights to my books but also in charge of all foreign languages. I had found this to be an efficient way of doing business inasmuch as the Laurence Pollinger agency had authorized sub-agents in every country on the continent of Europe as well as in Asia and South America.

Admittedly wishing to share in agency commissions abroad, it was Jim Brown's contention that he and I should not let the Pollinger agency have exclusive world-wide rights to my work outside the United States. And what Jim wanted to do during our travels abroad was first of all give notice to Laurence Pollinger of our intentions and then to visit Italy and France where we would make our decision about agency representation for those languages.

I made it very clear to Jim that I would not be in favor of giving up my association with Laurence Pollinger. Undaunted, and still hopeful that a compromise could be attained, Jim insisted that we should carry out our plan to visit the sub-agents in Milan and Paris in order to appraise their effectiveness. Since the trip was primarily in my interest, and not for the benefit of any of Jim's other clients, I was prepared to pay all our expenses from New York and return.

We arrived in London early one morning stiff-legged and glum after a night flight in the cramped seating of an early-model transatlantic airplane.

As Jim had arranged, we went directly from the airport to the small and elegant Brown's Hotel in the gloom of a foggy London morning. When questioned about the reason for our staying at Brown's Hotel, Jim explained that other than the name having a sentimental appeal to him it was chosen because it was typically British in furnishings and service from an earlier century. He praised it for not being modern-day British in atmosphere like the Savoy and the Mayfair hotels catering to American tourists who made insufferable demands for more creature comforts and pretentious amenities.

After a day-long nap and some recovery from the sleepless night over the Atlantic, we were having tea in the parlor of Brown's Hotel when Jim asked me why I had never learned to give the proper English pronunciation to such simple words as bath, half, rather, and radiator. When I replied that I had not had a privileged Harvard education, Jim whooped so loudly and with such delight that others in the parlor turned to stare at us Americans in their midst. Jim rarely made mention of his years at Annapolis and Harvard, but it always delighted him whenever a reference, no matter how oblique, was made by someone else.

The next day when we called on Laurence Pollinger at his agency office in Maddox Street, Mayfair, Jim stated that he had come to London with me, at my request, to act as interpreter or middleman to prevent any misunderstandings arising from conversations between Laurence and me.

With no indication of a smile, Laurence asked me to explain what Jim intended to say. For a moment, I thought Jim was going to burst into another loud whoop, but he remained strangely quiet for the next few minutes.

Later, after some random remarks by Laurence, Jim told him of our plan to go to Milan for a meeting with Erich Linder. Erich's Milan literary agency was the largest in Italy, although not Laurence's favorite, but it was with Laurence's tolerance the one that had represented me in Italy for many years.

The moment Erich's name was mentioned, Laurence was cooly indifferent to any further discussion about him. Our meeting ended shortly thereafter without a message, cordial or other, to convey to Erich Linder.

We had left Laurence's office and were on our way back to Brown's Hotel when Jim said that after getting to Milan he hoped to find out from Erich Linder the reason for what evidently was ill-will on the part of Laurence. He said he felt obligated for the sake of all literary agents to do his best to restore harmony and good relations between Laurence Pollinger and Erich Linder.

Nothing more had been said for several minutes when suddenly Jim grasped my arm. That was followed quickly by one of his explosive whoops of hilarious laughter.

"Now what, Jim?" I asked calmly.

"Oh, you!" he said, shaking my arm in his grasp. "You and Laurence! That stolid Englishman asking you to interpret my dialect! And with all his British mumbling I hardly understood a word of what he was saying. It's incredible. And I must say that's British humor to be admired."

"That's when you should have let Laurence hear one of your famous whoops," I told him. "Hearing that, it might have made him feel less antagonistic toward Erich."

"And that's no laughing matter," he said seriously. "We have got to find out the reason for Laurence's hostility toward Erich. It could very well be having an adverse effect on your publication situation in Italy. We came to Europe to find out if anything of that nature existed."

At our first meeting with Erich Linder in Milan, the whole time was spent listening to Erich's detailed account of his successful efforts to arrange publication of all of my books in Italian translation. From the earliest novelette to the most recently written novel this was accomplished by his alternating the offering of rights to the two largest publishing houses in Italy. These were Valentino Bompiani and Arnoldo Mondadori.

Although Bompiani and Mondadori were competitive to an extreme, Erich had been able to act as a pacifying intermediary for several years and the result was that he and I were on friendly terms with both Valentino and Arnoldo. However, as Erich admitted, he had been decidedly unsuccessful in establishing a personal or business friendship with Laurence Pollinger.

It was at a late lunch at Erich's favorite Milan restauant following an office meeting that he suggested that he may have offended Laurence during one of his visits to London.

The occasion in London had been when Laurence offered Erich the position of manager of an international literary agency vaguely planned to be established in Switzerland. As Erich recalled, he rejected the offer by saying in a carefree manner that he would rather work for himself as an Italian than work for an Englishman in Switzerland or anywhere else. It was a remark that had been bitterly resented by Laurence Pollinger.

Jim Brown's comment at that point was that he himself would have resented such a remark and could not blame Laurence for the attitude he had taken. More than that, Jim said he would never give Erich an opportunity to become an associate in his New York agency for fear that Erich would be so aggressive he would be in danger of being ousted from his own agency. Jim's outspokenness was not accepted lightly by Erich.

When Jim and I arrived in Paris, Jim said it was more important to see Jenny Bradley than anyone else and he made an appointment to take her to lunch the following day. Jenny, who was the widow of the long-time American literary agent in France, William Bradley, continued to represent many American and British authors. I had never met her and I fully expected to be invited to the lunch Jim had arranged.

A meeting with Jenny Bradley was not to take place, however.

In fact, I was not at all certain that Jenny Bradley was actually my agent in France. And when I asked Jim about the matter, he said it was important for him to discuss the situation alone with Jenny in order to clarify the agency rights before anything else was discussed. I was anxious to have a meeting with Marcel Duhamel, who had translated the dramatization of *Tobacco Road* for staging in France, and to go with Marcel to see Gaston Gallimard and his son, Claude Gallimard, at their publishing office.

When I did have an opportunity to speak to Marcel, and mentioned the lunch from which I had been excluded, he reminded me that another agent, Michael Hoffman had arranged several book contracts for me with French publishers. This complicated matters in Paris to such an extent that I wondered if Laurence Pollinger himself knew who was my authorized literary agent in France. I decided to wait and ask Laurence to inform me by letter about the true status of Jenny Bradley.

Being as curious as I was, I tried to find out what had been discussed when Jim and Jenny met for lunch. He would say no more than that my interests had been protected and that I had nothing to worry about. Ignoring my next question, Jim's face flushed with an instant glow.

"Look here, Skinny," he said sharply. "We're good friends. Let's stay that way."

"I intend to," I told him at once.

"Then stop pushing me. I've told you all you need to know."

"It was not enough. I want to know more."

"All right then. You asked for it. You were not invited to lunch because Jenny Bradley prefers to speak French and not English. I still have enough to get by. You don't have the first word. It would've been downright awkward and silly for you to be there and have to have every word translated for your benefit. Now you know why you weren't invited to lunch. And I hope we are still friends."

"Why didn't you tell me in the beginning why you didn't want me at lunch?" I asked.

"Maybe it was retaliation," he said. "My pride was hurt at the beginning of this trip in London when Laurence asked you to interpret my British-by-way-of-Harvard accent."

"But you laughed about that later and gave the incident one of your loudest whoops."

"Maybe I'll give a big whoop about this incident—later."

$$= 2 =$$

I experienced a wonderful sensation of freedom from care when I came home from Europe after my travels with Jim Brown.

That was when I realized I would be able for the first time in many years to write without hindrance as many hours of the day and night as I felt like doing. And for weeks at a time without unwanted interruptions, too. It was as if miraculously I had been granted a continuation of the early days of tranquil living in Mount Vernon.

Betty Pustarfi came and went unobtrusively, leaving behind notes for my information and checks to be signed. Mrs. Heald, at least once a week, never failed to leave a pan of freshly-baked soda biscuits for me in the warming oven. Occasionally I would see John-Henry Rushmore mowing the lawn or trudging past my workroom window with a few wilting stems trimmed from one of the oleander bushes.

What I was doing week after week was writing fiction to my heart's content. First of all, I finished *Love and Money*, a novel I had been working on in starts and lapses for a long time, and I was very happy with what I had accomplished. Next, and a return to my long-standing esteem and warm feeling for the short story, I began writing brief fiction for current magazine and eventual book publication.

Twenty-one related episodes when completed were to be published by Little, Brown under the title of *Gulf Coast Stories*. And even before the series of short stories had been completed, I was making preliminary notes for the next novel I planned to write and which would be published with the title of *Gretta*.

What was happening away from my typewriter during the months when I was writing the twenty-one short stories was that it soon became a habit for me to take leave of absence for two or three days—or, actually, nights rather than days—between the time one story was completed and the next one begun.

This routine became such a pleasantly rewarding one that I found myself being so eager to comply that I would pack an overnight satchel and leave home immediately no matter what time of day or night the story was finished. My destination when I boarded a plane at the Phoenix airport was always Las Vegas.

My reason for being in Las Vegas was to relax and clear my mind of the recently completed short story so that I could undertake to begin writing the next one without a mingling of content and confusion of characters. To that end, I had found that the ideal time for relaxation and the free play of thoughts was from dusk to dawn. In Las Vegas, sleep became a sometime thing.

By experience, I had determined that I was best suited to eating and drinking lightly and leaving the long dinners and lengthy cocktail shows for others to enjoy. For my part, it was much more fitting to take a meager serving of finger food early in the evening, a small helping from a midnight chuckwagon, and an early morning breakfast at dawn. Between times, I would alternate bar drinks with bottles of soda water in a lounge and now and then play a few hands of blackjack.

And that became my way of eliminating a recent story from my mind and preparing myself for the next one to be written.

At various times I had stayed at several of the hotels on the Las Vegas Strip, including the Sahara, the Desert Inn, and the Tropicana, and in all those years the most memorable night was spent at the resplendent Flamingo Hotel shortly after its opening.

The Flamingo was the hotel and casino that had been built by Bugsy Siegel and his backers to be the gambler's paradise on the Las Vegas Strip. It was there that I saw Bugsy for the first and only time in my life. He was dead on the blood-stained white carpet of a Beverly Hills mansion with carbine bullets in his body a short time later.

Bugsy's appearance that night in the casino bar of the Flamingo, accompanied by two ever-ready, gray-suited bodyguards, was not without considerable notice and attention. And then likewise later in the evening at a blackjack table his presence did not have to be heralded. If Al Capone and Lucky Luciano, with some of their troops, had walked into the Flamingo at that moment, they would have had to make a slam-bang entrance to be able to attract as much attention as Bugsy did merely by quietly appearing with his ever-present, half-smoked cigar clutched between two fingers of his left hand.

With his glowing personality, his handsome physique, and his expensively tailored dark-blue suit worn with a white-on-white monogramed shirt and black silk necktie it was a magical combination that stated Bugsy's presence in unmistakable terms. Bartenders, cocktail girls, busboys, porters, and even hard-drinking barstool customers recognized Bugsy either with lingering glances of awe or with unconcealed signs of apprehension.

Loud conversation at the long bar suddenly became subdued as Bugsy ordered drinks for the small group around him. While waiting for his drink, Bugsy blew a puff of cigar smoke at one of the briefly-costumed cocktail girls. She stopped as if mesmerized and stood there panting with a heaving of her breast until he motioned for her to go away.

Later in the evening, I was one of several players seated at a blackjack table when Bugsy decided to deal a few rounds of twenty-one for the house. His cigar clutched between two fingers of his left hand, he took charge of the game by silently dismissing the dealer at the table with a flip of his thumb.

With the flicker of a smile barely visible through the pale skin of his face, Bugsy deftly shuffled the deck of cards several times with the ease of a magician demonstrating how the hand could be quicker than the eye. After each shuffle, the cards were cut and the first one to be turned face up each time was an ace. Some of the players applauded with polite smiles while others regarded him with tight-lipped suspicion.

"Don't worry, friends," Bugsy said with reassuring glances and smiling pleasantly for the first time. "This is the Flamingo. What you saw can happen somewhere else in town. But never at the Flamingo. When you want an honest game, always come to the Flamingo for it."

Presently, after a long winning streak by several of the players, a chubby-faced, middle-aged man at the table spoke up in a loud voice and demanded to know if Bugsy could actually be Mr. Siegel. The man who had asked

241

the question had not used the detested nickname that Bugsy had acquired in New York. There had been several reported instances when a careless speaker had received a broken arm for his indiscretion.

"Are you really Mr. Siegel?" was the way the taunting question was asked.

Bugsy's reply was swift and brief.

"Yes, I am Ben Siegel," he said in an even tone of voice.

"The real Mr. Siegel who owns the Flamingo?"

"The same."

Moments later, one of the other players leaned forward and stared intently at Bugsy's face. He was a mustached man, about forty years old, with a shiny glow on the bald crown of his head. He had a vivid purple scar an inch or longer on one side of his face.

"I've heard about you," the man with the purple scar said to Bugsy. "And I've seen your picture in the papers, too. I know who you are. You're Bugsy Spiegel—that's who! Calling yourself Ben something else won't fool me—Bugsy!"

Bugsy fanned the deck of cards on the table with a sweep of his hand. His face was taut and whiter than ever.

"I'm pleased to meet you, too," Bugsy said with only a slight movement of his tightened lips. "Good-by!"

"What's the 'good-by' for, Bugsy?"

"It's for you—punk!"

"Now, hold on here," the scar-faced man said defiantly. "What makes you think I'm leaving? I ain't going nowhere till I make up my mind to leave. I came here to play some blackjack and I'll leave when I'm ready and not before. Now go ahead and deal those cards, Bugsy. Keep that deck warm. I don't like no cold decks when I'm playing this game."

Turning quickly to motion to the two gray-suited bodyguards with a single nod of his head, Bugsy stepped away from the blackjack table and left the game unfinished. The dealer stepped forward to take Bugsy's place.

Moments later the two muscular bodyguards were standing beside the taunting gambler. Quickly they stuffed his stack of chips and silver dollars into his pockets and lifted him bodily from his seat at the table.

"Leave me alone—take your hands off me!" he protested in a loud voice. "I ain't going nowhere!"

Nothing more was heard from him while, with feet dangling high above the floor, he was being hustled from the casino and into the night.

By then, Bugsy had gone back to the bar and had calmly relighted his cigar. After calling for a drink, he blew a puff of smoke at a passing cocktail girl.

= 3 =

Back home on North Central Avenue in Phoenix, after falling asleep one night confident with the thought that life had become a delightful carefree existence and routinely favorable for my writing, I woke up the next morning with the uneasy premonition that something unforseen was going to disrupt my well-ordered way of living.

Watchful as I was for many days, I could detect no signs for a long time to indicate that my foreboding was the result of anything more than a passing reverie in the night.

Then it happened. My worry had been justified.

I had known far in advance that Betty Pustarfi was going to graduate from Arizona State University in the spring and heedlessly I had expected her to continue her secretarial work for me for some time to come.

Consequently, I was totally unprepared when Betty informed me with much delight that she had enlisted in the Women's Army Corps and would be going to Fort McClellan in Alabama for basic training a few days after graduation. With a feeble smile, I invited Betty to go to dinner with me and at the restaurant I ordered a bottle of champagne to toast her in gratitude for her faithful secretarial services as well as for her patriotism.

Even though Betty had given me a full month's notice that her immediate future was to be that of a WAC and no longer my secretary, I was to no extent prepared, besides being decidedly unwilling, to go through the tedious and time-consuming ordeal of trying to find someone with her ability and proven responsibility to replace her.

For a long time I was utterly depressed, dejected, downcast. Whatever it was I was trying to write stubbornly resisted all efforts to make it acceptable by my standards. I probably spent more time at the bar of the Press Club during that period of failed accomplishment than I did at my typewriter.

Fortunately, as it proved to be for my own good before any lasting harm was done, Virginia Fletcher moved to Arizona from Florida. This was an event that not only had the immediate effect of eliminating the troublesome matter of replacing the loss of editorial and secretarial help but also Virginia's unexpected advent was responsible for a new and more settled way of life for me.

Not only being a calming influence in a recklessly inclined period in my life, the combination of Virginia's presence, her wisdom, and her congenial nature was an inspiration from the moment of her arrival in Phoenix from her home in Florida. Moreover, the attractive, dark-haired, swimsuit-slender young woman was a charming companion with an appealing personality. Whether during a late evening dinner or a midnight skinny-dipping in the pool, she was an eager listener to the most trivial of remarks and her contribution to the conversation was always interesting and perceptive.

As Virginia and I became better acquainted, we found that there was a distinct likeness in our lives. Our fathers had been ministers, our mothers had been teachers of English, our parents had moved from state to state every few years, and we had sons of the same age.

Years earlier, I had met Virginia for the first time in the countryside near Baltimore. Victor Weybright, the New American Library editor and publisher, had restored his family's Hollow Rock Farm and he frequently brought authors and editors on weekends to enjoy Maryland hospitality.

I was introduced to Virginia Fletcher on the weekend that June and I were house-party guests. Virginia had been invited to dinner, being one of the very few local residents Victor considered worthy of associating with his New York celebrities, and our meeting had been fleeting but memorable and pleasant. The occasion had remained vivid in mind because at the time June's conduct indicated that she was bored to the extent of being indifferent and unresponsive in the presence of other guests while Virginia was gracious and vivacious in contrast.

My next meeting with Virginia took place in Florida when I happened to be in Sarasota on one of my periodic treks here and there around the country. Brought together by mutual acquaintances, this time I had the opportunity to find out that she had been a premedical student at the University of Maryland at one time and had abandoned that pursuit to study painting and drawing at the Maryland Institute of Art.

Following her divorce, Virginia and her son, Drew, had moved to Sarasota where she was attending the Farnsworth School of Art. At that time, she was not certain that she would continue living in Florida after completing her course of training and was contemplating whether to move to the West— possibly Santa Fe or Colorado Springs or Arizona.

And now, much to my delight, Virginia was living in the Phoenix suburb of Scottsdale. Even though she had no secretarial experience, we were confident she had sufficient ability to assume the duties performed previously by Betty Pustarfi. It was decided that she would continue to work as editorial assistant until another person could be selected without haste and then trained in a normal manner for the job.

No mention was made of it, but I was inclined to think that we might prefer postponing the selection of another secreretary indefinitely.

During the long Arizona summer that followed, it seemed to become less and less desirable to find another person for the work that Virginia was doing so well. The swimming pool midway between the main house and the guest house was a convenient place for relaxation at any time of the day or evening and the grill was only a few steps away when the time came for charcoaling hamburgers or steaks and corn-on-the-cob.

Freed from schooling for the summer, my son Jay made frequent trips by bus from Tucson to Phoenix and Virginia's son Drew came to North Central Avenue for the two of them to swim and splash hour after hour. Later, as a special reward for being such efficient pool attendants and lifeguards, Jay and Drew were enrolled for several weeks in a rustic ranch camp for boys only in the highlands of Central Arizona.

At the end of summer, Virginia asked me in a casual manner one evening at twilight if I had ever considered leaving Phoenix and moving to San Francisco to live. The question was a startling surprise because I had thought of the very same thing many times without mentioning such a possibility to anyone.

The immediate effect of the question was the realization that life had become unusually delightful, existence routinely pleasant, and that I was in danger of becoming a victim of self-satisfaction. I knew at that moment that, as it had happened often in the past, I was being challenged to give up the old and to seek the new by changing my place of living again.

When I readily admitted that I had had serious thoughts about moving to San Francisco, Virginia smiled understandingly. And we then began discussing plans for Virginia to go to San Francisco to search for a suitable place for me to live and work. She was so confident that I was going to move that she enthusiastically began making detailed notes about location, duration of lease, and rental prices for apartments and houses.

And so San Francisco it was to be.

Chapter Twenty-Five

WITHIN A WEEK'S TIME IN San Francisco, as a result of luck, perseverance, and good judgment, Virginia had succeeded in obtaining, at a favorable price, a year's lease of a house with a superb location on the northerly slope of Twin Peaks. I immediately put my Phoenix compound on the market and began making plans to move to San Francisco without delay.

My new home was a large, wide-windowed, three-level dwelling that had been designed by the owner to provide a view extending from the Pacific Ocean in the west to the Golden Gate Bridge, the Embarcadero, North Beach, the Bay Bridge, the City of Oakland, and all the towns climbing up the mountains of the East Bay.

Even when the fog came creeping inland from the Pacific, obscuring parks and buildings and street lights and silencing the noise of the city, there was always the view from on high of the towers of the Golden Gate Bridge and the penthouses atop Nob Hill, Telegraph Hill, Russian Hill, and Pacific Heights. It was like a magic kingdom floating high above the clouds on another planet.

Indeed, the view from Twin Peaks was so spectacular that until I could become accustomed to such entrancing splendor I had to force myself to draw the curtains over the windows day and night when I was determined to concentrate on my writing.

As it continued to be after many years, I was not easily distracted by circumstances when I felt the urge to write a story or novel. Some of the less than kind accusations over the years had been that I was hardheaded, perverse, single-minded, stubborn, selfish, and took delight in inflicting mental cruelty on other persons by insisting on having my own way without compromise.

True it was, the compulsion to write with all my might had become an obsession that was driving me to success or failure in the end at the cost of endangering my own happiness and probably the happiness of anyone close to me.

The book that was almost finished was *Certain Women*, which was to be published the following year by Little, Brown, and I was beginning a preliminary draft of *Claudelle Inglish*. And as usual, I never hesitated to stop working on a novel when the idea for a short story came to mind.

This was during the time when I was working behind the drawn curtains at Twin Peaks. Virginia was living downtown in a residential hotel, The Gaylord, the same place my mother stayed during a short visit from her home in South Carolina where she had been living since the death of my father. Virginia was reviving her familiarity with French at Berlitz in the mornings and in the afternoons she came to Twin Peaks to restore order to files and records that were in a state of confusion after having been tipped upside down while in transit from Phoenix.

Living in San Francisco came to be a pleasant experience when Virginia and I went out to dinner and at other times to spend several hours in the evening at various bars and clubs in Chinatown and North Beach.

But there were other times, and increasingly so, when I was very lonely at Twin Peaks without Virginia's presence. Alone late at night in the large three-level house after work had been put aside and the curtains opened to city lights below, I often had a strong yearning to be with her and be able to express my feelings intimately and without reticence. Being good companions was always temporarily gratifying but I knew that before long a merely pleasant association with her would not be sufficient to satisfy my yearning.

Finally, late one evening at Shanghai Lil's, and a few weeks before the end of the year, I proposed marriage for the fourth time—vowing it would be the last time—in my life.

Surprised or not, and I was unable in the dim light of the lounge to see the expression on her face clearly, Virginia hesitated for a few tantaliz-ing moments before making known her response with a spontaneous hug and kiss.

Before the night was over, we had decided that we would go to Reno on New Year's Eve in time to obtain a marriage license for the ceremony at midnight. Actually, what we had in mind was to begin our life together at the beginning of the new year by being married precisely at one minute past midnight. That matter settled, I suggested that we go from Reno to New York and there take a ship across the Atlantic to Europe and after a few days there return by airplane to Florida to continue our honeymoon.

With all travel plans made and confirmed, including passage on the *Queen Mary* and a suite at the Riverside Hotel in Reno, nevertheless, as a precau-tion since it was the heavily traveled holiday season, I telephoned Lee Frankovich the day before leaving for Nevada.

Lee and I had known each other for many years and he was currently the manager of the Riverside Hotel. I wanted assurance from him that a suite would be available when Virginia and I arrived the next day.

As it happened, the negligent travel agent had not reserved a honeymoon suite as I had specified. However, Lee said he would cancel the reserva-tion for a twin-bedded suite and instead we would have king-size accom-modations. Also, he said he would make all arrangements for the marriage ceremony at the Park Wedding Chapel which was situated across the street from the hotel.

We arrived in Reno in the middle of the afternoon of New Year's Eve in ample time to obtain a marriage license at the stone-faced Washoe County Courthouse next door to the Riverside Hotel. Even at that time of day there was much activity inside the courthouse where both marriage licenses and divorce decrees were issued with proficiency and friendliness.

After waiting in line with many other couples to receive our license, the clerk presented Virginia with a small volume having the title of *The Bride's Cookbook*. It was a gift from "The Biggest Little City In The World, Reno, Washoe County, Nevada."

In early evening, a light snow began falling in a slight westerly breeze and on the north side of the hotel the Truckee River was flowing as usual in dark currents down from Lake Tahoe and the High Sierra.

Later, walking slowly through the swirling snow to the Park Wedding Chapel in sufficient time for the midnight ceremony, we were serenaded step by step with the sounds of whistles and horns and the echoes of bursting firecrackers already heralding the coming of the new year.

Brushing the snow flakes from our coats and stamping snow from our feet, we then went into the chapel. And there in the company of the night manager and his wife to serve as legal witnesses we stood at the candle-lighted altar waiting tensely for the stroke of midnight.

Suddenly, emerging from the shadows and moving into the flickering candlelight, Brother David was standing before us in a flowing white-silk vestment that was edged with purple piping. His costume sparkled with red and blue rhinestones as he began reciting the solemn-voiced words of the marriage ceremony. Unmistakably, he was the the same person I had known many years earlier when he was wearing a dingy clerical collar and a shiny dark-serge suit and drinking neat rye in a roadside bar between Reno and Silver City.

I had no intention of mentioning the previous meeting, preferring to wait to tell Virginia about it later. However, the moment Brother David concluded our marriage ceremony he stepped down from the altar and eagerly began shaking hands and wishing us future happiness in our married life.

Just as he was turning to leave, Brother David stopped and looked at me closely as if recalling at last that I was somebody he had known previously.

"Well, well!" he said with a broad smile. "Bless my soul!"

Reaching forward, he shook my hand vigorously.

"Here you are again! What a surprise! It makes me feel good to know that you would come back to me a second time to be married. I truly appreciate that. I do, I do! Now tell me something. What happened to that other young woman?"

Virginia had turned away and was leaving the chapel. I ran after her without a word in reply to Brother David. Hurrying hand-in-hand through the snowy New Year's night, I found that I was recalling over and over the remark Brother David had made concerning Margaret. As though it were inevitable, I could not keep my mind from wondering if Virginia like Margaret, would before the night was over perform what both Helen and Margaret had said was a purification ceremony. I realized that the uncertainty in my mind was caused by the fact that June had never indicated in any manner that she had a desire to engage in such a ritual.

= 2 =

Virginia and I were pleasantly at ease on our voyage to Europe while enjoying the privacy and comfort of our spacious cabin on an upper deck of the _Queen Mary_ after our hurried trip from Reno to board the ship in New York.

It was one of the very few times since my early years as a newspaper reporter when I was traveling without a standard-size or portable typewriter. So unusual it was, there were several times when I had to remind myself that I had purposely left anything of the kind behind me.

A few weeks before leaving San Francisco I had bought a light-weight writing machine that was the newest model on the market and was as easy to carry as an ordinary briefcase. However, realizing in time that it would not be suitable to take a typewriter on a wedding trip, I left it behind with some reluctance. Instead, I packed pencils and paper since making notes for future use in some manner was a habit I could not abandon by that time in life.

During the five days at sea, Virginia and I made several brave efforts to find enjoyment on deck chairs at various locations on the ship. Time after time, though, no amount of hot bouillon and layers of steamer blankets under the overcast gray sky had been sufficient inducement to suffer the icy winds of the North Atlantic Ocean in January.

After our leisurely voyage on the _Queen Mary_, and as previously planned, we spent several days in England before going to Italy and France to complete our brief European tour. In London, we were so pleased with the view of The Embankment and the Thames River from the balcony of our suite at the Savoy Hotel that we spent much less time than originally planned to visit shops and arcades during the day or to attend the theater at night.

The day before leaving for Italy we spent several hours at lunch with Laurence Pollinger at his favorite restaurant in Soho and it was a pleasant occasion until the final moments when it was time to say farewell.

While shaking hands with Laurence, and carelessly unmindful of his long-standing contention with Erich Linder, I asked him if he had a message for me to take to Erich in Milan.

"No!" Laurence said at once with a tightening of his lips. "Of course not! Never!"

"I'm sorry I mentioned it," I was quick to tell him by way of apology. "I forgot how you feel toward Linder."

"There's nothing for you to be sorry about," he said. "Stay out of it.

It's my concern, not yours. I can carry on alone as much as need be."

With a pleasant smile on his face and a friendly pat on my arm, he turned away to go back to his office leaving me to wonder if I should mention the incident when I saw Erich in Milan. A long time had passed with no lessening of resentment since Laurence had been offended by Erich's disdainful rejection of the offer to appoint him manager of a projected branch of Laurence Pollinger Limited in Switzerland.

Due to the excitement and confusion resulting from our arrival at the Milan airport the next afternoon, as well as constant activity during the two days to follow, Laurence Pollinger's expression of animosity toward Erich Linder did not come to mind a single time. Consequently, that unpleasant matter was never mentioned to Erich during our Milan visit.

Virginia and I had been greeted at the Milan airport not only by Erich Linder with a warm welcome but also by separate contingents representing the publishing houses of Valentino Bompiani and Arnoldo Mondadori. Pushing and shoving through a group of photographers and curious onlookers, both Valentino and Arnoldo were striving to be the first to present Virginia with large bridal bouquets of red roses. Unquestionably, the tumultuous scene was the result of careful planning by Erich Linder.

The flowery greeting, however, was only a prelude to the activity to follow.

Whether or not it had been planned by Erich, nevertheless the Mondadori group of greeters surrounded Virginia and, sweeping her off her feet, soon had her seated in a limousine that went speeding toward the city. While Virginia was being kidnapped by the Mondadori group, I was being taken by the Bompiani people to another limousine.

The competing publishers had planned simultaneous receptions with elaborate offerings of food and wine and the kidnapping of Virginia was declared to have been justified in order to insure a successful Mondadori event. After more than two hours apart, Virginia and I were united by Erich and taken to our hotel.

The bridal suite at the Duomo Hotel was filled with numerous vases of long-stem red roses from both Valentino Bompiani and Arnoldo Mondadori. Virginia was so overwhelmed when she saw the enormous display of roses that she was helpless to keep tears from her eyes.

I had looked forward to seeing Marcel Duhamel in Paris but for a longer visit than it was to be. As it happened, Marcel and Germaine were preparing to leave for the south of France to spend two weeks at their villa near Antibes. And since they were to take the train the day following our arrival from Italy, the only time Virginia and I could be with them was at dinner the evening before they left Paris. It soon became evident that Marcel and Germaine were as anxious to leave the snow and ice of Paris behind and get to the sunny Riviera as Virginia and I were in a hurry to be on our way to the sunshine of Florida.

After reconfirming our airline reservations to return to the United States, and with only two days to wait for departure, Virginia was delighted to have the opportunity to visit several of the high-fashion dressmaking houses and some of the art galleries. In the evening, the Lido and the Crazy Horse Saloon were entrancing places of entertainment.

= 3 =

Our first week in Florida was spent traveling leisurely by automobile down the east coast of the state to Miami and from there through the Everglades to Naples on the west coast.

It was in Naples that I telephoned Al Manuel in Beverly Hills to ask what progress was being made as the result of his efforts to form a partnership to produce a film of *God's Little Acre*.

Before leaving San Francisco, Al had told me that he expected to reach an agreement within a few weeks for me to participate in a partnership with Phil Yordan, the screenwriter, and Tony Mann, the director, for the production and distribution of the motion picture by United Artists and financing by the Bank of America. Al's first words over the telephone indicated that he was in an optimistic mood.

"Relax, Skinny," he said. "The trouble with you writers is that you-all worry too much when there ain't nothing worth worrying about. Take a deep breath and think about that some. Your job is to do your writing and honeymooning and let me take care of the important matters. By the way, how was your and Virginia's trip to Europe?"

"It was cold over there at this time of year," I told him. "Florida feels better. But what about our film, Al?"

"Give me a week or ten days, Skinny, and I'll have the good word for you," he said. "Now in the meantime stop worrying. Do some more honeymooning. Buy some picture postcards. Pick some grapefruit. Things like that—anything to keep busy and not worry. Then phone me in a week or so like I said. Good-by."

Exactly a week later, Virginia and I were in Alpine, Texas, in the Big

Bend region of the Rio Grande, and about midway across the continent on our way home to San Francisco.

The place selected in the small town of Alpine from which to make a pay-station telephone call to Al Manuel was an owner-operated little grocery store attached to a weather-grayed bungalow. The store had no name lettered on the windows or over the entrance, but there was a conspicuous sign at the doorway that was plain for all to see. The wording of the sign was explicit in meaning. POSITIVELY THE DRINKING OF BEER OR WHISKY ON THESE PREMISES IS FORBIDDEN ABSOLUTELY.

The large-breasted, gray-haired women in her sixties who was sitting on guard at her cash drawer did not hesitate to frown disapprovingly when she was asked to give us quarters for several dollars which were to be inserted into the coin slot of the pay-station telephone.

In a testy manner, her voice sharp and belligerent, the unsmiling woman said she could not spare more than eight quarters and doubted that anything in this life on earth was worth spending more than two dollars to talk about on the telephone.

Not knowing the name of the querulous Texan, and not inclined to arouse her wrath unnecessarily, we decided to devise a suitable name to use when referring to her. In subdued voices, we decided that she would be called Mrs. Fussy.

Midway through our lengthy conference, after explaining why it would be necessary to hang up the phone and for him to call me, I asked Al to telephone me at the pay-station number at the grocery store.

After a few minutes Al did call me. In the meantime, Virginia had bought two ice-chilled bottles of Coca-Cola from Mrs. Fussy and had managed to pour out most of the soft drink without being observed. Shielded behind the opened top of my briefcase, but in full view of the stern-faced Mrs. Fussy, I emptied a full flask of bourbon into the two bottles.

As Al had assured me the week before in Florida, the final details for forming the partnership and filming of *God's Little Acre* had been completed to his satisfaction. That known, Virginia and I felt we had good reason to celebrate happily with sips of bourbon from the Coke bottles.

For a long time, alternately talking on the phone and drinking bourbon while at any moment expecting the wrath of Mrs. Fussy to be hurled upon us, the pungent odor of whisky fumes floated airily throughout the small grocery store.

Finally, as we were preparing to leave, and while she was sniffing suspiciously, we were told by Mrs. Fussy in an accusing tone of voice that there was something mysterious about our presence in her grocery store that made it smell like an old whisky barrel.

"If you people ever come to Alpine again," the store owner told us, "I want you to remember that there are other pay-phones in town. You don't have to come here the next time."

By the time Virginia and I had returned home to San Francisco after our lengthy trip to Europe and Florida, Al Manuel began telephoning frequently to say he wanted me to be prepared to leave on short notice to search, with Tony Mann and others, for a suitable location in the Georgia countryside near Augusta for the filming of *God's Little Acre*.

During that long period of waiting, I revised my short story for children, *Molly Cottontail*, to be published as a book with suitable illustrations. Following that, I wrote several more short stories for a collection with the title of *When You Think of Me*. Both books were scheduled for publication by Little, Brown during the next year.

There were two novels in mind that I wanted to write, also, and I was impatient to get to work on them, although I knew better than to begin writing either of them while being involved in the filming of *God's Little Acre*. That was a project that was important to me since it was my hope that the new film would be far superior to the earlier one, *Tobacco Road*, which had suffered much harm when a false ending had been imposed on the story by Twentieth Century-Fox Films.

Finally, a meeting with Tony Mann was arranged and after a week in Augusta a forty-acre farm had been rented for one of the location sites and verbal agreement had been reached with the owners of a small cotton mill for filming interior scenes and adjacent company-owned streets and housing. In another day or two, the movement of cameras and other filming equipment from California to Georgia, together with actors and crew, would have been under way.

It was early evening when our Augusta attorney, who until then had arranged business matters for us with ease and without delays, came unexpectedly to meet with us at the Bon Air Hotel. His customary smile no longer to be seen, the lawyer was grimly serious when he stated at once that there would be no filming of scenes for the motion picture at either the cotton mill we had selected or at any other cotton mill in the area. From the beginning, he shook his head firmly from side to side to impress upon us how hopeless was the situation.

"I'm very sorry about this situation," he said. "I'm deeply sorry. But there's nothing I can do. I live in Augusta and I practice law here. And I am not going to cut my own throat by opposing the business and political power of my clients and associates in this community. Yes, I am sorry but it can't be otherwise."

During the next half-hour, we listened to an explanation of the reason for the ban being imposed by agreement among the owners of cotton mills in Augusta on the Georgia side of the Savannah River and owners of mills in Horse Creek Valley on the South Carolina side.

Again and again, we were told it had been decided that it would not be in the best interests of millowners to permit the filming of a novel that was not critical of workers striking against the owners of a cotton mill.

In the end, convinced that no appeal would succeed in reversing the decision to oppose the filming of the novel, we left town saddened by the rejection but determined to find a way to make the film somewhere else.

A few weeks later from the open cockpit of a small airplane while flying over the San Joaquin Valley in Northern California, Tony Mann found an ideal site for the outdoor scenes for the filming of *God's Little Acre*. And in Stockton nearby, a small spinning mill was found to be satisfactory for the interior factory scenes.

Less than a year from that time, with the principal players being Robert Ryan, Tina Louise, and Buddy Hackett, the film was completed and on the way to Italy in mid-1958 for its first public showing at the Venice Film Festival.

Chapter Twenty-Six

IN THE YEAR 1958, which was the time of my coming to be fifty-five years old, I had reached the stage in life where my interest wavered back and forth between a compelling desire to write as a storyteller and an overwhelming urge to travel across the world as an observer of people and places.

Fortunately, instead of becoming subjected to the harassment of conflicting demands, I found it to be an ideal opportunity to devote half of the year to writing and the other half to travel.

During the next three years, I was able to follow the plan I had devised for myself by maintaining a realistic balance between my two ambitious activities.

After a few months at my typewriter in San Francisco at the outset, Virginia and I traveled to Italy for the showing of *God's Little Acre* at the Venice Film Festival. Having yielded to considerable pleading by each of our teenage sons, Jay Caldwell and Drew Fletcher, Virginia and I had taken them with us so they could have the satisfaction of seeing some of the celebrated American and European actors and actresses in person. After a brief stay in Europe, I was in good spirits and ready to return to my typewriter day and night to finish the first of the novels I had set myself to write before the end of three years.

In those years the need to write fiction had come to be as demanding as the craving for food when hungry. When not traveling, and at the same time being prevented by a perverse fate from being able to transfer mental images to the reality of paper and ink was certain to bring about distress of body and acute frustration of spirit.

A variety of scenes and themes, together with innumerable faces of people either brought to mind for the first time or recalled from the past, could result in total confusion until order could be established by ruthlessly eliminating subject after subject until the final choice would receive exclusive attention.

I had never known a time under those circumstances when I was unable to write a short story or novel for lack of an idea and suitable material. There were occasions, it is true, when I was utterly lazy or preferred some other activity temporarily, but even then I was always careful to store in mind or in notebooks my thoughts and impressions for future use.

In March of 1959, with the preliminary draft of *Jenny by Nature* completed and put aside for the customary seasoning before I went to work on the final draft, I was eager once more to go traveling. Several days later, with little time lost following our decision to spend several weeks abroad, Virginia and I boarded the *Liberte* in New York.

After the first night and part of a day at sea, with most of the magazines and newspapers read from start to finish, it was logical enough to begin reading the ship's passenger list that our room steward brought to us with our eleven o'clock breakfast.

In the beginning, the long listing of fellow travelers contained a few recognizable names, mostly those mentioned from time to time in Hollywood or Broadway newspaper gossip columns. However, it was near the end of the alphabetical listing that I saw the name of anyone I actually knew. And there it was in bold print: MR AND MRS JOHN STEINBECK.

A few brief messages were sufficient to arrange for a meeting with John and Elaine later in one of the ship's lounges.

That meeting came to be the first of many times the four of us gathered for cocktails, lunches, and dinners before landing at Southampton. Only once before had John Steinbeck and I happened to meet while traveling outside the United States. That meeting had taken place in a restaurant in Cuernavaca where both of us were complaining about the effects of drinking water at random in Mexico.

John had recently finished writing what was still an untitled novel and, like me, was taking one of his frequent trips to Europe to relieve himself of stress resulting from long hours at work at his typewriter. Even after such a brief time at sea, he was relaxed and in good spirits. No matter how humorous or satiric were some of his remarks at times, there were moments when he was characteristically outspoken and critical. This was evident once when he complained to a lounge steward about the pale color of the olive in his martini and demanded that it be replaced by a fresh olive of natural greenness.

It was when we had gathered near the end of our voyage on the *Liberte* that John announced he had discovered after diligent research that without exception all the classic novels of the past hundred years had been written by authors with peptic ulcers. Satisfied with having made that unchallenged announcement, he next proposed that he and I collaborate on a project to startle the literary world by creating an imaginary young American novelist whose soon-to-be published first book of fiction would result in his fame immediately spreading world-wide.

Abounding with enthusiasm, both of us quickly agreed that our youthful American author would be a fifteen-year-old prodigy who was still too young to shave but would have prematurely gray hair and be untainted by contact with sophisticated older authors and unprincipled book reviewers. Try as we did, however, we could not decide immediately if he should have a given name and surname or an added middle name or two initials and a surname.

Finally, in the late evening of our last night at sea, it was decided that in order to perfect the hoax more time was needed for our collaboration to be successful. We assured each other that during our next meeting abroad, wherever that might be, we would make every effort to provide the prodigious young author with an impressive name to inspire students in creative writing courses to imitate assiduously for the purpose of gaining approval and accolades from their instructors.

When the four of us arrived in London the next day, all we would say to newspaper reporters was that we were collaborating on a project that was still in a preliminary state of development. After that, John and Elaine went immediately to spend the weekend with friends in the country and Virginia and I spent all possible time in shops and at theaters before leaving to meet James Oliver Brown in Paris.

As I had expected, the first thing Jim asked me was when would I finish the novel on which I had been working for several months. When I told him it would be ready for him soon after I returned home, he was very pleased and said he planned to take it to Little, Brown in Boston as soon as possible and demand a new contract with improved terms and a larger royalty advance than we had received in the past.

$$= 2 =$$

The recently built Istanbul Hilton Hotel was surrounded by luxuriant gardens, the largest of which was situated at the rear of the tall building, and all the park-like areas were crisscrossed by winding footpaths through flowers and shrubbery.

The location of the hotel of four hundred rooms was within walking distance of many of the street markets and bazaars. And in addition to being not far from the Blue Mosque, most of the guest rooms provided an unobstructed view of the Bosphorus.

Virginia and I had arrived in Turkey from Greece late in the evening after visiting several European publishers and translators and it was midmorning before we had breakfast served on our balcony overlooking the vast expanse of flowers and foliage in the rear garden.

It was shortly before noon when I looked down from our tenth-floor balcony and was surprised to see several women of various ages and physiques strolling unhurriedly along the paths through the shrubbery. Each of the women carried a rug folded over her arm or draped over her shoulder.

The guide book in our room had an entire page devoted to the Turkish cottage industry of rug weaving and it stated that homemade rugs were on sale in many of Istanbul's bazaars. Not a word, though, was said about the availability of similar rugs in the city's parks and gardens.

Late that afternoon, returning from a visit to some of the street markets, it was startling to see dozens of women, the youngest evidently in the earliest teens and the oldest being stout and gray-haired, walking slowly and singly, and obviously purposefully, along the paths.

From the street, and walking briskly and singly, men were going into the park-like garden where they were immediately approached and surrounded by several women from the youngest to the oldest in age. After animated discussions of various lengths, one of the women, unfolding her rug and shaking it vigorously as she went toward the bushes, was soon out of sight with the man who had negotiated for the rental of her rug. One by one, as the women returned to strolling on the footpaths, there would be more shaking of rugs to free them from twigs and wrinkles before being folded to carry on arms or draped over shoulders.

On our way to and from the markets and bazaars, Virginia and I had passed several kiosks and newsstands that displayed many Turkish-language paperback books with recognizable names of American and European authors. Among the various displays we found translations of twelve of my novels and short stories. Copies of each title were bought for the Turkish equivalent of fifty cents American and they had been brought back to the hotel for closer inspection.

Laurence Pollinger had told me in London that the pirating of books in the Middle East was a flourishing business and that American and British publishers and literary agents had had no success in attempting to put an end to the practice for the benefit of their authors. Laurence was firm in his belief that an individual bookseller should not be blamed for selling unauthorized translations when it was the unscrupulous printer and publisher who should be held to account for pirating a book and distributing copies to dealers without payment of royalty to the author.

Unhappy about what I had seen at many kiosks and newsstands, it seemed to me that it would be worthwhile to confront the pirating Istanbul publisher of my books and make an attempt to persuade him to make an agreement with the Pollinger agency for the payment of royalties. At my request, the hotel interpreter arranged for the publisher to meet with me the following day at the Hilton.

Promptly as promised, the amply fleshed and jovial mannered publisher arrived at the hotel with his darkly handsome, English-speaking attorney and proceeded immediately to present Virginia with a bouquet of flowers and to me a carton of Turkish cigarettes. After ordering a dark and bitter tasting drink for all of us in the hotel lounge, the affable Turk conveyed to us through his lawyer a warm welcome to his country.

Not a word was said about the unauthorized printing of some of my books during the next quarter-hour. It was then that I asked the lawyer to tell the publisher that I had seen some of my books displayed for sale at several kiosks and newsstands in Istanbul and regretted that they had been translated and published without permission from me or my literary agent in London.

Smiling and nodding genially, and then speaking at great length to his attorney, the publisher responded to my complaint as though I had congratulated him for his astuteness as a businessman.

"He wants me to thank you for your remarks," the lawyer said, "and to tell you that he plans to issue more and more of your books as fast as you can write them. And he said to be sure to tell you that he is very proud to be the publisher of your books in our country."

"But he is pirating my books," I protested. "My books are copyrighted. He can't print them for his profit and not pay me royalty. And I'm sure I'm speaking for other American authors whose books are being pirated, too."

"I agree with you," said the lawyer. "You are absolutely right. He's nothing more than a thief. But as his attorney, I am ethically bound to defend his business activities. I could never do otherwise."

"Then I should have a Turkish lawyer to represent me."

"That would be a wise procedure."

Pausing then, the young attorney glanced thoughtfully first at the middle-aged publisher and then at me. I was sure he was seriously considering the thought of suggesting a compromise or perhaps some alternative that would not endanger his relations with his client but at the same time enable him to take advantage of the opportunity to act on my behalf.

"I'll sue the rascal for you—that's the best way to handle this situation," he said bluntly, sitting up erectly. "That'll teach him a lesson to remember."

He pointed his finger directly at the publisher who immediately began smiling and nodding his head in an approving gesture.

"But you couldn't do that," I protested. "That would amount to a conflict of interests. It would be unethical."

"Nonsense," he said at once. "This is Turkey. This is not America or Great Britain. You must listen to me."

The publisher continued to smile and nod while he listened to our conversation with no indication of comprehending what was being said in rapidly spoken English.

"If you did do such a thing," I asked tentatively, "how much would it cost me?"

"My fee would be arranged to your satisfaction. Payable in American dollars or British pounds of course."

Listening with an eager expression while the lawyer spoke to him briefly in Turkish, the publisher then smiled approvingly as he stood up and came forward to shake hands before leaving.

"I'll gladly come back alone to discuss our private matter," the lawyer said aside in a lowered tone of voice. "Would tomorrow morning suit you?"

"I'd rather not do that now," I told him. "I'd have to consult my agent in London before doing anything like that. But I feel sure he will not approve of your representing both the publisher and me. Thank you for your offer to help, though."

"Well, if you ever decide you want me to sue him for you, just remember I'll render my best efforts. As your attorney, I'll be as conscientious as you'll find any lawyer to be anywhere in the world."

He handed me several of his embossed professional cards with the suggestion that I could pass them along to other writers who might be interested in seeking his services.

= 3 =

Two days after the meeting with the Istanbul publisher and the lawyer, having searched without success for other titles of mine that may have been pirated and disappointed for not having succeeded in finding a way to prevent further infringement of copyright, Virginia and I left Istanbul for our final destination before returning home. This was to be Moscow where I looked forward to seeing a number of persons I had known while a correspondent during the German-Russian War and where Virginia looked forward to a visit for the first time.

When we arrived in the Soviet Union, we were met at the Moscow airport by Elena Romanova, who had been a helpful friend in wartime, and by Frieda Lurie who, like Elena, was a deputy commissar in the bureau of the Foreign Commission of the Union of Soviet Writers. We were greeted with flowers and chocolate candy and taken swiftly through passport control and customs. From there, we went by car to the National Hotel where a room facing the Kremlin and Red Square had been reserved for us.

The aging, dingy-yellow National Hotel had been untouched by raiding German aircraft and the original brown carpeting had become more faded and threadbare than I remembered it being in the past.

Shortly after breakfast the next morning our interpreter, a sprightly young woman from the Writers' Union, arrived with instructions to take us first of all to one of the state publishing houses. There I was handed an account of sales of one of my books amounting to more than a hundred thousand copies and a bundle of ruble notes so large that the one way it could be carried was in Virginia's tote-bag. After that, our sightseeing tour was a short one and came to an end when Virginia, loaded down with rubles, suggested that it would be more interesting than viewing the sights to go shopping for jewelry and objects of art. Our young interpreter was quick to approve of the suggestion.

Several times during the next few days we were stopped by grim-faced, pistol-armed militiamen at entrances to shops and museums and ordered to present passports for identification. As I recalled, even in wartime during the Stalin regime there had been much less surveillance of foreigners whereas at this time anyone with a camera was followed and closely observed by plainclothes men and others in uniform. Once Virginia was forbidden to take a photograph of children playing in a park and at another time we were sternly waved away by two militiamen from a grassy plot surrounding a monument.

There were no restrictions imposed on the amount of good food and Georgian champagne available, however, and our friends at the Writers' Union made an effort to find out if Boris, my wartime driver and bodyguard, could be found for a reunion. After a thorough search of records, it was determined that he had been a casualty of German air raids.

Unaccustomed to being subjected to the strict prohibitions and constant surveillance imposed by a military state, Virginia soon began counting the hours until we would be leaving for home. On the morning of our boarding of a Scandinavian Airlines plane for Copenhagen, which was to be our only stop on the way to California, we were sitting in the departure lounge at the Moscow airport with Elena Romanova and Frieda Lurie when Virginia impulsively stood up and took her small Minnox camera from her purse.

Other departing passengers sitting nearby stared at Virginia in amazement while at the same time an armed sentry stood in rigid posture at the departure gate. Fortunately, the sentry was facing the airfield and not the passengers in the lounge.

On bold lettering on the wall, it was proclaimed in several languages, one of them being English, that it was forbidden to take photographs anywhere at the airport and stating that violators were subject to arrest and imprisonment.

Waving their arms excitedly, both Elena and Frieda called to Virginia cautiously in loud whispers to put her camera out of sight at once.

"Virginia! Virginia!" they said urgently. "No! No! Hide that spy camera! Hurry! Please!"

"But I want to have a picture to remember you by," she told them. "Just one picture will do. Please let me. It'll only take a moment."

"Listen to me, Virginia," Elena begged. "You must do as I say. Hide that camera! Hurry!"

Before I could reach her, Virginia had reluctantly put the miniature camera back into her purse. It was just in time, too. When the sentry turned around, the camera was no longer to be seen.

Later, when our airplane was rising from the runway, Virginia, covering her face with her hands, began weeping with anguished sounds. Presently, as her sobbing diminished, she tried to explain with eyes filled with tears why she had been unable to keep from crying.

"It's because I'm so glad to be going home, I suppose," she said in an uneven tone of voice and trying to dry her tears. "Maybe for one thing I'm homesick and maybe, too, I didn't realize how different it would be in Moscow. I'm glad I went, but I became so tense and felt so unwanted. And then at the last minute I was not allowed to take a picture of Elena and Frieda. And now at last to be going home. Maybe I just couldn't keep from crying for joy."

$$= 4 =$$

After having lived serenely atop Twin Peaks in San Francisco for almost three years, a splendid townhouse on Nob Hill was found to be for rent. I was immediately ready to exchange the view from ocean to city to mountains and the ideal seclusion for the opportunity to live on intimate terms with the sights and sounds and distinctive atmosphere of Chinatown, North Beach, Maiden Lane, Union Square, the Tenderloin, and other well-defined neighborhoods in downtown San Francisco.

Our new home, which had been designed by Willis Polk and was owned by Gwen Walkup, had an ivy-walled courtyard at street level, winding stairways, a snug two-person elevator, and a roof garden and greenhouse on the fourth level.

The rented house on Mason Street, which had been available for only a short term, was on one of the steepest inclines in the city and was situated opposite the towering Mark Hopkins Hotel. Our infrequently invited guests, sometimes being Herb Caen, Truman Capote, Shelley Berman, Nevin Busch, and visiting editors and publishers, often arrived huffing and puffing even after having been advised to take a taxi or to walk backward like most native pedestrians were accustomed to doing.

Selfish it probably was, and no doubt offensive to many persons, but I never hesitated to withhold invitations to friends and strangers alike in order to compensate for so much time spent traveling. The allotted time for travel could always be changed at will but six months for writing was fixed and an unalterable house rule.

This meant that plausible excuses sometimes had to be devised on a moment's notice in order to decline invitations from friends as gracefully as possible. Rude and discourteous I may have been, but my selfishness did enable me to go about my writing at any hour of the day or night and without the bane of interruptions.

It was not long after moving to Mason Street that I was satisfied with the final draft of *Jenny by Nature* that I had written following its seasoning while I was abroad. With revisions completed and the novel typed, it was ready to be delivered to Jim Brown when he arrived in San Francisco after visiting several authors in Los Angeles. With the book in hand, Jim left for New York saying Arthur Thornhill, Sr., had asked him several times when Little, Brown could expect it to be sent to them. Relieved to have the novel completed, Virginia and I began immediately to make plans for a long delayed trip to Japan.

Visas in hand and reservations at the Imperial Hotel in Tokyo confirmed, we arrived in Japan in the latter part of January 1960 for what was a memorable sojourn.

Charles Tuttle, my literary agent in Tokyo, with the cooperation of two publishers who had issued translations of some of my novels and short stories, arranged to have me autograph books at several shops the day after our arrival.

Although World War II had been over a long time, there was still lingering antipathy towards Americans among the older Japanese. This was particularly evident where some of the ubiquitous saki bars posted signs in English stating that the premises were off-limits for Americans.

However, the younger generation of Japanese, most of them being students, were avid readers of books by Americans and crowds of eager young men and women sought autographs or permission to take photographs wherever I appeared. In fact, during the entire length of our visit, from early morning until late at night, there were few times when several polite but persistent students were not waiting in the hall of the hotel for Virginia and me to leave or return to our room.

The greater part of an entire day was spent at Waseda University at the invitation of Professor Tatsu to visit with his twenty-two young women students of English. Accompanied by our young interpreter, Toshi Niikura, himself a professor in the English department at another Tokyo university, we went to Waseda in late morning and where we were entertained at great length by the group of smiling young women dressed in elaborate variations of traditional Japanese kimonos.

First there was a lengthy musical recital performed with modern versions of ancient Japanese harps and other stringed instruments. This was followed by group and solo dances, some being demure and sedate, others being as sensual as an unrestrained Hawaiian hula-hula. The remainder of the day's entertainment was devoted to a program of vocal music, recitations of poetry in Japanese and English, and finally at the close of day there was the performance by the twenty-two young women of the elaborately staged traditional Japanese tea ceremony.

Undoubtedly incited by the singing and dancing of the twenty-two girls in Professor Tatsu's English class, I suggested to Toshi Niikura on the way back to the Imperial Hotel that Virginia and I would like for him to arrange for us to visit a geisha house of entertainment.

With a startled expression coming to his face, Toshi hesitated for a long time before making any reply. When he did speak at last, he said he would have to ask his brother who, unlike him, had been a visitor to a geisha house and would know if Virginia would be permitted to enter.

The next morning Toshi told us that his brother, having obtained approval, had arranged for the three of us to go that same evening to one of the most renowned geisha houses in Tokyo.

At some hour after midnight, in an evening of leisurely dining combined with native refreshments, Virginia was saying she was enjoying one of the most delightful times of her life. I thought I was having a pleasant time, too, until I realized I was experiencing the sensation of gradually losing my sensibilities. In other words, I was passing out.

This embarrassing situation occurred when suddenly I was overcome by the exotic music rendered by two of the geisha girls on their formidable, unearthly looking, stringed instruments. Both Virginia and Toshi advised me to close my eyes and recline on the cool, smooth-as-silk, rice straw matting that covered the floor. It was their assumption that I had been overwhelmed by the combined effects of late hours, exhaustion, ear-piercing music, unfamiliar geisha customs, seductive surroundings, and an overabundance of warm rice wine.

After half an hour's rest on the soft matting with a pillow placed under my head by one of the geisha girls, I had recovered enough to accept an offering of more saki but asked that no more geisha house music be played for the remainder of the night.

All the way back to San Francisco a few days later I had moments of wondering why the same music played on similar instruments by both the Waseda students and the geisha girls had had such distinctly disparate effect on me. I was still unable to think of a satisfactory explanation when I arrived home and telephoned Jim Brown in New York to find out if he had succeeded in obtaining a better contract with improved terms when he delivered the manuscript of *Jenny by Nature* to Little, Brown. Jim's matter-of-fact reply was so unexpected that it was a long time before I had any further thoughts about the mystifying effects of Japanese music on me.

What had happened in Boston was that the current editor-in-chief for Little, Brown had curtly rejected Jim's request to revise the existing contract and Jim, with equal abruptness, had snatched the manuscript from the editor's desk and had taken it back to New York. Evidently Jim had been affronted and so severely that he did not wait to let Arthur Thornhill have an opportunity to intervene.

There was silence over the phone while I tried to recover from the effect of having heard the startling news from my literary agent and at the same time wonder about the publication of my books in the future. In addition to that, then came the recollection of having changed publishers several times in the past and that left me wondering why it had to happen again. James Oliver Brown was an astute businessman in his field and a loyal protector of the rights of his authors. However, he was easily offended and when aroused to anger he often made life difficult for both himself and others.

"Jim, what's going to happen now?" I finally asked.

"Don't worry, Skinny," he answered assuringly. "You have a new publisher. One of the best. There's nothing to lose and everything to gain. It's all been arranged with Farrar, Straus and Giroux."

"How did that happen?"

"I did it."

"Are you sure?"

"Of course I'm sure—James Oliver Brown is always sure," he said at once. "A new and better contract is being drawn right now. When are you coming to meet Roger Straus?"

"Jim, I've already met Roger Straus. I've known him for several years."

"Then hurry to New York and become reacquainted. Roger wants to talk to you. He's very pleased that you're going to be one of his authors. He wants to have a big cocktail party for you and make an announcement about your new novel."

Several moments of silence followed before I could say anything.

"All right, Jim," I told him then. "I'll be seeing you."

Chapter Twenty Seven

WITH THE PUBLICATION of *Jenny by Nature* scheduled by Farrar, Straus and Giroux for 1961, I had postponed until later in the year a trip to New York to meet with Roger Straus. Instead of going there immediately after the new contract had been drawn, I preferred to stay at home and work steadily on the novel to follow. The title of the next book was to be *Close to Home* and I wanted to have a satisfactory preliminary draft finished before Virginia and I left on our next trip abroad. This was to be a tour of Northern Europe that had been planned to begin early in the year.

Two weeks before leaving for Europe on the first day of February, the final few days of work on the novel-in-progress had to be disrupted when Al Manuel, persuasive as usual, induced me to take a hurried trip to the Warner Brothers studio in Burbank.

Al had sold Warner's the film rights to *Claudelle Inglish* the year before and now that it was in production he was worried about the quality of the motion picture. He said he had visited the set at the studio several times and was in no manner pleased with what he had observed. And as a result of his visits, Al blamed everybody at the studio for indifferent performances, including not only the producer and screenwriter, the director and cast, but also the hairdresser and the costume designer. It was Al's hope that my presence would inspire everybody concerned to strive to make better efforts to produce a film of superior quality.

After a lengthy afternoon visit to the sound stage in Burbank, during which I had a pleasant but unfulfilling conversation first with the director, Gordon Douglas, and then with Diane McBain, the featured actress in the title role, I left for home in San Francisco depressed and feeling that little could be done to prevent *Claudelle Inglish* from being a mediocre film version of the novel.

In full agreement with Al Manuel, it was my judgment that the story had not been properly adapted and prepared for the screen. And ever afterward, as advised by Al, I never went to see the completed film at a theater and avoided watching it on television.

When Virginia and I left for Denmark, it was my good fortune to be able to leave behind the greater part of my unpleasant experience of having witnessed a portion of the making of a wretched film of one of my novels. Moreover, during the next few days in Scandinavia I was stricken with enough distress to relieve my mind of all remaining displeasure about the motion picture being made in Burbank.

Our first few days in Copenhagen, many hours of the visit being spent with Edith Kellerich, my Danish agent, were agreeable enough. However, the time would have been more pleasantly remembered if Virginia and I had not indulged ourselves at a feast that included servings of oysters on the half-shell. Even though we did not feel well or sleep well that night, the penalty for eating tainted oysters was not fully imposed until later the next day in Norway.

The disastrous aftermath of the oyster assault began at seven o'clock in the evening at a reception and dinner at the Grand Hotel in Oslo and did not end until almost five hours later when it had finally run its course. The dinner for fourteen guests had been arranged by Harold Greig, the Norwegian publisher, and the highly-regarded specialty of the country, smoked salmon, was served often and abundantly.

Virginia was seated next to the affable publisher and I sat facing them across the flower-decorated table. Whether it was the sight of the colorful salmon, or the pungent aroma of it, there was no doubt about the immediate effect of its existence on our plates.

Before taking one bite of the salmon, Virginia hastily excused herself and went with a lively step to the ladies' retiring room. Many minutes later when she returned to the table, her usual faintly tanned face had become as pale as chalk and her distinctly animated expression had vanished completely.

With spirited conversation and moments of carefree laughter resounding from one end of the long table to the other, Virginia and I were striving as best we could to keep from calling attention to the discomfort we were enduring as the result of eating the polluted oysters the night before.

With a brave gesture, I took the first bite of smoked salmon. And it was only moments later when I was on my feet gagging as I raced to the men's room to relieve my upset stomach. At the end of almost two hours, I had abruptly left the table three times with unrelenting nausea.

Virginia was combating her distress in an entirely different manner. Frequently urged by Harold Greig to have another serving of the highly prized salmon, Virginia would slowly take a morsel to her lips but no farther and then, adroitly concealing it with her napkin, dispose of it under the table. While evidently none of the other guests observed her in the act, I was quite sure that one of the waiters had detected her method of disposing of several unwanted servings of the food. By the end of the evening, the waiter's glance and mine, both accompanied by a partly suppressed smile, had been met across the table several times.

With the passing of another twenty-four hours, Virginia and I had fully recovered from the misery of the previous night and were enjoying a hearty fare of sandwiches and beer. This time we were guests of Carlotta Frahm, my Norwegian literary agent, at her home in the countryside a few miles from Oslo. This memorable occasion provided an introduction to a long-established Scandinavian custom that until then I had not known to be in existence.

Shortly before midnight, which I expected to be the end of a pleasant evening, I began to wonder how soon Virginia and I, along with the other half-a-dozen guests, would be returning to the city. An hour later, at the time of another serving of sandwiches and beer, I cautiously asked Carlotta in a lowered voice how much longer we would be staying.

"Oh, it's much too early to think of leaving," she said with a bright smile. "I thought you knew—I should have told you. This is February, deep in our Norwegian winter, and we must celebrate our long dark nights. It's an age-old tradition for us to stay up all night long several times during the winter when clouds obscure the moon and stars and celebrate with sandwiches and beer. These nights are as much of our lives as the short white nights of summer. Celebrating like this is our way of rendering homage to our heritage. Now, you wouldn't want us to stop celebrating only halfway through this long dark night, would you?"

Several days later in Stockholm at a dark night dinner in a restaurant where we were guests of Bo Wahlstrom, the Swedish publisher, I was better prepared to stay awake at another night-long celebration. And this time no explanation of the Swedish version of the wintertime custom was necessary.

Later, in Helsinki, when I inquired, I was told that the custom of celebrating a similar tradition in Finland would not exist because saunas were preferable and available every night of the year. It was inferred that the taking of saunas was much more healthy and civilized than the practice of dark-nighting.

It was in Finland that I became acquainted with the world-wide activities of the United States Information Service, a bureau of the Department of State, and afterward for several years I was to serve as a volunteer speaker on tours in Europe and Asia. The activities of the USIS appealed to me not primarily because of any political ideology involved but basically because I could come in contact with readers and other writers.

As a result of my meeting with students at the USIS library in Helsinki, I was asked to make a similar appearance in Germany at the Hamburg USIS library. Still impressed by the midwinter celebrations in Norway and Sweden, I asked Henry Miller, who also was at an USIS library reception in Hamburg, if he had ever had the experience of dark-nighting anywhere in the world.

Knowing of Henry's familiarity with night life of Paris, which had been apparent in some of his writings, it had been interesting to know that he then was engaged in a lengthy program of research in the night life of Hamburg. His reply to my question was not surprising.

"I've heard of that primitive pastime," he said, "but it wouldn't be for me. Why wait for night? If you find a congenial partner, why would you want to postpone bedmating till wintertime?"

= 2 =

My long delayed meeting with Roger Straus, following the signing of the publishing contract that had been negotiated by James Oliver Brown, finally took place at the Farrar, Straus and Giroux office in lower Manhattan. Any displeasure on Roger's part that might have resulted from several postponements by me was in no manner evident when I delivered the completed manuscript of *The Last Night of Summer*.

As it was, Roger may have been so pleased to have in hand the next novel called for under the terms of our agreement that he was immediately enthusiastic when I proposed the publication of a nonfiction book.

The proposed book was to be a volume of American travel observations and impressions with text by me and illustrated with pencil drawings by Virginia Caldwell. It was agreed that the title of the collaboration would be *Around About America*.

For many months, I had been subjected to numerous distractions that had occurred while I was striving to maintain my usual pace and tempo of writing. In particular, I had been determined not to let an excessive amount of European travel interfere with any plans I wanted to make for work on novels and short stories. But a number of events, some welcomed and others deplored, were time-consuming and demanding of special attention.

One of the distracting events, although one that was never regretted, was of my own making. After two years of pleasant living in the comfortable townhouse on Mason Street in San Francisco, I decided that it was time for Virginia and me to have a home as owners and not as renters. This was when we bought a newly built, seven-room, one-story, California ranch-style house situated eastward beyond Oakland and Berkeley in the rolling palomino-colored hills near Orinda and Walnut Creek overlooking Rheem Valley.

This time, not forgetting the trauma on the three occasions in the past when I was divested of homes in Mount Vernon, Darien, and Santa Fe, I wisely made provision to forestall a repetition in the future.

This was accomplished by having the deed to our Orinda home recorded in Virginia's name as her separate property. In doing so, I was making a light-hearted jest of not tempting villainous fate to see to it that my happy marriage to Virginia would not remain solidly intact.

A financial settlement, entailing the division of community property, which included the proceeds from the sale of the Tucson house, had left me with a meager amount of money at the time of my divorce from June. From that time onward, expenses had to be paid from current royalty income and accumulating a reserve in savings had not been an easy task. The decision to buy the Orinda house was the result of Virginia's expression of confidence in our ability to increase our savings in the future.

The move from San Francisco to Orinda had been completed without much loss of time when later it became necessary to prepare for another trip to Europe. Preparations included passport renewals, selecting seasonal clothing for Europe, travel reservations, and charging a part-time secretary with the duty of promptly paying utility bills and making correct replies to important letters in the mail.

This particular journey was urged upon me by two of my publishers, the New American Library in New York and William Heinemann in London, for the chore of appearing in person for promotional purposes at the Frankfurt Book Fair.

While plans were being made for travel by Virginia and me to Germany, the European director of the United States Information Service, Morrill Cody asked me to spend ten days appearing at USIS libraries and local universities in the Balkans. The cities to be visited in Yugoslavia were Belgrade, Zagreb, and Ljubljana. In Bulgaria, Sophia was the only place to be visited. I was told that I would receive per diem payment for living expenses in addition to the usual small fee for lectures.

It was my first visit to the annual Frankfurt Book Fair and I found it to be less a celebration of books of the world on exhibition than it was an orgy of eating and drinking from midmorning to midnight. Publishers from nations of the world were so deeply engrossed in trading language rights and making intricate deals that for almost an entire week few of them ever left the restaurants and bars of the Frankfurterhof to walk the short distance to the exhibition hall to inspect the display of their own publications.

The ten days Virginia and I spent in Yugoslavia and Bulgaria gave us the opportunity to recover from the wearying week in Germany. We were in such good spirits by then we did not object to listening to the suggestion that, instead of our waiting another week in the Balkans until it was time to leave for Milan and Rome for the USIS, we could travel to Italy by way of Moscow.

The inducement that appealed to Virginia was the prospect of having an opportunity to spend a day in Leningrad looking at the famous collection of paintings in the Hermitage.

We did visit Leningrad and Virginia had her day at the Hermitage. Then came the day before we were to leave Moscow for Italy when there was an unexpected meeting with Elaine and John Steinbeck. It was the third time we had met abroad accidentally following the previous meeting in Mexico and on board ship while traveling to England. John, like me, was on a tour of duty for the United States Information Service.

It was immediately arranged for the four of us to have dinner in our sitting room at the National Hotel. John and I soon agreed, since we were unprepared, that it would be wise to postpone until a future meeting the unfinished business of giving our fictitious, teen-age, gray-haired prodigy a suitable name and choosing a title for his yet unpublished novel.

Later in the evening we entertained two young journalists from Kiev whose interviews, when published, were probably enlivened by John's audacious humor and satiric comments. Too late it was then but it undoubtedly would have given credibility to the introduction to the world of our mythical young novelist if we had been prepared to let the journalists from Kiev make the announcement.

During the interviews, there had been a constant and abundant serving of caviar and Georgian champagne by waiters but with an ample supply of rubles that could not be have been spent otherwise before leaving the Soviet Union there was no concern. With so much champagne available, the two waiters who were serving us happily accepted the invitation to join us in offering toasts to various causes in the world.

The two journalists from Kiev left shortly before midnight and it was less than an hour after that when Elaine and John decided it was time for them to return to their hotel in another part of the city.

There were no taxis available on the street at such a late hour and John asked the night manager of the National Hotel to help obtain transportation to the other hotel. John was told that since it was after midnight it was too late to call a taxi and that he and Elaine would have to walk the distance of nearly two miles.

In protest against the indifference of the hotel manager, John went to the street and lay down in front of the entrance to the National.

Presently a late performance ended at the Bolshoi Ballet theater nearby and a large group of people gathered around John where he lay in the middle of the street.

As reliably related by Elaine later, one of the persons in the group around John pointed at him.

"I know who he is!" the man said in English. "That's Hemingway the American writer! I know what he looks like with that beard!"

While several others in the group were loudly speaking in Russian, John raised himself on his elbows and shook his head vigorously.

"Hemingway, *nyet!*" he said. "Steinbeck, *da!*"

Another English-speaking Russian asked John if he had been knocked down by an automobile.

John said he had not been hurt and that it was his way of protesting against the treatment he had received from the hotel manager. At that point, one of the men came forward and grasped John's hand to help him to his feet.

"I know you really are Steinbeck the American writer," he was told. "You look like your pictures. And you have a better beard than Hemingway. Come with me. I'll take you in my car wherever you want to go."

$$= 3 =$$

The field trips to gather material for *Around About America* were searches for the unknown in regional byways from the Atlantic to the Pacific. The busy highways will always lead to the hurly-burly of a metropolis where people have no time for strangers. However, in the hinterland there will be many times when an act of human kindness rarely fails to be offered to friend and stranger alike.

During our unhurried trek across the United States with portable typewriter and drawing pencils there were many instances of unexpected offerings of kindly feeling and goodwill. Among them were:

Item—We arrived in Bluefield in the soft-coal region of West Virginia in late afternoon to find that every available room in the city, as well as for miles around, was occupied by people attracted to a miners' convention. The owner of one of the motels with no vacancy explained that the reason for the city to be overcrowded was because people from all sections of the state, and many of them with no interest in coal mining, had come to see a parade of many young women in a beauty contest for the selection of Miss Bituminous Coal.

The friendly motel owner offered to telephone a friend who operated a small motel about forty miles north of Bluefield. We were told that there was only one room available there and that it could be held for one hour— or maybe two hours if we were reliable people.

Leaving Bluefield immediately, we drove through drizzle and fog in the dark night over narrow, winding, mountain roads in time to claim our room. When we left Bluefield, the very helpful motel owner there said if the room forty miles away had not been held for us, we should come back and he would somehow find a place for us to sleep for the night. He did not say so, but he probably would have found two cots somewhere and let us sleep in the motel office.

Item—In the heat of summer, we were in the Imperial Valley near the California-Mexico border where hundreds of acres of watermelons and cantaloupes were ripening on the vine as fast as crews of harvesters could load them on trucks. We had seen large piles of melons at markets in Calexico that were either culls or overripe and had been rejected for shipment out of the state. Stopping at a melon field where scores of workers were harvesting melons, Virginia immediately began making sketches of the scene. When the owner arrived, I asked him to sell us one of the delicious-looking melons. He said the crop had been bought by a wholesaler and, while he could not sell us a melon, he would be glad to give us all we wanted.

Instead of one jumbo-size melon, dozens of them were placed in our car. When the back seat was full, others were put into the trunk until we had enough melons to stock a supermarket.

The owner's parting remark was that if we wrote about his melons and drew pictures of them for publication we were entitled to have as many as we could carry away. We did have so many of them that after sharing with the manager and all the maids at the motel where we were staying there were a few left over to give to surprised tourists. A comment by a suspicious tourist was to say that the melons were too perfect to have been bought from a local market so they probably had been raided from one of the nearby farms.

Item—He was a retired Basque sheep rancher, nearing eighty years old, who had holdings of Nevada grazing lands probably as large in acreage as the average county elsewhere in the United States. Now wealthy in land and money, he and his wife had left the range and came to Winnemucca to live in a small brick cottage surrounded by a white-painted paling fence. Their married children lived in similar unpretentious homes in other parts of Winnemucca.

The rancher had not been wealthy earlier in life. He had come from the Basque Provinces of Spain when he was eighteen years old to work as a sheepherder to pay for his passage to the United States. His wife had been a mail-order bride also from the Basque Provinces.

When Virginia and I were invited into the family's comfortable country kitchen, it was soon to be mealtime. The rancher's wife, wearing a hand-stitched apron that was frayed and faded after many washings and she herself adorned with huge diamond earrings, was cooking a Basque lamb stew.

The rancher immediately began pressing upon us glass after glass of Picon

Punch. With an expression of deep concern on his range-weathered face, he began urging me to work diligently while I was still able and without fail week after week to save earnings to invest equally in land and Bank of America bonds and common stock. With that advice accepted gratefully, it was then his wife's turn, her dangling diamonds constantly sparkling, to advise Virginia that the most nourishing and least expensive food anyone could cook and serve was Basque lamb stew. A recipe for preparing the stew was given to Virginia as we were leaving.

With the completion of the text and drawings for *Around About America*, and already planning for the writing of the next nonfiction book, which was to be *In Search of Bisco*, I was again without a literary agent in the United States. James Oliver Brown and I, both of us stubborn and steadfast in our determination to have our own way, had agreed in a friendly manner to discontinue our association as agent and author.

Jim had been ill for a year or longer and his tolerance for what probably were excessive demands was completely exhausted. The aftermath of a serious attack of hepatitis clung to him tenaciously month after month and nothing seemed to be effective in relieving his distress mentally or physically.

In the past, Marcel Duhamel and Claude Gallimard had suggested to Jim that the Chinese needle, or acupuncture, should be seriously considered as a method of treatment but Jim would have none of it.

Regrettably, our previously pleasant association came to a sudden end when Jim insisted that I would have to pay the salary of an additional secretary in his New York office to relieve him and his staff of an overburden of work performed for me. His reasoning, firm and uncompromising, was that otherwise he would be unable to give adequate attention to the other authors he represented.

Reasonable Jim's demand may have been, but nevertheless I insisted that if I paid the salary of a full-time secretary she should work in my office and not in the office of James Oliver Brown. Our friendly parting was toasted many times with martinis in the years to follow.

I was in need of a literary agent for many months but the selection of a new representative was delayed for a long time. My concern was that I wanted to be sure that my next agent would not bring upon me in the future the anguish and disruption and confusion that had been my lot in the past.

It was during this period without an agent that I took it upon myself to sign a contract for the writing and publication of another book for children.

I was offered the opportunity to write the child's story for a series of illus-trated books edited by Louis Untermeyer and published in New York and London by Collier-Macmillan. While writing the story and for a long time afterward I had the pleasant thought that Louis Untermeyer, by commis-sioning me to contribute to the series, was rewarding me for having taken his earlier advice to devote myself to the writing of prose and not poetry.

I never regretted having acted as my own agent but I was glad when I could turn all such matters over to my next representative. This was to be the agency of McIntosh and Otis, Inc.

Many years earlier I had met Mavis McIntosh and Elizabeth Otis in a casual manner at a publisher's cocktail party. Now, following the retire-ment of Mavis from the agency, I continued to hear much praise of Eliza-beth Otis as an author's representative and I was pleased when it developed that we were acceptable to one another. Afterward, following Elizabeth, I was fortunate to receive the advice and attention of Patricia Myrer and Eugene Winick as successors to Elizabeth within that same firm.

Chapter Twenty Eight

AS THOUGH HE THOUGHT I had so little to do that much of my life was being wasted by long intervals of lassitude, Roger Straus proposed and then relentlessly drove me to undertake going on a lecture tour.

This project obligated me to appear and speak at a number of colleges and universities from coast to coast as arranged by the W. Colston Leigh lecture bureau. The first tour was scheduled for the month of February 1965 and subsequent tours were planned for that month in the two years that followed.

At the end of that period of three years, I gladly admitted to Roger that it had been a worthwhile experience and I thanked him for having urged me to take to the lecture circuit. By then, it did not matter that what he had done was to send me on tour to promote the sale of my books published by Farrar, Straus and Giroux and not for my own pleasure. The opportunity to meet students throughout the United States and to hear them express various attitudes relating to political and social problems of the world was of lasting value to me.

Other than being disinclined to expose myself as an unqualified and often inarticulate public speaker, I had not been inclined to interrupt necessary travel and investigation I was anxious to do in order to complete two books of nonfiction that meants so much to me.

The first of these books was *In Search of Bisco*. This was to be a book of observations concerned with the violent era of integration in the South and the changing relations between blacks and whites in American life.

The second book, having the title of *In the Shadow of the Steeple*, was devoted to my observations of the practice of evangelical religion, and its excesses, in the Southern states. This book was being written as a tribute to my father and was a celebration of his differing point of view in the land of the WASP.

I was soon to discover that the domestic lecture circuit was the most physically tiring and mentally oppressive of all my varied experiences in life. And that included opposing coal miners on the football field and contending with college calculus examinations.

My first professional speaking engagement in the United States had been a shaky performance on the evening of February 1, 1965, at the Library of Congress, Washington, D.C. The fee for the lecture had been provided by the Whittall Poetry and Literary Society.

As fate would have it, a few hours before the time for the lecture to begin the Washington radio stations began broadcasing warnings of an impending blizzard and residents were advised to stay at home that night. Only a very few persons ignored the storm warnings by coming to the auditorium. However, as it was explained to me later in the evening, the purpose of the lecture was not to have me appear before a large audience but only to have my talk recorded for the archives of the Library of Congress.

By the time I had concluded my short career as a public speaker, I had appeared at seventy-two colleges and universities from Fairbanks, Alaska, to San Juan, Puerto Rico, and from Boston to Los Angeles. Each engagement had been a one-night stand. It was only when I was writer-in-residence at Dartmouth College for six weeks that I spent enough time to become better acquainted with students on a campus.

There were some incidents along the way that were to become unforgettable. One of these occurred when my wife and I boarded an airplane in Kalamazoo, Michigan, in a snowstorm at midnight for the scheduled twenty-minute flight to Detroit and landed there three hours later after first having landed by mistake in the blizzard at some other airport.

Then there was the time when I left the reading copy of my lecture in a hotel room and, with not enough time to retrieve it, I had to deliver as much of it as possible from memory. And not to be forgotten was the occasion when I was assigned to sleep in a girls' college dormitory and I lay awake most of the night listening to the laughter and intimate conversation of two girls in the adjoining thin-walled room.

Of all the questions asked by students, the most frequent one put to me was such a difficult one to answer that often I had to rely upon the advice given me many times by my maternal grandmother.

The often-asked question was this:

"What is the best way to learn to be a writer?"

Quoting my grandmother, I would say:

"What is the best way to find a needle in a haystack? Look for it, of course."

There were many occasions, though, when flippant replies to sincere questions were uncalled for and were to be avoided. There were times, especially late in the evening after a lecture, when several interested students would want to gather, most of us with mugs of beer in hand, to discuss the proper study and practice of writing. With all formality aside, I would then talk about my personal concept of writing as a profession.

My contribution to the group for thought and debate would be what I have come to consider as being the four necessary elements for achievement. In order of importance, in my way of thinking, these elements are: talent, desire, determination, and luck. I realize this is an uncommon combination and one that is not easily defended. But I do deem it to be realistic and worthy of consideration by a young person with the ambition to be an author.

It was inevitable that my career as a perennial performer on the lecture circuit would come to an end at the conclusion of the third February tour.

The preparation and the performance and the necessary period of recovery before, during, and after a month's tour prevented me from being at my typewriter for two or three months of the year. That became unacceptable. And in the end, as a person who wanted to experience all facets of life, excepting those that were physically and ethically harmful, I was grateful for the opportunity to hear about and appreciate the fears and aspirations of the younger generation of Americans.

My decision to discontinue the annual lecture tour came at a time when Colston Leigh and I were less friendly in our relationship as client and lecture agent than we had been in previous years. This was a situation that had been brought about by mutual dissatisfaction concerning a lecture engagement Colston had arranged for me at the University of Hawaii.

I had forced the cancellation of my appearance in Honolulu by refusing to travel via air from Seattle to Honolulu to New Orleans with only five hours allotted for sleep on land during a period of two days. Both Colston and I were probably restrained by the realization that our resentment was of equal intensity. Otherwise, our parting might have been with much harsher recriminations.

= 2 =

In the Shadow of the Steeple, an apology for having rejected the principles of organized religious practice, was completed and the manuscript submitted to Farrar, Straus and Giroux shortly after the publication of *In Search of Bisco*.

Promptly came word from Roger Straus that he did not consider my most recent book one that he would want to publish. The rejection did not void any existing contract because my pledge to Roger's publishing company did not include books of nonfiction. Other than that, the last of the three books of fiction already published had fulfilled the terms of the original agreement as negotiated by James Oliver Brown and, consequently, our contract was no longer an obligation.

I had previously sent a duplicate copy of the manuscript to Laurence Pollinger in London and within days of the rejection by Roger Straus I received words from Laurence that *In the Shadow of the Steeple* had been accepted by William Heinemann for publication in England. Laurence said the British publisher was particularly pleased to publish a book that had such inherent implications in its title.

I could not quarrel with Roger Straus about his decision not to publish the book in the United States, since he had the right to accept or reject any book submitted to him, but I was never able to discover the underlying reason for his decision.

Throughout that decade, there was widespread controversy and debate regarding the influence of white Anglo-Saxon Protestantism in American society, from which the derogatory acronym WASP had been derived, and I assumed that Roger was fearful that my observations would be interpreted as being an approval of its existence.

If called upon, I would have defended the results of my observations of excessive religious fervor by referring the reader to scenes in the book that could only be satirical in effect.

One of the examples would be an exhibition of dozens of worshipers rolling in the aisles of a church with cries of ecstacy and rolling in the aisles not because the pastor had told a very funny joke but because they had abandoned themselves to the throes of coming-through.

Another example I would have cited was the exhibition staged by a long-bearded preacher with a croquet mallet in hand and hitting himself on the head with painful blows as if it were a baton being used to direct the tempo of the organ music and accompanying moans of joy from the congregation.

Like most publishers, and rightly so, Roger Straus could have refrained from issuing any book that might have aroused antagonism amoung churchmen of various faiths. Religion being a subject that requires delicate handling, Catholics, Jews, and Protestants alike are quick to retaliate and seek revenge by boycotting any publisher who offends them.

During the time that I was writing the book that Roger had rejected, Victor Weybright had begun pressing me to let New American Library be the original publisher of all the novels I would write in the future. Victor insisted that I owed allegiance to NAL for having issued all my books in paperback editions and should acknowledge my gratitude by giving his company the right to publish my books of fiction in both hardcover and softcover editions.

I was well aware that Victor and his associate, Kurt Enoch, deserved all the thanks and consideration I could offer. Printings of several of my novels and volumes of short stories amounted to millions of copies in paperback editions. No pressure had ever been put upon me to change or eliminate anything I had written and NAL had never hesitated to defend my work when charges of obscenity were directed at a book of mine. However, I hesitated to give up my association with a solidly managed publisher, as was Farrar, Straus and Giroux, in favor of a company that never before had published a novel in a hardcover edition.

In this period of indecision, I consulted with Elizabeth Otis many times for advice. Elizabeth had not negotiated any of my contracts with Roger Straus, all such agreements having originated with Jim Brown, and as an experienced literary agent she was careful not to disturb any existing good relations between author and publisher.

In effect, Elizabeth Otis's position was that she wanted me to indicate how, where, and when I would feel most comfortable as an author. I was confident that when I made the decision, she would see to it that I was well protected by the terms of a new agreement.

My friendship with Victor Weybright had extended over a long period of time and, combined with my gratitude for his having circulated paperback editions of my books by the million, I was not an unwilling listener to his earnest entreaties. There had been several meetings in New York, a number of telephone conversations and, finally, Victor came to see me in California. By then, he was anxious to reach an agreement without further delay.

Well aware of Roger Straus' rejection of *In the Shadow of the Steeple*, Victor offered to publish the book in the United States in return for my granting New American Library all rights of publication to my future novels. It was clearly stated that the nonfiction book would be published by a company not affiliated with NAL. It was then revealed that a company bearing his name was being organized and would soon begin publishing books in hardcover editions.

I failed to wonder why Victor was so anxious for me to agree to have NAL publish my novels in both hardcover and softcover editions when he was organizing a company of his own. It was not until much later that the reason was clearly revealed. That occurred when it was made known that Victor and Kurt had been negotiating for the sale of New American Library for an enormous amount of money. By the time the sale was completed, I had become convinced that the value of their company, and the sale price, had been enhanced to some extent by the gaining of rights to my future novels.

And so thus it was that once more I changed publishers. I immediately delivered to NAL the completed manuscript of *Miss Mama Aimee* and soon after that I finished writing *Summertime Island*. Four other novels followed in as many years.

And so to what end came *In the Shadow of the Steeple*?

In unequivocal terms, Victor Weybright stated that his new company would not publish the book with the title I had given it.

"I must be frank and firm about this, Skinny," Victor said. "I've been in the publishing business for many years now and I know from experience that it would be utter folly—yes, absolutely an assured disaster—to put a book with that ominous title on the market. Believe me, I know what I'm saying."

"Why, Victor?" I asked in protest. "Why should it?"

"Because readers will avoid reading any book that bears the slightest suggestion of being a religious tract. The people with an emotional devotion to their personal religious beliefs don't want to risk having their tranquility disturbed by reading comments and observations by somebody who may have persuasive beliefs differing from their own."

"But not everybody has a closed mind about such things."

"Look here, Skinny," big, jolly, rotund Victor said. "You may be right in theory but you're wrong in facts. If you could make a survey, you'd be greatly surprised to find out how many people who do not go to church or make a show of their religious beliefs really pray and pray zealously in secret."

"Well, if you win this argument and have your way," I said, "what will be the title of the book."

"*Deep South*."

"Is that good?"

"It's safe."

= 3 =

Yes, again. I moved.

I had been told at the conclusion of a routine physical examination that I was the victim of emphysema. My only hope for the future, the doctor said, was for me to move as soon as possible to a semi-tropical climate where swimming daily the year around would retard the progress of my affliction.

Both Virginia and I being familiar with various regions of Florida, we decided to go house-hunting in the central part of the state and hoped to find a house we liked in a small town on the Gulf of Mexico. The place selected for our search was Dunedin in the end. After several days, we had become disappointed to find that all available houses for sale were too small or too large or were in undesirable locations.

Our desperate search for a place to live ended early one morning when Virginia came upon a builder who was pouring cement for the foundation of a house he was going to offer for sale as soon as it was completed. Agreeing to Virginia's changes in design, the builder altered the blueprints, widened the foundation, and made provision for a swimming pool. Five months later we left foggy Orinda and moved into our new Dunedin home in a day of Florida sunshine.

Shortly afterward, a reputable emphysema specialist in Florida informed me that my ailment was nothing more than ordinary chronic bronchitis and that I should not aggravate my condition by swimming in water unless heated to body temperature. Having no intention of ever going to such an extreme, I was tempted to fill the pool with dirt and gravel and send the bill to the California doctor who had made the erroneous diagnosis in the beginning of it all.

Comfortably settled in our Dunedin home, we soon decided to plant a hedge on each side of our one-acre lot that would grow to a height of five or six feet within a reasonable length of time. A local nurseryman suggested viburnum, saying that, in addition to being a glowing tropical green in color, it also would provide the quickest growth for our purpose.

The knee-high nursery stock was transplanted on a drizzly afternoon and that same night the rains came. A few days later we left home for an extended visit to Dartmouth College, at the invitation of Edward Connerly Lathem, the librarian, to attend an exhibition of books and manuscripts I had donated to Baker Library. After our stay in New Hampshire, and a lengthy tour of Northern New England by automobile, we returned to Dunedin to find the flourishing, proliferous, luxuriant wayfaring plants were already waist-high and in need of immediate trimming and shaping.

But that was only the beginning. All summer long I was constantly trimming and pruning the viburnum, often on a stepladder and sometimes wearing a raincoat during the afternoon thunderstorms, in an effort to keep the overnight growth from shooting higher than my head.

Eventually, the wayfaring bushes became stabilized at the height they were destined to grow from the beginning. That occurred at the same time of the great banana uprising at the rear of the lot that was excessively watered by a spring and by frequent tropical deluges.

The great banana uprising was the unfortunate result of our having transplanted a single tubful of banana roots from a nearby grove that was being replaced by a shopping center. The transplanting had been done during a heavy downpour of rain and the roots were buried in the soggy ground at the rear of our property. By the end of the first week, the roots had sprouted in the fertile dark loam and soon there were thriving stalks racing upward to reach their intended height of about fifteen feet.

The pods of blossoms on the luxuriant foliage were soon transformed into tiny green fingers of bananas and that was when my caretaking became much more of an arduous task than had been my struggle with the wayward viburnum.

This was at a stage in the growth of finger-size bananas when, simultaneously with the bearing of fruit, roots began spreading in all directions, new sprouts burst through the earth, and the quickly maturing stalks had to be cut down. The fully grown stalks, thick as a gallon jug and heavy as a slab of stone, had to be removed after one bearing of fruit in order to prevent a horde of large red ants from coming to feast on the sugar-sweet pulp of the stalks and then stay to multiply and establish an acre-size colony.

As time went on, I tried by various means to persuade some of our neighbors to help me stop the spreading of the voracious banana roots by digging up a few tubfuls to transplant on their lots. After observing the struggle I was having with my grove, not one of them was interested in my offer.

Ernie Harwell, the master of radio broadcasting for the Detroit Tigers baseball club, and his brother, Richard Harwell, the University of Georgia librarian, took one look at my rampaging banana grove and politely declined to have anything to do with it.

Dan Rowan, who had ample acreage to grow bananas at his Manasota Key vacation home, and who always had been exceedingly friendly when we would meet at a nightclub where he was performing, rejected with emphatic amusement my appeal to him to take away a few tubfuls of banana roots.

And even normally gracious Roscoe Fawcett, who as a sales executive had distributed more of my books than anyone else in the business, flatly refused without even an apology to take a single tub of banana roots to transplant on his Florida estate.

I had been asked by the United States Information Service to go on another tour in Europe. This time the itinerary was limited to a few cities, these being Oslo, Stockholm, Milan, Amsterdam, and London, and only two weeks of time would be required for the trip. Before leaving Dunedin, I had asked the friendly nurseryman to do his best to find somebody who would remove every stalk and root of the finger-size banana grove from our property.

When we returned to Dunedin from Europe, there was a much larger spread of bananas than there had been when we left home. The first thing the nurseryman said was that I should have asked for his advice before transplanting a single banana root in the beginning. Then he told me that I had the choice of doing one of two things since nobody in his right mind would dig up the roots and duplicate my mistake on his own lot.

"This is what you can do," the nurseryman told me. "If you want to spend the money, you can bring in some heavy earth-moving equipment and end up with a hole in the ground big enough to bury all the elephants in the circus. That's one choice. Or you can wait till somebody wants to build a supermarket here and they'll pave every inch of your land for a parking lot and choke the cussed bananas to extinction."

Chapter Twenty-Nine

AFTER PREVIOUSLY COMPLETING A term of six weeks as writer-in-residence at Dartmouth College, I was asked early in 1971 by Edward Lathem to sit for a portrait to be hung in Baker Library on the campus. I assumed that the purpose of having the portrait painted was to enliven the prosaic display of books and manuscripts in the Caldwell Collection and I willingly agreed to do so without further discussion.

At the same time, I had assumed that the portrait would be painted by an American artist in the United States. Several weeks later Ed Lathem informed me with great enthusiasm that a highly regarded British artist had been commissioned to paint the portrait in England.

Fortunately, I was planning to meet with Laurence Pollinger and his son Gerald in London in October and from there Virginia and I expected to travel to Japan where it had been arranged by the USIS for me to appear at several universities in Tokyo and Kyoto. Since the distance from London to Tokyo was approximately the same in either direction, east or west, we had decided to travel through the Middle East.

The Weather Shelter had recently been published in England by Michael Joseph and *The Earnshaw Neighborhood* was the next novel to be published there. After a lengthy and very pleasant meeting with the Pollingers,

Laurence and Gerald, I was then ready to begin sitting every morning and every second afternoon for a week in the studio of John Gilroy on Holland Park Road, Kensington.

All through the tiring ordeal of trying to maintain a rigid posture in the unheated studio, I was promising myself that I would never sit for another portrait. In the end, looking at the figure on canvas, I was very pleased at the sight of the new suit I was wearing, which had been bought in Clearwater, Florida, but a hurried glance at my own likeness was sufficient unto itself.

The day before we were to leave for our first stop in Asia, Lulu and Ernie Harwell of Detroit and Dunedin arrived in London. They were on an European tour, it being the end of the baseball season, and they were so impressed by our three-room-and-balcony suite at the Hilton Hotel on Park Lane that Ernie said he knew we were forced to eat cheese and crackers for breakfast in order to be able to pay for such luxury.

Ernie's jesting remark about cheese-and-cracker breakfasts was the absolute truth. When we arrived in London, what we sought was a room in a hotel on Park Lane with a spectacular view of Hyde Park. The costly large suite was the only accommodation then available with the preferred view.

After Beirut in Lebanon, abounding with Arabic-language pirated editions of some of my novels, our next stop eastward was in Pakistan.

In Karachi, Sardar Kahn, the affable manager of the Inter-Continental Hotel, who asked question after question about American cowboys, insisted that we stay a day longer than we had planned so he could have a handle on one of our suitcases repaired. We soon found out that the real reason for his wanting us to stay for an extra day was to have us go with him to a distant park to ride camels. His curl-brim hat and rawhide boots looked as if they might have been bought at a ranch-supply store in Wild Horse, Wyoming.

When we got to the camel park, where Sardar Kahn kept his own camel tethered, and where I had a close-up view of one of the hulking creatures, I insisted on being an observer and not a rider. Virginia, however, was thrilled to have the opportunity to ride a camel and eagerly took to the airy ride. An hour later when she returned to earth, she was smiling bravely even though her face was pale and her step was faltering as if she had been stricken with seasickness.

There had been many areas of poverty and privation visible in Karachi but the ultimate scene of human misery and wretchedness was in Calcutta.

It was our first trip to India and, although we had been forewarned what to expect, neither of us was prepared for what we saw. I had seen hunger and suffering in the meanest shacks and hovels in the United States but none of that was as deplorable as what was commonplace in Calcutta.

Among millions of people in the sprawling city on the Hooghly River, the course of life was not hidden behind curtains and walls. There life constantly was on public display day and night on the sidewalks and road-ways. It was where birth and procreation and death took place side by side when nature decreed. It was where life came and went at all hours amid the stench of urine and feces in the gutters and the ever-present swarming of flies and revered dung of wandering sacred cows.

Rangoon in Burma and Bangkok in Thailand were astoundingly differ-ent worlds in contrast to Calcutta in India. Bangkok was a city that better could be called Tourist Junction. It was a crossroad where eastbound and westbound tourists could pause on their journey to watch nonstop oriental dancing, dash eagerly from gift shop to gift shop, compare afternoon mas-sages with the nighttime version, and along the way have the choice of buying opium or cannabis.

With Tokyo our destination since leaving London, we arrived there on schedule on a misty November afternoon and were met at the airport by Warren Obluck of the American Embassy who was in charge of my USIS mission. On the way to the New Japan Hotel, we went zigzagging through the city to avoid as much as possible the thousands of Japanese who were demonstrating in the streets against the government's unpopular policy regarding the return of Okinawa from American occupation.

When we reached the New Japan Hotel, Charles Tuttle and Tom Mori, my literary agents in Japan, were waiting for us. They had made tentative plans for meetings with Japanese publishers which were subject to adjust-ment in order to avoid conflict with the USIS schedule.

Registering alongside us at the hotel were several professional wrestlers from California who were in Tokyo to give exhibitions of American-style wrestling. The beefy athletes had immediately drawn an admiring crowd of chambermaids, waitresses, and hotel clerks. There was a large group of students in the lobby with cameras and notebooks and Japanese transla-tions of some of my novels and short stories but only two of them succeeded in making their way through the crowd to ask for autographs.

The following three days in Tokyo were spent in the usual manner when plans were made by the United States Information Service for appearances for a writer who had volunteered to go on tour abroad. In this instance, it had been arranged for me first of all to take part in a roundtable discussion and reception at the American Embassy that was attended by sixty or more professors and journalists. That session lasted almost five hours and I was hoarse and weary through the afternoon and far into the night.

Other duties performed included interviews mornings and afternoons and visiting five universities to speak to students. All the trips through the city were taken in a roundabout manner in order to avoid being stalled and delayed by one of the many daily protest demonstrations that often blocked the streets.

On the fourth day after our arrival in Tokyo, it was a relief after almost constant activity during waking hours to take the Bullet Train to Kyoto for a relaxing three-hour trip that was much more comfortable than travel in an airplane for the same length of time.

On the train, there were no bumpy landings, no turbulence aloft, no stuffing of bodies into crates for seating. As if it were standing motionless, the speeding train created a sensation I had never before experienced. When watching the changing landscape through the window, it was like seeing the earth itself rapidly moving backward instead of the train speeding forward. In the distance, only the fabulous white-clad Mount Fuji maintained an eternal stillness.

The two days in Kyoto were similar to the time spent in Tokyo. The schedule there included receptions, seminars, and brief talks at Sophia University, Doshisha University, and Kyoto University. The American Cultural Center, acting for the USIS, was in charge of our visit in Kyoto.

After returning to Tokyo on the Bullet Train, we had one full day to spend as we wished before leaving for home. Following a farewell lunch with Charles Tuttle and Tom Mori, we decided to go to one of the nearby bathhouses for a few hours of relaxation. The one we selected was advertised in a weekly entertainment guide. Its name was Tokyo Hot Springs.

At Hot Springs we were introduced to the unfamiliar custom of being repeatedly soaped, sponged, splashed with hot water, rinsed with tepid water, sprayed with icy water, and vigorously massaged by several giggling eighteen- and nineteen-year-old girls. The young women now and then interrupted their soaping and massaging to walk barefooted up and down the customer's back.

Becoming pleasantly relaxed by the unaccustomed treatment, I soon began to wonder if the American wrestlers we had seen at the hotel would be coming to Tokyo Hot Springs while they were in Japan. That thought then led me to wonder if the girls who were massaging Virginia and me had been the same ones who had soaped and massaged four American Indians the previous year and had had to be rescued by the police.

I had been told about the incident involving the Indians by Al Manuel. Al had heard the full details of what had happened from a client of his who wrote the screenplay for a typical cowboy-and-Indian film. The four American Indians, as the incident was told to me, were from a reservation in Montana and had been taken to Hollywood to appear in one of the scenes in the motion picture. Afterward, the Indians had been taken to Tokyo on a promotional tour by the film company.

To help make life more bearable for the four homesick Indians in a strange country, they had been taken by the film company representative to the Tokyo Hot Springs for an evening of relaxation.

What took place at the bathhouse, as told by Al Manuel, was that the four Indians from the Montana reservation, all soaped and massaged, grabbed the girls who had been walking on their backs. Then, stripping the clothing from the girls, the Indians began soaping and massaging them until their screams brought the bathhouse manager to the scene.

Being physically unable to restrain the brawny Indians and prevent the girls from being raped, the manager ran to a sub-station a block away and sent a small squad of policemen with clubs running to the aid of the screaming bathhouse attendants.

At the end of our evening at the Tokyo Hot Springs, Virginia and I, both of us pleasantly rinsed and towel-dried and pampered with dabs of talcum powder, reluctantly left the giggling girls and their long-to-be-remembered smiling faces and the farewell waving of dainty hands.

= 2 =

Once more I entered the Mayo Clinic for a precautionary physical examination.

For many years prior to 1972 I had been an annual visitor to the clinic and the month of February had become my favorite time of year to stop whatever I was doing elsewhere and take to the snowlands of Minnesota. One reason for choosing to be there in the coldest month of all was that I still had a nostalgic feeling for the deep snow and icy wind of the season after many rigorous winters in the state of Maine. Another sentimental reason for treking to Minnesota at that season was due to the fact that

Virginia had a favorite fur coat that we felt was deserving of homecomings to its habitat.

In the beginning, and during the period when my home was in Tucson, I entered Mayo Clinic with the hope of being relieved of an insidious and persistent case of lingering amoebic tourista that had plagued me for many months following a ten-day visit to Mexico. I was not disappointed. I was permanently freed of my discomfort.

A few years later, Dr. Llewelyn Howell, a Mayo consultant, informed me that there was a blocked artery in my left leg and that something had to be done to save the leg from amputation sometime in the future. When I asked what could be done about it other than surgery, his reply was immediate and explicit.

"If you take my advice, you will stop smoking cigarettes," he told me. "And if you do, your leg can be saved."

"That's not easy to do," I told him. "I've tried several times to stop and I've always gone back to it."

"It'll be easier to do than walking through the rest of your life on one leg. Besides, what would the girls think of a young man like you hobbling along on one leg and a crutch?"

"I don't care what the girls think," I said. "But I do want to stop, anyway."

"Then do it."

"All right, I will stop."

The tall and somber-browed Llew Howell, striding back and forth in the small consulting room, spoke to me gravely in a concerned voice.

"Good for you, Mr. Caldwell. I know you've got the willpower to stop smoking. Let's see you prove it. You can start by telling yourself that before this day is over you will have smoked your last cigarette."

After fortifying myself with two fingers of bourbon and one last cigarette in the nearest bar, it was there that I commanded myself to quit smoking cigarettes forever. And I signified my determination by blowing a gigantic last smoke ring as high as I could over the bar.

A few years later, following the retirement of Dr. Howell, another Mayo consultant, Dr. Richard Weeks, further extended the years of my life by persuading me to forestall alcoholism by abandoning bourbon and replacing it with wine in moderation.

There were times to come, however, that were equally as critical as any in the past. Meanwhile, blissfully confident that I was in good health, I had left Mayo's in the early spring of 1972 feeling fit and hardy enough to be able to spend several stressful weeks of activity in France.

Much to my surprise, I had received a telephone call from my new literary agent in Paris, Michelle Lapautre, telling me that I was going to be invited to be a member of the ten-person jury at the 25th International Film Festival in Cannes. Michelle, speaking excitedly in French-accented English, said my official invitation and all details would soon be sent to me by Maurice Bessy, the director of the festival.

I was so surprised by the unexpected news that I was not immediately able to decide what to do. When I told Al Manuel about Michelle Lapautre's telephone call from Paris, and that I was not certain what I wanted to do about the invitation, first of all he prefaced his advice with a few of his favorite expletives.

"Are you crazy or something?" Al said excitedly moments later. "Don't you know nothing no more? Don't be a fool, Skinny. Get yourself over there. You and Virginia will be traveling first class on Air France and staying in hotels with carpets on the floor and curtains over the windows and running water in the bathrooms. And you won't have to spend a dime of your own money, neither, when you want something to eat."

"But I've got an idea in mind about a book—"

"Listen here," he interrupted, raising his voice. "Put that storybook writing away for a while and you can go back to it later and pick it up again where you left off. There ain't no sense in staying at home and piddling around on a story when you can go to that important Cannes film festival and see all the great films from all over the world. It'll be educational—like going to school again. See?"

"I can understand how you feel like that about it, Al," I told him, "but I don't know anything about films. That's not my field."

"Then educate yourself, Skinny," he pleaded. "Go over there and learn something for your own good. Someday there won't be no more books and everybody'll be looking at pictures. If all you can do is write stories for books and not know how to write stories for films, then there won't be no future for you. Ain't that right, Skinny?"

Marion Manuel, Al's fashion-conscious wife, told Virginia that no matter how much she had to nag me it was important for me to accept the invitation to be a jury member at the film festival. Then Marion said emphatically that Virginia should at once begin assembling a fashionable new wardrobe because the latest styles would be necessary when we attended the social events with the film stars and directors.

Combined with Michelle Lapautre's persuasive enthusiasm, Al and Marion's insistence made me feel that I was duty-bound to accept Maurice Bessy's invitation.

When we arrived in France in April, a full week was scheduled to be spent in Paris at the Lancaster Hotel for daily conferences with the film festival's organizing committee. Aside from the conferences, however, there were opportunities to see Claude Gallimard and Marcel Duhamel; Pierre Belfond, the publisher of the French translation of *The Weather Shelter*; Georges Lucas, publisher of Portuguese translations in Lisbon; Morrill Cody, formerly the European director of the USIS; Michelle Lapautre; and Thomas Quinn Curtis, the long-time oracle of the *Paris Herald Tribune* and patron of La Tour d'Argent restaurant.

Judging the merits of the many films in competion began immediately upon arrival in Cannes and an arduous task it was to be from the opening day of the festival. For a person who ordinarily would see two or three motion pictures in a year's time, I was confronted by the screening of two full-length features daily and that amounted to a total of twenty-eight films in fourteen days.

Being the casual film-goer that I was, I sometimes made flimsy excuses when some of the other members of the jury, more addicted to the cinema than I, proposed going to see a film that either was not in competition at the festival or was a pornographic feature at a small theater on a back street of Cannes.

The proceedings at the 25th International Film Festival were not confined to the daily screenings and jury conferences. Nightly there would be one or more receptions at hotels and casinos. These affairs were given by film-makers from many different countries and in some instances they were far more entertaining than the films that they had entered in competition for festival honors.

Of all the receptions that Virginia and I attended, the most lively affair was presented by the Israelis. The lavish buffet was of great length and depth. The folk dancing with accompanying music was continuous. And the champagne never ceased. When we left the reception at two o'clock in the morning, there was no indication that the gala would end before dawn.

During the daylight hours, the afternoons on the broad terrace of the Carlton Hotel provided a continuous spectacle of filmdom on parade. There it was that the established stars and aspiring starlets alike promenaded slowly down the terrace in scanty attire on the way to the beach for suntanning and photography in near nudity.

Among the commentators and observers on the terrace from time to time were Alfred Hitchcock, Robert Redford, John Huston, Arthur Rubenstein, and Groucho Marx. Tom Curtis, a practiced observer of the Mediterranean beaches from Nice to St. Tropez, frequently could be seen pointing out from where he sat in his favorite terrace chair which of the bikini-adorned starlets had or had not yielded to the lure of silicone.

At the conclusion of the two weeks of the screenings of films, I decided I had enough confidence in my judgment to state before the jury that my preference for first prize was the Robert Redford film with the title of *Jeremiah Johnson*.

I was satisfied with my decision even though I still wondered how a novelist and short-story writer could possibly become a qualified, instant critic of motion pictures in fourteen days and be able to render wise judgment. However, I remained steadfast with my decision even though the majority of the jury was in favor of awarding first prize to an Italian film with the title of *A Workman in Paradise*. Every member of the jury did agree that *Slaughterhouse Five*, a film of the novel by Kurt Vonnegut, was worthy of being awarded a special prize for excellence.

It was the night before we were to leave Cannes to return to Florida when Michelle Lapautre, with another of her many surprises, telephoned to say that I had been invited to go to Nice the next day to be a member of the jury to select the author to be honored at the five-day International Book Festival.

While I was trying to think of any plausible excuse for not staying in France any longer, Michelle said with her usual assurance that a car would come to the Carlton Hotel for us at ten o'clock the next morning to take us to the Negresco Hotel in Nice.

Chapter Thirty

FOR THE FIRST TIME in many years there was sufficient reason for Virginia and me to stay at home in Dunedin at the very beginning of 1973 to celebrate our wedding anniversary.

Usually we had planned in the past that this annual event, the purpose of it being to commemorate our one-minute-past-midnight marriage in Reno, would take place in various chosen locations from New York to Honolulu.

As memorable as each occasion had been, my wife and I agreed that the most practical and healthful anniversary of all was the one that came about when we entered the Mayo Clinic in Rochester on New Year's Eve for checkups and tests. Three days later when we were discharged, both of us were declared by the consultants to be ideally fit for another year of living.

By the end of the first week in 1973 we were completely rested after our mildly active celebration at home and well prepared to begin a rigorous winter trip to Europe lasting for six weeks from early January until the middle of February.

This winter trip had been planned by the United States Information Service and the schedule had been arranged for me to spend several days in the capital cities of Scandinavia and eastern Europe and to conclude the tour in Moscow. Unlike earlier tours, when usually I was expected to attend receptions and give readings or speak at libraries, this time my assignment was to speak only at universities along the route. As usual, I was to receive per diem government allowance for expenses and a small fee for each lecture.

Beginning in Copenhagen, I was immediately aware of an unconcealed coolness—and in some instances outright animosity—toward Americans. This was something I had never experienced before in Europe and I soon found out that the reason for the display of ill will was because the Danish people were almost solidly opposed to American participation in the Vietnam War. More than that, people did not hesitate to let their disapproval be known.

This was an attitude that I was in full sympathy with and made no apology for my country's actions. Perhaps the USIS staff felt that my presence as an American writer, together with the public expression of my personal convictions, would help ameliorate the existing widespread anti-Americanism among the Danes. Evidently this was in keeping with the official policy because not once in the past had this government agency ever suggested what I should or should not say in public or in print while abroad on a mission for the USIS.

In Helsinki, the Finnish people were even more outspoken than the Danes in their opposition to a continuation of American warfare in Vietnam. However, even though it had been expected by the members of the USIS staff, I was not booed when I spoke to students at the University of Helsinki.

The only unpleasant incidents encountered in Finland involved minor physical mishaps. Virginia suffered a bruised knee when she slipped on an icy sidewalk and I soon recovered from a mildly frostbitten ear. Continuing the tour to Warsaw and beyond, there were no other unfortunate accidents, other than spraining my ankle in Prague on the way to deliver a lecture at Charles University, until much later when we were on our way from Bucharest to Moscow.

In Poland, Czechoslovakia, Hungary, Yugoslavia, and Bulgaria it was only in a few scattered instances that the Vietnam War was mentioned and by the time we reached Romania there were no longer any instances of overt anti-Americanism.

It had been a long and tiring trip for Virginia and me when we reached Bucharest at the end of the first week in February. A few days later we were looking forward to a restful journey when we boarded an airplane for the U.S.S.R. and my final lecture at the University of Moscow.

Less than an hour after leaving the Bucharest airport in the darkness of nightfall, I thought for a terrifying length of time that I was going to be responsible for bringing the ancient Romanian Airlines plane down to earth in flames.

According to custom, the cabin stewardess operated a small booth in the rear of the plane where she sold beer and mineral water in bottles. That was all she had for sale and she was not required to perform any other duties. This had been made evident when I asked her to help me adjust a faulty seat and she had refused with a frown and a toss of her head.

With that incident concluded, I immediately asked an English-speaking passenger across the aisle to trade a cigarette for a stick of chewing gum. That accomplished, I lit the cigarette and with puff after puff blew as much smoke as I could at the stewardess without inhaling any of it. She received my message with another scowl and a toss of the head.

A short time later I stuffed the partly smoked cigarette unto what I assumed was an ashtray under the window. It was the first—and was to be the last—cigarette I smoked since making a vow to quit the habit. In blowing a retaliatory cloud of smoke at the uncooperative attendant, I was very careful not to let myself inhale a single whiff of it.

The opening under the window was not an ashtray. Instead, it was a rip in the soundproof padding of the cabin that may have been the result of a slash of a knife, and smoke from the unseen material indicated that it was burning. I tried to smother the fire by stuffing newspapers into the opening, but that intensified the fire and a greenish haze of smoke began billowing upward to the ceiling.

A frantic call to the firm-chinned stewardess brought no help whatsoever. She merely shook her head with another scowl on her face and refused to leave her booth. Probably she thought I had lit another cigarette and was trying to annoy her with more clouds of tobacco smoke.

In desperation, I went to the booth and hurriedly bought a large bottle of mineral water. Fortunately, the smoldering fire was soon extinguished by being thoroughly drenched.

The stewardess had instructed me to return the water bottle to her as soon as it was empty. And I did so, and without comment from either of us.

= 2 =

My most recent novel, *Annette*, had been published by New American

Library and I was busily engaged in trying to control the persistent growth of wayward viburnum and proliferous bananas on our Dunedin acre when I received an urgent call from Dick Drost in Indiana.

What was wanted of me, I was soon to find out, and on my own terms, was to be the final judge at Dick Drost's Miss Nude America contest at his Naked City nudist resort near Roselawn. My first reaction was to decline the invitation by saying I was not a practicing nudist and, since my wife traveled with me on all occasions, I doubted that she would consent to appear in public without clothing.

That excuse was quickly put aside by Dick with his saying that we would be exempted from the requirement to disrobe when entering the Naked City compound. He argued, also, that since I had been a judge at a French film festival I was a well-experienced observer of young womanhood. Dick was so insistent that his pleading manner finally persuaded me to say I would discuss the matter with Virginia and let him know my decision if he would telephone me the following day.

What Virginia and I did decide right away was for me to telephone Edward Butler, a long-time friend and the marketing executive for New American Library, and ask him what would be expedient. Ed did not hesitate to state his opinion.

"Go ahead and do it," he said in his decisive manner.

"Are you sure I should, Ed?" I asked.

"Of course, Skinny. What makes you undecided?"

"Well, it's unusual, for one thing. I'm not accustomed to anything like that."

"Neither am I but it will promote the sale of your NAL books. And we'll sell them to nudists just as quickly as we will to people walking around in raincoats. So what's the difference? Authors are always expected to show themselves at bookstores to autograph their books to stimulate sales. So why shouldn't judging a contest be equally as honorable for a writer?"

Four days later a Naked City limousine, its interior from front to rear flocked and upholstered in a bright shade of pink, arrived at the Ambassador East Hotel in Chicago to take us to the nudist resort an hour and a half away in Indiana.

In the heat of the August noonday sun, hundreds of panting nudists were crowded closely in the arena where the twenty-eight selected contestants for the crown of Miss Nude America were waiting to parade one by one in front of the judges.

Already in progress in the arena were the precision parachute landings from airplanes by nudist couples. The winning couple was awarded a complimentary week's occupancy of a guest suite at Dick Drost's resort. The elaborately decorated suite, like the interior of the limousine, was dazzling pink from carpet to ceiling and, according to Dick, the shades of coloring were designed to resemble skin tones. The centerpiece of it all was a king-size round water-bed in a subdued hue of peach-blossom pink that slowly revolved around and around on the raised flooring in the middle of the large bedroom.

By the time the judging and the selection of Miss Nude America had been completed, I had found it difficult to distinguish one body from another. The only features that varied were the colors and lengths of hair and those variations were strictly limited in number. As far as I was concerned I could just as easily have closed my eyes and pointed at random at any one of the contestants in the group of young women and felt fully justified in making my choice. Unlike the parachuting couple, the only rewards the winning Miss Nude America received were a queen's paper crown and, reportedly, an offer of a job as a cocktail waitress in a Gary, Indiana, bar.

After returning to Chicago from Naked City, it was not easy to become readjusted to seeing everybody in clothing. This was particularly evident that evening in the hotel restaurant when it seemed odd that all the people there were completely clothed. All through dinner I expected at any moment to see a nude young woman enter the restaurant and be escorted to a table in the room.

Several weeks later after the experience of being a judge at a nudist contest in Indiana I was at Dartmouth College in New Hampshire to attend the unveiling of the portrait by John Gilroy. Following the ceremony in Baker Library, I told Edward Lathem about my presence at Naked City. He nodded gravely for several moments and then said it was time for me to divert my energies to a task more compatible with the obligations of an author.

"What are the obligations of an author?" I asked him.

"To write books, of course," Ed answered.

"It seems to me that I've been doing that for many years."

"That's true. Fiction. And good fiction, too. But the writing of good fiction can become better fiction when interspersed with meaningful nonfiction. And I would like to offer my services to aid and abet the work on your next book of nonfiction whatever the subject may be—an encomium for nudist colonies excepted. But be aware that this is a moment of confession. And the confession is that I have an unquenchable thirst to devote what talents I may have to the honorable profession of editorship."

"What work of mine would you be aiding and abetting with your editorship, Ed?" I asked him.

"That is a matter for you to decide, Erskine," he replied.

Edward Lathem had assembled material and had been the editor of several important books. Among the most notable of these had been a highly regarded anthology, *The Poetry of Robert Frost*, and also *Interviews With Robert Frost*. I knew of Ed's association with Dodd, Mead and Company as an editor and I was not unwilling to have my next book of nonfiction taken there for publication.

With the publisher decided upon, Ed had no objection to my having the publication contract negotiated by Elizabeth Otis, and by the time I was ready to leave Hanover, Ed and I were in full agreement about how we would proceed in the future.

The book was to be a volume of observations of life in the United States, confined in scope to a smaller area and more intense in concept than *Around About America*, but likewise it would be illustrated with drawings by Virginia Caldwell.

= 3 =

Not a word had been written but the title for the new book had already been chosen when Virginia and I, our automobile loaded with typewriters and drawing materials, left Dunedin one morning in July during a tropical downpour. This was to be the first of two planned field trips, the purpose being to gather material, that we would take over a period of two years. The title of the book was to be *Afternoons in Mid-America*.

The region that had been of interest to me as the scene I was setting out to write about was part of the original territory of the Louisiana Purchase. I had wanted to travel more extensively in that area of the United States to see the people and the land ever since having read about it in a high school history textbook.

This part of America bordered the Mississippi River northward from Arkansas to Minnesota and extended southward from the Dakotas to Oklahoma. What eventually was to become the State of Louisiana chose to remain separate and let the vast lands in the north and west that had been acquired from France be divided into many territories which later were admitted to statehood.

There were two minor incidents in the beginning of our travels through Mid-America that were of so little significance at the time that I failed to consider them to portend a third occurrence of a more serious nature. I should have known better and been prepared for what might come, because my maternal grandmother often had warned me to expect a third incident, whether fortunate or unfortunate in effect, to follow two of a kind.

The first of these two events took place one afternoon while we were driving along the landside base of a Mississippi River levee in Arkansas near the town of Marked Tree. This was in the fertile delta plantation region of the state where cotton and soybeans were the principal crops.

What happened there was that I carelessly drove the car over a splintered board from which protruded a rusty twenty-penny nail. My reaction was too slow to swerve the wheels in time and the right front tire was punctured. When I pulled the nail out of the tire, there was no sound or other indication that air was escaping and I decided to drive as fast as possible back to Marked Tree and try to get there before the tire went flat. It was an exciting twenty-minute drive over narrow roads and bumpy bridges. However, in the end, even though we reached Marked Tree before the tire had lost all its air, it was rim-cut and so damaged otherwise that a new tire had to be bought.

A week later, we were in New Madrid, Missouri, a few miles from Arkansas and still in the plantation country of cotton and soybeans. It was here that Virginia came upon a friendly, white-haired grandmother whose coloring was the blackest of black. Virginia thought she was an ideal subject for a drawing and the elderly woman eagerly consented to sit for a portrait.

The light was rapidly failing at the end of a preliminary drawing and it was agreed that Virginia could come back the next morning and finish the sketch.

When we went back the following day to the small cottage in the segregated part of New Madrid, there was no response to our knocking on the door. For a long time, voices could be heard inside the plank-sided cottage but no one opened the door.

Presently, the elderly woman's middle-aged daughter came to the corner of the house and with a stern frown, waved for us to go away. When we did not leave immediately, she walked to the edge of the porch and waited for us to come down the steps to the sandy yard. Hesitantly then, she told us why her mother could not let Virginia finish the drawing.

As it was explained, the white owner of a neighborhood grocery store in the black section of town had observed us the previous afternoon and, seeing our car with Florida license plates, had warned the elderly black woman to stay away from us. The reason for the warning, we were told, was that we were from Florida where most of the people were Yankees from the North and that we should not be permitted to draw pictures or take photographs of anybody in New Madrid.

The incident in New Madrid, which was the second setback to happen to us since leaving home, was a minor annoyance at the time and quickly dismissed as being of little consequence.

After leaving Missouri, we had been traveling for two weeks when we arrived in Waterloo, Iowa. A few days later it was decided that I should return to Mayo Clinic in Southern Minnesota for another of the tests that Dr. Richard Weeks had been conducting periodically for the past year and a half. I considered the tests to be merely routine medical procedure although Dr. Weeks himself several times had expressed concern about his findings.

Following five full days of esophogoscopy, bronchoscopy, and x-ray tests among others, it was determined by Dr. Weeks and associates that cancer had developed on my right lung and that surgery was necessary. It was a Friday, though, and Dr. Spencer Payne, the lung surgeon, did not operate on weekends. I was instructed to return to the clinic Monday morning. As I was leaving, and with unstated understanding between Dr. Weeks and me, I knew he could be saying that I would not have cancer now if I had stopped smoking cigarettes many, many years sooner.

Virginia had been talking on the telephone to Elizabeth Fawcett in Brainard, Northern Minnesota, where she and Roscoe had a summer home on Gull Lake, and when Elizabeth found out that I was to undergo surgery the following week, she and Roscoe had insisted that Virginia and I be their guests over the weekend.

It was a very pleasant two-day outing in the lake country of Minnesota for several of the other guests. For my part, I was glum and apprehensive about life thereafter. I am sure that everyone else thought Roscoe's ringing of the big dinner bell on his float boat was highly mirthful when he wanted Elizabeth to bring him another drink. The best I could do was to smile occasionally while most of the time wondering, if I did not survive lung surgery, what momentous events might take place in the world after my life had ended.

At six o'clock on Tuesday morning I was taken to surgery and six days later I was released from intensive care and placed in a hospital room. By that time, and confident that I actually was alive, I was so glad to be able to look at the pictures on the wall and admire the colorful curtains over the window that I had no interest whatsoever in knowing what might be happening that moment anywhere else in the world.

Time and time again, I thought of the discovery of cancer on my lung as being the third and final incident in the series of unfortunate events that had its beginning alongside the Mississippi River levee in the Arkansas delta. With my grandmother's observation in mind, I wondered if a series of fortunate events would be as likely to occur as unfortunate ones.

= 4 =

A few days after leaving the hospital, I was eager to leave Minnesota in our car for Florida, seventeen hundred miles distant, and both Dr. Payne and Virginia persuaded me solemnly to promise not to attempt to drive the car one foot of the way. As much as I wanted to sit in the driver's seat, and envious of Virginia for having that privilege, I managed somehow to be moderately pleasant as we went southward through the states to Dunedin.

Much of the time before leaving Rochester had been devoted by Virginia to answering telephone calls far into the night from persons who had seen a brief newspaper item about my surgery for lung cancer.

There had been calls from Dabney in Boston, Janet in Raleigh, Pix in Los Angeles, Jay Caldwell from Anchorage, and Drew Fletcher from Ashland. Other calls came from former neighbors in Tucson, Orinda, and San Francisco. There were calls from Ed Lathem, Al Manuel, Eddie Lewis, Eddie Schwartz, Forrest MacMullen, Adriana and Dan Rowen, Julius Weiss, publishers, literary agents, and many more.

One of the most unusual messages was a telegram signed Anonymous which stated that a donation had been made and arrangements completed to have prayers offered for me in a Catholic church in Cleveland for a year. I was never able to find out the name of my benefactor so I could thank him for his act of kindness.

After a full month's rest and recuperation in Florida, we left in our car—with me driving—to complete our first field trip for *Afternoons in Mid-America*. Virginia expressed happiness to be able to relinquish the steering wheel and resume her knitting, reading, and letter writing as usual when traveling by car.

This investigative trip was resumed in the tall corn country of Iowa and ended a few weeks later in the Oklahoma Panhandle. The most exciting incident that occurred during that portion of travel was in Oklahoma while attending the annual Cow Chip Festival in the dust bowl at Buffalo and watching the cow-chip whirling technique of contestants of both sexes and various ages from five years to ninety-five years. As an out-of-state visitor, I was offered the opportunity to whirl a chip.

Almost half of the text for our book had been completed by the end of the year and it was soon after the early part of 1975 when Ed Lathem came to Dunedin to have his first reading of the material in his capacity as editor. He had no suggestions and little comment to offer, saying only that he was pleased to see what I had done and wanted to wait until later to consider any editoral suggestions.

It was early spring then and, too soon to begin the next field trip, Virginia and I were easily persuaded by Kazimierz and Wanda Piotrowski, my Polish translators, and Czytelnik, one of my Polish publishers, to go to Warsaw to appear and autograph books at the Polish Book Fair. There was no difficulty about meeting the expenses of the long weekend trip, which was to be at the height of the flowering lilac season in Warsaw, since my blocked royalty accounts were more than ample to pay for round-trip flights on LOT, the Polish airline between New York and Warsaw.

Our Polish weekend, every moment spent in the swirling perfume of lilac blossoms, was strenuous but pleasant. My stint of book signing took place under a shady tree in a park where I was to sit for two and a half hours autographing books at the rate of thirty every five minutes for a total of nine hundred copies. A Soviet novelist from Moscow, seated at another table nearby, with a smiling challenge raced with me to see which of us would have signed the largest number of books by the end of our allotted time.

After returning from Poland, our final field trip was planned to begin in the middle of June in the Dakotas. First, though, we stopped at Mayo's in Minnesota for the routine twice-yearly tests and x-rays. As a result, Dr. Weeks found cancer on the other lung. I insisted that we had to finish our field trip as planned before the heavy weather of winter set in but did promise to come back for the operation within a short time. The disapproving Dr. Weeks said he had no authority to force the operation for cancer upon me but he did wish me good luck and urged me to hurry back to have the cancer removed.

Work on the book which by that time I was anxious to finish had been interrupted the previous year by the discovery of cancer and I was not pleased by the prospect of another disruptive delay. I promised to return to Mayo's in about six weeks when the field trip had been completed and then to stay at the clinic as long as necessary.

With permission reluctantly granted, Virginia and I left Rochester for Brookings, South Dakota, and then later to travel westward to Mobridge to visit the Standing Rock Indian Reservation.

After spending several days at the Hutterite settlements near Brookings, I was convinced that the members of that religious sect were among the most industrious and persevering of all American workers. In contrast, it was distressingly depressing to see drunken young Standing Rock Indians sprawled in stupor along the roadside between Mobridge and the reservation.

And equally depressing was the sight of drunken Indian women, young and old, staggering on a Mobridge street or clinging to a telephone pole.

At the end of six weeks we had returned to Mayo's and twenty-four hours later I was again operated on by Dr. Payne for the removal of half of my other lung.

The second long period of recuperation in Florida provided all the time needed to complete the text for *Afternoons in Mid-America*. Virginia's pen-and-ink drawings were finished, also, when Ed Lathem arrived in Dunedin to see the results of our work of almost two years on the book.

He declared immediately that our work was superb in every respect and, as advisory editor for Dodd, Mead, he saw the book as being ready for publication in the next season.

Chapter Thirty-One

I WENT TO EUROPE IN the budding spring of 1976 and there began and brought to an end my fifth and final tour for the United States Information Service.

My reason for giving up the opportunity to continue visiting countries where many of my books had been published in translation was that I felt I had amply fulfilled a desire to mingle with readers abroad. In addition, I had felt called upon to serve my country as a writer inasmuch as I had been too young to serve in the armed forces in World War I and too old to serve in World War II.

But that was not all. Looking forward to the conclusion of my final tour, it was my feeling that the younger American writers should be given the opportunity by the USIS to take my place after so many years as a volunteer in the service.

Beginning with the first one, each tour of duty had provided me with entry into the complex society of Europe that I would never have known as an occasional traveler on the London-Rome-Paris tourist circuit. Perhaps my contribution to the enhancement of friendly relations among peoples may have been slight whereas I, for my own benefit, was well rewarded with enduring friendships and offerings of good will beyond the bounds of political ideologies.

This terminal trip, starting in Milan and Rome and ending in Paris and London, was similar in a routine manner to previous ones. What made it much different during the middle of the tour were unexpected events incited by university students in Denmark, Norway, and Sweden.

University students in each of these Scandinavian countries were staging strikes and boycotts as a sign of independence and with demands that aging professors be retired and replaced by younger instructors.

This was a wave of protest that probably was generated by an inevitable outbreak of spring fever that coincided with that time in life when youth can no longer be constrained, as in early childhood, and demands the right to abandon the old and to establish new rules and regulations for its own generation.

In Denmark, it was at Aarhus University where students attended my lecture and where professors were barred from the same auditorium. A few days later at Odense University, the situation was reversed when students boycotted the lecture and it was attended only by members of the faculty.

My third appearance in Denmark had been scheduled for the University of Copenhagen and there it was that students had left the classrooms and had gathered in the large cafeteria. I was asked not to appear in the auditorium where faculty members were waiting and, instead, to sit at a cafeteria table where I would be visited by interested students for discussions.

The student boycott at the University of Oslo in Norway did not apply to visiting speakers although when the time came for me to appear in the auditorium the members of the faculty outnumbered the students by far.

After Norway, the student strike at Upsala University in Sweden was firmly enforced but without threats of violence or even shouted insults directed at faculty members as had been heard in Denmark.

Upon arriving from Stockholm at Upsala University in the rainy spring afternoon, Virginia and I were taken to a cavernous, underground restaurant by Professor Olov Pryckstedt for a leisurely dinner and to hear an apology for the cancellation of my talk that evening in a university auditorium. Professor Pryckstedt, a teacher of English, tall and trimly clothed in brown tweeds, was not yet forty years old and one of the few who had not been called upon to resign by striking students.

The rosy-cheeked, middle-aged waitress attending to us in our alcove in the cavern was an attentive listener to the conversation at our table. And while almost constantly pouring wine, or contemplating doing so, from one bottle to the next she would nod approvingly or frown with disapproval. In fact, the waitress was so pleased with our sympathetic attitude toward student demands that I would not have been surprised if she had reached forward and patted one of us on the shoulder.

Instead of sending us immediately back to Stockholm in the drizzly gloom of night, Professor Pryckstedt took us to what was evidently a previously arranged meeting place on the campus where a three-student committee was waiting for us.

From there, Virginia and I were taken to a brightly-lighted aboveground reception hall where there was a riotous gathering of beer-drinking, strike-happy young people. It was almost midnight when the students, with much reluctance, let us be on our way back to Stockholm.

Little notice was taken of the student strikes and boycotts beyond the Scandinavian countries but I did hear from travelers that the protests had gradually dwindled in intensity and scope until campus life there was soon normal and uneventful.

I was in Paris a week after visiting Upsala University and nearing the end of my final USIS tour. With one full day free of any obligation to the USIS before leaving for London, I was to find out that Marcel Duhamel had made elaborate plans for a meeting with Alexander Calder.

This was a complete surprise to me. And I did not know until later that Marcel and Virginia had secretly arranged the meeting to reveal to me that Sandy Calder had illustrated a French edition of *The Sacrilege of Alan Kent* with twenty-five full-page aquatints. The large folio-size book had been translated by Marcel and published by Galerie Maeght.

This was the same book that Pablo Picasso earlier had agreed to illustrate as soon as he could find time for it on his schedule. Shortly after Picasso's death, Marcel and Virginia found that Galerie Maeght still wanted to publish the book and after that Sandy Calder agreed to furnish the illustrations.

The meeting with Calder had been arranged to take place at a luncheon given by Aimee Maeght in his spacious apartment in the shadow of the Eiffel Tower on Avenue Elysees. Soon after a bear-hug greeting by Sandy, followed by toasting with an abundance of red and white wine, the dozen guests were entertained with the disclosure of some of Sandy's working habits while drawing the illustrations. This was related by a Maeght associate, Jacques Duprie, who was present in Sandy's studio during working hours.

At the beginning of each day's work, Sandy would ask Jacques to read aloud a few paragraphs of *The Sacrilege.* When emotionally moved by some image he had visualized, Sandy Calder would then ring a small, tinkling, tea-table silver bell as a signal to stop reading. Later, with a sketch completed, he would ring the little bell for more reading until he was inspired to execute another spontaneous impression.

Throughout the detailed and often humorous descriptions of Sandy's working habits by Jacques Duprie, the burly artist, whose favorite greeting of men and women alike was a bear-hug, with a mischievous wink would frequently reach for a cookie or one of the constantly replaced wine glasses on the broad cocktail table.

Louisa Calder, with constant watchfulness, often spoke up and reminded Sandy not to mix red and white wines. Germaine Duhamel, likewise concerned, did not hesitate to tell Marcel several times that he had already taken more wine than usual. While I was receiving similar admonitions from Virginia, at the same time I was gently reproving her in return by advising her to be aware of the large quantity of chocolate cookies she had been taking from the bowl on the cocktail table.

This mention of chocolate cookies by me did not go unnoticed by Sandy Calder. With bold glances, and pretending he was not being observed in the act, he reached into the cookie bowl and, with much ado, shyly passed one chocolate cookie after the other to Virginia over his shoulder or behind his back. After each successful passing of a cookie, he would reprove himself with a brisk slap on his cheek.

= 2 =

At midnight on the occasion of another wedding anniversary, Virginia and I solemnly resolved that soon in the new year of 1977 we would move from Florida to somewhere west of the Mississippi River.

Even though, as in many years past, we continued to spend as much as half the time away from home engaged in a variety of projects, I was still restless enough to want to make another change of residence. And as for Virginia, she admitted that Florida's damp climate was making frequent twinges of arthritis increasingly painful.

This was not the first time in recent years for us to have thoughts of moving in mind. What had happened previously was the result of my having written an article for publication in *Family Weekly*, a syndicated Sunday newspaper supplement inserted in newspapers nationwide, in which I speculated about the advantages and disadvantages of moving from place to place during a lifetime.

I had received letters of advice, more than two thousand of them, from every state and with every imaginable reason to move to the letter-writer's own region. Among the many letters, though, there were a few that offered dissenting views about the advisability of moving to another part of the country. One such letter stated with forthright candor:

"In your picture in the paper you look tired. You should stay right where you are and get some rest."

A land developer in East Texas was so aggressive in trying to get us to move to Tyler that he sent us airplane tickets for a weekend visit. For several days before leaving to visit Ben Fitzgerald in Tyler, Virginia received from him each morning a dozen red roses and I had a telegram stating the expected temperature and cloud conditions there for the next twenty-four hours.

After arriving in Texas, and being almost continually entertained from early morning until late at night by Margie and Ben Fitzgerald, we were made to feel so welcome among friendly people that we were tempted to buy a house immediately and move to Tyler from Dunedin.

Before anything was said to indicate that we would consider moving to Texas, though, Ben told us he had a word of advice about building a house in Tyler.

"Be sure your house has a she fireplace," he said. "That's very important in East Texas."

"What kind of fireplace is that?" I asked him.

"That's one that your wife can carry wood in for."

It was at that point that I told Ben Fitzgerald we might be interested in buying an existing house but not one that had to be built.

"That's not the purpose of your visit here," he said with an unexpected frankness.

It was then revealed that Ben was interested in our moving to Tyler only on the condition that we would accept the gift of a lot in one of his real estate projects and, moreover, build a house on it and live in it. The offer was declined with thanks. After expressing our appreciation for the opportunity to come to Tyler, back we went to Dunedin.

Still in search of a drier climate than Texas could provide, it was later in the year when we left home for Colorado Springs. All the way to Colorado on the airplane, it was our hope to find a suitable new home in a climate that would help alleviate the pains of arthritis. There had been a recent snowfall in Colorado Springs, followed by thawing, and patches of dingy snow were scattered over lawns and parkways. The overcast winter sky hovered over the rooftops like a gray canopy waiting for the moment it would be lowered over the city with the gloom of night.

In the daylight hours, we had been taken on tours of vacant houses for sale by a grumpy real-estate broker, who was a retired army colonel, and he was much more critical than we were of the unfurnished houses we inspected.

Surprisingly, the salesman appeared to be pleased when he was told that none of the houses interested us as a possible future home. And at the end of two days we were ready to return to Florida. That was when the salesman said he had made a mistake when he retired in Colorado Springs instead of doing so somewhere in Florida. It was that remark that put us to wondering if we had made a mistake when we put our Dunedin home on the market.

A month after our unsuccessful hunt for a house in Colorado Springs, and still hopeful, we were in Albuquerque, New Mexico, in a search there for a suitable new home. This time, wary of real-estate salesmen, especially retired army colonels, we used newspaper advertisements by individual homeowners to guide us in our search.

Visiting an occupied home by appointment, instead of walking into a vacant house, usually resulted in personal contact with the owner that prevented a prospective buyer from being completely objective in his evaluation of a property. During the three days Virginia and I were house hunting in Albuquerque, we were entertained in many ways by homeowners anxious to get us to make an offer to buy their property.

In one house, we were tearfully begged to listen to a piano solo by the grandmother of the family for almost half an hour longer than we wished to stay. At another time, a three-course meal had been prepared for us and only by being offensively rude could we have avoided sitting down at the table. There were several occasions, too, when beer, wine, or whisky—and once even home-brew—was pressed upon us.

The hospitality offered us in Albuquerque was much appreciated but no house was found to be acceptable. We were sent on our way back to Florida thoroughly discouraged when the last house we inspected was a splendid modern dwelling with a spectacular view of the city but in which the large and well-equipped kitchen did not have a single window.

When we returned to Dunedin, there had been no offer made to buy our house and the broker insisted on lowering the sale price. Then as an additional incentive for someone to buy the house, he persuaded us to agree to vacate the property two weeks after the sale had been completed.

It was early March then and time for preparing income tax returns. As had been the custom for several years, Owen Golden, my tax accountant, and I met in Scottsdale, Arizona, for the annual ordeal. While this unpleasant task was being performed in a hotel room, Virginia was blithely engaged in a search for a suitable house for us to buy in Scottsdale.

One particular house had appealed to Virginia very much and, although all houses were beginning to look the same to me, I was pleased with her choice and was glad we had not bought a house elsewhere. In some manner, Virginia and the affable young real estate agent, Jean Chapin, had managed to obtain an option on it.

After the week in Arizona, we returned to Florida only to leave almost immediately for Santo Domingo in the Caribbean where I was to serve for two weeks in seminars conducted by the Southern Consortium For International Education. Our need to find a new home somewhere in the western part of the United States was easily banished from mind temporarily in the sensuous tropical climate in a land abounding in colorful flowers, varieties of luscious fruit, and endless balmy weather.

Within an hour after we had returned home from Santo Domingo, the real-estate broker informed us that our house had been sold the week before and that, as previously agreed, we would have to remove all our furniture and other belongings within the next few days. The only helpful thing the broker did after that was to promise us that a cashier's certified check in full payment would be handed to us at a bank the same day we vacated the house and turned the keys over to the new owner.

An urgent telephone call from Virginia to the real estate agent in Scottsdale secured the house there on the terms specified in the option. For hour after hour, this was a tense and enervating period that left us dazed and exhausted.

I was wondering what mishap could occur that would make our move across the country difficult when the moving company's van arrived to load our furniture. The van was already partly loaded with another person's household belongings. A second van had to be sent and that was cause of a long and worrisome delay in the beginning.

When both vans were loaded, with our furniture divided between the two, one was dispatched by way of St. Louis and the other by way of New Orleans. The two drivers smilingly assured us that in all probability our furniture would be consolidated in one van somewhere between Dunedin and Scottsdale.

Three days later, in possession of the check to make payment on our new home in Arizona, we raced across the country in an attempt to reach Scottsdale before our furniture arrived. We were delayed for almost half a day in Lafayette, Louisiana, when in haste I slammed a car door on a thumb and had to wait several hours in a hospital for x-rays and stitching.

When we arrived at our new home in Scottsdale, the moving van containing all our furniture was at the gate and the driver and his assistant were sitting on the doorstep.

"You people got here just in time," the muscular driver said in a friendly greeting. "Me and my helper had started arguing about whether to turn around and haul your stuff back to Florida or whether to set fire to the van and collect insurance. But now that you're here to unlock the front door, I guess what we'd better do is stop talking and start unloading."

$$= 3 =$$

The year of my seventy-fifth birthday began with a second trip to the Dominican Republic to participate in another seminar in Santo Domingo. Several weeks after that I went to Guatemala in Central America with a different group of sociologists, economists, and other specialists to take part in a similar two-week seminar.

The visit to Guatemala City was made memorable by the display of colorful weavings in the market, the endless number of ancient buildings, and, in particular, the excitement in the night each time a nearby volcano suddenly erupted in flames and smoke.

Later in 1978, I was invited to spend the last week of September at Dartmouth College. In the past when I was in residence there for a longer period of time, it had been arranged for me to visit fraternity houses and student dormitories for conversations with interested students in late afternoons and early evenings.

While the talks were always friendly and pleasant, the results were often less than worthwhile when an excess of beer prevailed. There were times, also, when literary matters were of less interest as topics of conversation than Ivy League football and week-ending Wellesley and Smith College girls.

During this latter visit at Dartmouth, though, it had been arranged for me to meet students one at a time by appointment in a quiet reception room in Baker Library. This was a more satisfactory arrangement for students, whether serious in purpose or merely curious, and after such interviews

I always felt that my time and that of the student had been well spent.

With the advice of Maxwell Perkins firmly in mind, my parting words to an aspiring writer were always the same. These were:

"Don't talk about your writing. It's better to let your writing speak for you."

It was October again and the autumn foliage season was aflame with forests of vivid colors in Northern New England where the maples and birches painted the countryside in unending shades of reds and yellows. From Vermont through New Hampshire and into Maine, every hillside and meadow had been splashed with the magic paints of autumn. It was difficult for us to leave Northern New England when the time came for Virginia and me to be on our way to the pavements of New York and from there to the chilly winds of Washington.

Farther ahead was to be a birthday party on December 17th in Charlottesville, Virginia. But more immediate was a reception to honor the Performing Arts in Washington at the White House.

There were many guests at the White House reception and, since most of them were unacquainted with each other, it was an occasion for one stranger either to introduce himself to another stranger or for both to stand aside in silence.

When I was greeted by President Jimmy Carter, I was immediately made to feel welcome by his remark that he had looked forward to meeting a fellow Georgian whose public life was as controversial as his own.

"I suppose we were born to be what we are," I said, "and whether writer or statesman we must live out our fate."

There was a quick smile on his face when he remarked that we would have an excellent opportunity to change our lives by being born again.

When it was Virginia's turn to be presented to President Carter in the receiving line, she impulsively leaned forward and kissed him on the cheek.

There was an immediate flurry among members of the security force and she was hastily encouraged with stern gestures to step lively and shake hands with the president's wife. It was not known what Mrs. Carter said to Mr. Carter about the incident.

Several days after the visit to the White House, we arrived in Charlottesville to attend the birthday celebration at the University of Virginia. It had been my understanding that the occasion would be informal and attended by only a few persons. The gathering had been arranged by Waller Barrett, the genial bibliophile and donor of the Barrett Library of American Literature to the university.

The reception preceeding the dinner in the Barrett Library was attended by more than a hundred persons and other guests had arrived when seating for the dinner was announced. I had already begun to wonder what was the purpose of such a large gathering of people when, to my surprise, the president of the University of Virginia, Frank Hereford, was standing before me and welcoming me back to the campus of my youth.

I was still in deep thought about what I, the former United Daughters of the Confederacy scholarship student and poolroom attendant, could say to express my appreciation for such unexpected attention when Waller Barrett announced that I would give a reading of a recent essay.

This announcement was the second surprise of the evening. The year before, the University of Georgia had published an essay of mine under the title of *Recollections of a Visitor on Earth*. And now with the pamphlet in hand, I stared at it as if I had never seen it before in my life.

Presently in the silence of the room I realized that I was expected to read aloud in public the many pages of strange-looking words that had been gleaned mostly from the dictionary. Nervously slurring pronunciation and heedless of cadence, I somehow managed to read to the end of the essay that had been written only for the silence of print.

Other than being marred by my inept pronunciation and elocution, the evening was a pleasant one to be remembered by a nongraduate alumnus and former racker of billiard balls in an off-campus poolroom. The next morning the *New York Times*, fortunately omitting any mention of my performance as a public reader, reported in its news columns that I had been rehabilitated as a Southern writer by the University of Virginia at a reception and dinner on my seventy-fifth birthday.

Rehabilitated or not, I was grateful for Waller Barrett's manifest esteem for the writing I had done as a Southerner and an American. And I was no less grateful for the tolerance of the university that had not deprived me of its privileges when I ignored the strict requirements of the classroom to be in pursuit of my own scheme for learning.

Chapter Thirty-Two

AFTER MANY YEARS OF crisscrossing the United States by various means of travel, and crossing the North Atlantic Ocean first on ships and latterly in airplanes, it was not easy to restrain myself and reduce the length and frequency of travel following my seventy-fifth birthday.

Offered the slightest encouragement, I found it not at all difficult to prepare myself for another journey at home or abroad. The appeal that travel and movement had for me no doubt was similar to that of the bus driver who often went for a ride in a bus on his day off from work.

Item—Only a few months from the time of having attained the privilege of still being alive after three-quarters of a century, little thought was necessary for me to agree to go to France when invited by Editions des Autres to perform the usual extracurricular duties of a writer. Among the duties required were autographing books and shaking hands with strangers and smiling for photographs. The occasion was the publication of the French translation of *The Bastard*.

The trip began with the three-and-a-half-hour flight on the supersonic Concorde from New York to Paris. Thereafter, a six-day tour of France and Belgium by automobile, train, and airplane began with my signing copies of *The Bastard* at book festivals in Bruxelles and Lille and ended at an industrial fair in Marseille and a wine-tasting celebration in Bordeaux. How many books were sold by the publisher was probably a trade secret.

Our hours of sleep during that week being from long after midnight until five or six in the morning, it was evident to both Virginia and me that we were thoroughly exhausted and yet still travel-happy when we returned home.

Item—The next opportunity for travel came about when Ljerka Radovic, my Serbo-Croatian translator, and Minerva, my publisher in Yugoslavia, urged me to help celebrate Minerva's publication of a twelve-volume library edition of my fiction. All expenses were payable in dinars from my unconvertible royalty accounts and, as a further inducement, the visit would take place in the very pleasant Yugoslavian month of September.

But there was to be a delay in Portugal on the way to Belgrade. To begin with, our suitcases did not arrive with us on the airplane from New York to Lisbon and it was three days before we were able to retrieve the baggage. During that long waiting period, the restaurant workers at the Ritz Hotel went on strike and we were served a carafe of tepid coffee and a cold, paper-wrapped, sausage sandwich by the management three times a day. Finally, with our baggage in hand, I lost our airplane tickets at the Lisbon airport. What would have been the third calamity in a series of misfortunes was averted when half an hour later an airline pilot found our tickets on the departure lounge floor and returned them to us.

After our arrival in Yugoslavia, our visit to Minerva in Subotica lasted exactly twenty hours from four o'clock Monday afternoon until twelve noon the next day. During that short afternoon, a long night, and the brief morning, we were taken to table five times by the Minerva editors and publishers. These dining occasions provided a banquet, a brunch, two buffets, and a roasted suckling pig for midnight snacks. The twelve-volume library edition of novels and short stories was published as scheduled. And as for Virginia and me, we returned home with gains of many unwanted pounds of excessive weight from bountiful meals averaging one every four hours.

Item—Once more at the friendly behest of Edward Lathem, I was in residence at Dartmouth College as a Montgomery Fellow in midsummer 1980. Ed Lathem was then an established administrator of many titles at Dartmouth and, other than being dean of libraries emeritus, he was the current Woodward Fellow, executive director for the Montgomery Endowment, and perennial advisor to each succeeding president of the college.

This time Virginia and I, instead of residing at the Hanover Inn or the Choate House, were assigned to the spacious Montgomery House. This comfortable guest house on Rope Ferry Road was a short walk from the campus with glimpses along the way of the Connecticut River and the Vermont countryside from its hillside location.

We had been greeted upon arrival by Betty and Ed Lathem with a chilled bottle of Schramsberg champagne and then often thereafter, on some pretext or other, Ed appeared at our door with another bottle of Schramsberg. The unfamiliar brand was Ed's most recent discovery of an obscure wine and, as in the past when meeting with him in Dunedin, Scottsdale, New York, or elsewhere, his current finding was always enthusiastically pressed upon us bottle after bottle as if there would be no more available in days to come. And so once more we were treated to Ed Lathem's champagne-on-the-rocks.

Item—With unrelenting efforts, first in cablegrams and next by overseas telephone, Kazimierz Piotrowski, my Polish translator, persuaded me to go to Warsaw in the autumn of 1981 to help celebrate the publication of his translation of *Episode in Palmetto*.

I was never indifferent to any situation having to do with the publication of one of my books anywhere on earth. However, in this case, what was equally of interest to me in Poland at that time was the opportunity to observe the increasing popularity and appeal of the Solidarity labor movement. This public approval of the cause was evident upon our arrival in Warsaw where the majority of the people with whom we came in contact were wearing Solidarity lapel pins and badges.

Kasey Piotrowski's motives had not been revealed in full to me. This was apparent when Virginia and I were taken to the hall of the Union of Polish Writers supposedly for a sampling of wine of the country.

Instantly upon our arrival, I was guided to an assembly of writers and there presented to a committee representing the Polish Ministry of Culture. In a brief ceremony that followed, I was decorated with the Republic of Poland's Order of Cultural Merit. All during the proceedings I could see Kasey Piotrowski on tiptoes grinning and clasping his hands above his head in a signal of victory. Only then did I realize how anxious he must have been while pleading with me to come to Warsaw.

Although the three government representatives at the ceremony that day at the Union of Polish Writers did not wear Solidarity pins or badges, every writer proudly wore the insigna in full display. Later, returning to the Inter-Continental Victoria Hotel, it seemed to be in keeping with the spirit of the popular labor movement to see several well-dressed young women strolling the bar and lobby-lounge with the brightly-enameled Solidarity emblem pinned to blouse or jacket. One of the enterprising young women, her Solidarity badge shining prominently on her breast, had stationed herself at the doorway of the hard-currency shop where foreign tourists and businessmen were given the opportunity to return her smile and, perhaps, exchange a few words as they emerged with Swiss chocolates or American cigarettes.

Item—For more than twenty-five years, beginning in 1956 at Kezar Stadium in San Francisco, I had watched and read about the trials and misfortunes of the San Francisco Forty-Niners as contenders for honors in the National Football League. And now at last the Forty-Niners were at the Super Bowl in Pontiac, Michigan, to contest Cincinnati for the 1982 championship title.

Shortly before the final game was to be played for the championship, Virginia and I had been in Hawaii for our twenty-fifth wedding anniversary. During our return to Los Angeles, the captain of our plane told the passengers that the Forty-Niners had just won their final game of the regular season and would be going to the Super Bowl. That was when Virginia said she was determined to find a way for us to get to the championship game two weeks later.

All seats in the Silverdome in Pontiac had been sold six months earlier and no travel agency could obtain a room for us closer than seventy-five miles from the scene. However, Ernie Harwell, from his observation post as radio announcer for the Detroit Tigers baseball club, found two tickets by some means and, somewhere in the Detroit suburbs, an unheated motel room. Ernie could not not provide any means to hold back the fury of the January winter, though. Snow and ice covered all. There was snow on top of ice. And there was ice on top of snow. Walking and driving a car were equally dangerous on the slippery streets and icy roads.

Tickets for shuttle busses to the Silverdome were being sold from the doorway of a trailer stationed in a parking lot in downtown Pontiac. Within minutes, a throng of clamoring ticket buyers—hundreds of shoving and shouting football fans—besieged the flimsy trailer with such force that it tottered precariously and was in danger of being overturned.

I was struggling in the midst of the mob to keep my footing on the ice-crusted pavement and at the same time trying to move closer to the ticket seller. Suddenly down I went with a painful thrust of an elbow and another person's tripping foot. Before I could get up, I was being lifted from the pavement by two strong arms. Turning, I could see the smiling face of a muscular-shouldered man of about forty-five years of age who was holding me protectively with a firm grip.

"I didn't like to see you take that fall," the stranger said in a familiar drawl. "In a mob like this, a man can get a bad trampling down there on the ground."

"Thanks," I said right away. "I appreciate your helping hand. It's lucky for me that you are a football fan. And you look like you may have been a football player yourself. With your accent—maybe a player on the Dallas Cowboy team?"

"No, not that," he said in a drawl that was unmistakably Texan. "I'm just a humanitarian—a doctor from Dallas."

Item—In the spring of 1982, and cherry-blossom-time in Japan, Virginia and I were in Tokyo again. This time we were not there for a college speaking tour or for geisha house entertainment or for massages at Tokyo Hot Springs. We had gone to Japan as guests at a banquet in the Okura Hotel for members of the Erskine Caldwell Literary Society. At the large gathering, we were in the company of Hisao Aoki and Fujisato Kitajima both of whom were university professors and translators of some of my books. It was a memorable occasion where many speakers had something to say and where I was not called upon to utter a single word. Consequently, there and then, I became a profound admirer of traditional Japanese consideration for letting me remain silent throughout the evening.

= 2 =

As usual, in 1983 I had dutifully submitted to the annual physical examinations in February and June at the Mayo Clinic in Rochester, Minnesota. We had taken another summer trip to Ashland, Oregon, for Virginia to visit her two grandchildren. And, as customary, Virginia and I had spent an August week in Santa Fe, New Mexico, where another of her oil paintings had been acquired at the Jamison Gallery by a perceptive collector of art.

With the coming of September, we were at home in Scottsdale and I hoped to have the year of my eightieth birthday expire quietly on the occasion of reaching the magic four score years of age. Then the phone rang.

Calling from Paris was Michelle Lapautre with the message that I was being invited by an organization of French writers to attend a gathering in Nice during the first week of October. Michelle would listen to no excuse I tried to make in order to decline the invitation and she insisted on having my immediate promise that Virginia and I would follow instructions implicitly and arrive in Paris on October 4th without fail. The travel arrangements would be made by Ruda Dauphin, administrator for *Journees Mondiales de l'Ecrivain*, I was told by Michelle, and she was as excited and insistent as Kasey Piotrowski had been when he telephoned me from Warsaw two years earlier.

We were met in Paris by Ruda Dauphin and, after a night at the Ritz Hotel, the three of us went by airplane to Nice. Michelle Lapautre arrived the next day.

By the beginning of the third day in Nice, I began wondering why I was not expected to appear at any meeting of the five hundred writers in the large civic auditorium. Both Ruda and Michelle assured me that plans were being made for me to take part in the program on the fourth and final day of the writers' convention.

At four o'clock in the afternoon, only an hour before the scheduled closing of the assembly, which was to be followed by a banquet in the evening, I was escorted from the Meridien Hotel to the stage of the crowded auditorium. I had no idea what would be expected of me as I stood facing the audience in a state of nervous perplexity until finally I was led to the center of the stage.

What followed immediately was a lengthy presentation speech by the director of the Ministry of Culture and at the conclusion I was decorated with the Republic of France's Commander of the Order of Arts and Letters.

The reason for the invitation to come to France and all the preceding secrecy was revealed so suddenly that the best I could do to express my appreciation for the honor was to mutter a few nervously spoken words of thanks. And, as I was to discover that evening at the banquet, the ceremony in the auditorium would lead to a tribute that was even more surprising to a grateful and appreciative American writer.

At ten o'clock that evening in the grand ballroom of the Plaza Hotel, slightly more than five hundred persons had gathered for a gala dinner. It was a colorful assembly of fashionably dressed men and women and the huge ballroom was filled with gaiety and laughter.

Following the serving of dinner, the lights were dimmed and the orchestra began playing the familiar Happy Birthday music. Then each person was handed a lighted candle by a waiter and other waiters brought in an immense cake decorated with eight large flickering candles. As I was being given a knife to cut the first slice of cake, everyone in the ballroom rose to his feet and began singing the birthday song in English.

It was an overwhelmingly sentimental moment for me, so unexpected and unbelievable that I could only gaze around me in silent wonder. Over and over in the twinkling candlelight the five hundred softly accented French voices sang the birthday song in English until everyone at our table was blinking with tears. And, like others and in view of all, I did not hesitate to dab at my eyes with my napkin.

Finally, near the end of the tribute, several shouts of *Vive! Vive!* were to be heard above the music and the words of the song. In response, I stood up and waved my arms to betoken my appreciation for the ever-to-be-remembered homage I had received in a foreign land.

Back home in Scottsdale on the actual date of my eightieth birthday, December 17th, I was completely surprised and overwhelmed for the second time within little more than two months. This occurred when Virginia presented me with the impressive results of an entire year's effort in secret to obtain and mount three hundred and more messages of good will and birthday greetings from around the world. It was remarkable, too, that she had been able to accomplish so much over a long period of time without my having the slightest inkling of any such activity. As I was to be told later, using a post office box in her maiden name, as well as having the cooperation of a friendly postmaster, contributed greatly to the success of her ambitious scheme.

In two huge leather-bound volumes with a combined weight of twenty-seven pounds, among the more than three hundred responses there were hearty greetings, in alphabetical order, from Edward Albee and Saul Bellow to Raphael Soyer's impressive mirror-painting and Richard Wilbur's pen-and-ink illustrated stanzas of verse. And, contributing to the weight of the collection, there were colorful tiles from Portuguese friends emblazoned with birthday sentiments.

After the two spectacular tributes, the first in Nice and the second in Scottsdale, I have had enough of the good things in life to satisfy the normal desires of any writer. Consequently, I would like to bequeath to the future young writers of the world any additional approbation that might be engendered.

= 3 =

From the first bright rays of dawn to the shade of evening, the day is done.

My goal from the beginning has been to be a writer of fiction that revealed with all my might the inner spirit of men and women as they responded to the joys of life and reacted to the sorrows of existence.

What I have resisted doing as a writer was glorifying the sensational and knowingly falsifying the anguish or the jubilation of men and woman who have been brought to life and were captives in a story of mine. Like the physical body of a person real or imaginary, the human spirit should not be ravished and outraged in print by ghouls at large.

Perfection in writing is rarely achieved and I would be reluctant to attempt to improve a published story with latterday revisions. Likewise, I would not willingly consent to relive my life for the purpose of rectifying the mistakes I have made and attempt to correct the errors I have committed along the way. I accept my own failings together with the knowledge that my writings and I must exist with all our imperfections to the end of my time.

EPILOGUE

THROUGHOUT MY MANY YEARS of living I have collected bits and whits of philosophy as befitting any sage sitting cross-legged atop Potato Hill. Here and now as I look to the future, after having experienced the past, I want to share one of my strongest convictions as expressed in the remarks that follow. These offhand although well-considered remarks were made at the Fifth International Meeting of Writers in Sofia, Bulgaria, on October 25, 1984.

•••••••••••••••••••••••••••••••

Friends:

It seems to me that history has been written, chapter by chapter, century after century, in praise of war and its accompaniment of death and destruction. If we look at the history of our war-ravaged world, these chapters have glorified the winning of wars, the number of people who have been killed, and the destruction that has occurred.

Between these chapters of horror there has been very little written about peace because there have been so very few intervals of peace to commemorate.

However, it is my belief that the time is coming—how soon I do not know, but inevitably—when war will have been banished from this planet.

It is not consistent with the ideals of liberal-minded people, people with foresight and intelligence, to let the horrors of war be perpetuated and encouraged to continue to exist in the future as they have been in times past.

I suggest that this meeting of writers offers the opportunity to inaugurate a crusade for peace. And I am confident that such a crusade would be successful because writers do possess a talent that enables them to contribute to the good of the world and the welfare of mankind.

As writers, we often try to make it seem as though we are dillydallying in a casual occupation, although those of us who are engaged in, and pursue, communication as a vocation know that it is no easy task to be a writer. Writing requires dedication and hard work to be successful and I am confident that we can be successful in the cause of peace.

As we know, every nation has a Ministry of War, a Department of War, which is charged with the duty to prepare for future wars during brief intervals of peace. It is my suggestion, and my hope, that in every nation the Ministry of War will be abolished and in its place be created a Ministry of Peace.

I realize that this is a farfetched, and even radical, idea and seemingly an impossibility. However, it was universally believed not so long ago that man could not go to the moon. So now that nothing is impossible, surely peace is possible and should not be withheld any longer from the people of our world.

In these closing words, I would like to repeat myself.

Over and over again I have said: "Enemies kill enemies, but friends do not kill friends." So let us be friends. All of us in every nation.

BOOKS BY ERSKINE CALDWELL

All Night Long 1942
All-Out on the Road to
  Smolensk 1942
American Earth 1930
Annette 1973
The Bastard 1929
Call It Experience 1951
Certain Women 1957
Claudelle Inglish 1958
Close to Home 1962
The Courting of Susie Brown 1952
Deep South 1968
The Earnshaw Neighborhood 1971
Episode in Palmetto 1950
Georgia Boy 1943
God's Little Acre 1933
Gretta 1955
Gulf Coast Stories 1956
A House in the Uplands 1946
In Search of Bisco 1965
Jenny by Nature 1961
Journeyman 1935

Kneel to the Rising Sun 1935
A Lamp for Nightfall 1952
The Last Night of Summer 1963
Love and Money 1954
Miss Mamma Aimee 1967
Moscow Under Fire 1942
Place Called Estherville 1949
Poor Fool 1929
Some American People 1935
Southways 1938
Summertime Island 1968
The Sure Hand of God 1947
This Very Earth 1948
Tobacco Road 1932
Tragic Ground 1944
Trouble in July 1940
We Are the Living 1933
When You Think of Me 1959
Writing in America 1967
The Weather Shelter 1969
With All My Might 1987

FOR CHILDREN

Molly Cottontail 1958
The Deer at Our House 1966

ANTHOLOGIES OF ERSKINE CALDWELL

The Black & White Stories of Erskine Caldwell,
Selected by Ray McIver 1984
The Complete Stories of Erskine Caldwell 1953
The Humorous Side, Edited by Robert Cantwell 1951
Stories, Edited by Henry Seidel Canby 1944

BY ERSKINE CALDWELL AND MARGARET BOURKE-WHITE

North of the Danube 1939
Russia at War 1942
Say: Is This the U.S.A.? 1940
You Have Seen Their Faces 1937

BY ERSKINE CALDWELL WITH VIRGINIA M. CALDWELL

Afternoons in Mid-America 1976
Around About America 1964

SPECIAL

The Sacrilege of Alan Kent, Illustrated by Alexander Calder 1976

BOOKS BY ERSKINE CALDWELL

All Night Long 1942
All-Out on the Road to Smolensk 1942
American Earth 1930
Annette 1973
The Bastard 1929
Call It Experience 1951
Certain Women 1957
Claudelle Inglish 1958
Close to Home 1962
The Courting of Susie Brown 1952
Deep South 1968
The Earnshaw Neighborhood 1971
Episode in Palmetto 1950
Georgia Boy 1943
God's Little Acre 1933
Gretta 1955
Gulf Coast Stories 1956
A House in the Uplands 1946
In Search of Bisco 1965
Jenny by Nature 1961
Journeyman 1935

Kneel to the Rising Sun 1935
A Lamp for Nightfall 1952
The Last Night of Summer 1963
Love and Money 1954
Miss Mamma Aimee 1967
Moscow Under Fire 1942
Place Called Estherville 1949
Poor Fool 1929
Some American People 1935
Southways 1938
Summertime Island 1968
The Sure Hand of God 1947
This Very Earth 1948
Tobacco Road 1932
Tragic Ground 1944
Trouble in July 1940
We Are the Living 1933
When You Think of Me 1959
Writing in America 1967
The Weather Shelter 1969
With All My Might 1987

FOR CHILDREN

Molly Cottontail 1958
The Deer at Our House 1966

ANTHOLOGIES OF ERSKINE CALDWELL

The Black & White Stories of Erskine Caldwell,
Selected by Ray McIver 1984
The Complete Stories of Erskine Caldwell 1953
The Humorous Side, Edited by Robert Cantwell 1951
Stories, Edited by Henry Seidel Canby 1944

BY ERSKINE CALDWELL AND MARGARET BOURKE-WHITE

North of the Danube 1939
Russia at War 1942
Say: Is This the U.S.A.? 1940
You Have Seen Their Faces 1937

BY ERSKINE CALDWELL WITH VIRGINIA M. CALDWELL

Afternoons in Mid-America 1976
Around About America 1964

SPECIAL

The Sacrilege of Alan Kent, Illustrated by Alexander Calder 1976